SECRET DEVICE

THE DONAVAN ADVENTURE SERIES
(VOLUME 2)

TOM HAASE

Copyright © 2018 Tom Haase. All rights reserved.

This book is a work of fiction. Similarities to actual events, places, persons or other entities are coincidental.

www.tomhaase.com

Secret Device/Tom Haase. – 1st ed.

To my son, Michael Anthony Haase

ALSO BY TOM HAASE

THE DONAVAN ADVENTURE SERIES

Secret of the Oil

Secret Device

Secret of the Thorns

Secret of the Bibles

Secret of the Icon

Secret Vengeance

THE COASTAL ADVENTURE SERIES

Betrayed Angel (Summer 2018)

Betrayed Devil (Fall 2018)

For the latest information on Tom's upcoming books, sign up for his free author newsletter at tomhaase.com/news.

FREE NOVELLA

To receive your free copy of the exclusive Donavan Adventure series novella *Secret of the Assassin* (not available anywhere else), visit **tomhaase.com/assassin.**

1

AIR FORCE ONE – 2:13 P.M

President Christopher Brennan relaxed his old frame in the comfortable leather chair on Air Force One. He rolled down his white shirtsleeves to prepare for the landing in Atlanta, still twenty minutes away. His personal cell vibrated, and on seeing the number of his special agent, he answered it.

"Hello, Matt. What's happened?"

The voice of the president's agent, who operated in an off-book capacity, came over the phone in a rush.

"Mr. President, you can't land in Atlanta. I'm convinced there'll be an attempt to detonate an improvised atomic device when you touch down. I know for sure the bastards got it into the country."

Brennan sat upright and leaned forward signaling his press secretary, Gary Fazio, who prepared to leave, to remain in his seat.

"Are you sure? We're only a few minutes from landing. What proof is there?"

"Sir, we've little time. I've tracked them from Savannah to Atlanta. The trail ended at the home of a female FAA flight controller. I believe the Russian kidnapped or murdered her to get access to the control tower. They know you're landing shortly." Matt made a gasping-for-breath sound over the phone with what sounded like the noise from helicopter rotor blades in the background. Matt continued, "The weapon is with him. Bridget and I are on the way to the airport to intercept him."

The president put the call on hold and ordered Gary, "Get Avery in here." Brennan swiveled to look out the window, where his image reflected a wrinkled brow and his wavy uncombed gray hair. He took off his glasses and swung back and forth in his chair. A few seconds later, Dean Avery, the national security advisor, entered the compartment. A short, stocky man, his face always exuded confidence, and his dress was immaculate, including the combed-over hair.

"One of my agents tells me there may be an atomic weapon detonated when we land in Atlanta," he said to Avery, trying to mask any trepidation in his voice. His right hand, however, tightly clenched the phone on which Matt waited on the line.

"What? Is this a joke? Surely, it has to be." Avery appeared calm.

"Mr. President," said Gary in rat-a-tat New York style speech, "we must go on. This is a crank. What proof is there of anything? No specific warning from the intelligence community about a threat in Atlanta. This will be a splendid opportunity for you in that city with the dedication of the new runway. Come on, you worked hard to get this." He walked back toward the president, going around the bulky national security adviser.

"Who is this report from? How reliable is the information?" Dean Avery demanded. He was not only the president's friend, but also his closest adviser on most matters. He wanted answers. Christopher Brennan did not respond to the questions.

"I hear you both. But the man on the phone is someone I trust. Dean, assuming the existence of a bomb, what's your input?" the president asked.

Avery put one finger under his collar and moved it from the right side of his neck to the left. Sweat formed on his forehead. "Your safety is paramount. We should return to Washington."

"No. Come on." Gary paused. "We need this appearance. You promised to support that Georgia governor. We are behind in the polls. This will help you. Besides --" The President signaled for him to stop talking. Gary Fazio was a young man to hold this important job, and the president valued his knack for accurately predicting any public reaction, but public relations weren't the issue here.

Brennan said, "If we mention this to the Secret Service, they'll want to turn us around. They've done this before with other potential threats. I'm still the boss, and I'll decide what to do."

Avery moved toward the president. His stern face started to redden. "If we proceed to Atlanta we could be vaporized." He paused, seemed to review his options, and in a more measured tone, continued, "If we don't land, your people may use this chance to find these terrorists before they can target you again."

The president heard the fear in his friend's voice, but Avery always gave a considered response, even in a crisis like the one now brewing. He remembered that Avery hadn't wanted to come on this trip. The president had insisted he come along because of some foreign policy matters he'd planned to address during a reception at the governor's mansion later today.

"You're assuming they won't set off the weapon if I'm not there." Brennan pushed his fingers through his hair.

"Mr. President, we don't even know if there is a bomb. The press is going to eat us alive. Do you really want to run?" Gary almost yelled at his boss.

"Mr. President," Avery said, "we should go back to Washington. It doesn't make sense for them to waste a weapon if they couldn't get you as well. The target they're after is you." After taking a moment, he continued at a faster clip. "Remember the intelligence briefings we received today on the Russians warning us of an attack, and on the recent calls for your destruction by the Iranian leader? You're the bull's-eye, and if you're not there, there's no reason for them to take action."

"I'll have to get a story together to cover the cancellation," said Gary, almost resigned to the decision being used against him.

"No cover story would hold up to the press scrutiny on this," Brennan said, and he took a few moments to think before continuing, "I can't. I don't want to turn tail and skedaddle, and not support the people running for reelection on my ticket." He closed his eyes for a moment, while noting that Matt remained on hold. Recently, Brennan had sent Matt and his partner, Bridget, to track down a suspected terrorist. He concluded there could be a direct connection between that incident and this new threat. He took in both men's countenances and rapidly shook his head side to side, then continued, enunciating every word, "I don't like giving in to a terrorist threat."

"Mr. President," Gary said, "you realize the press will have a field day, since by turning around, it would appear you fail to support your party's candidate for governor. They might speculate that your failure to show meant you believe in the unavoidable loss of another governorship."

Brennan barely heard Gary as he calculated that if Matt did not succeed in stopping the detonation, thousands would die, including everyone on board Air Force One. On the other hand, if his agent stopped the terrorists and the president failed to land, he could write off all the political capital he would have garnered at the dedication.

Matt, he thought, could not be certain about the weapon. They regularly received many terrorist threats. At the same time, with all the lives at stake, it wasn't worth taking such a risk.

"The only alternative... I don't like it, but right now it's the correct course of action. We go back to D.C.," the president said.

Fazio nodded and let his shoulders slump. He exhibited that pissed-off face a New York cabbie gives at a cheap tip.

"Good decision," Avery chimed in, "because I was coming to tell you that I learned from the National Security Council staff that they believe a Russian counterterrorist team is operating on our soil."

The president held up his hand to Avery, "Stop, let me finish this first. One bloody crisis at a time." He released the hold button on the speakerphone and put the receiver up to his mouth to tell Matt his decision. The red phone on the console next to his chair buzzed. He used his free hand to pick up the direct connection to the White House Situation Room. "Yes?"

"Mr. President, the Secret Service has notified us of the high probability of an explosive device planted on your plane."

"What? You are kidding? This can't be, damnit," the president shouted.

The two men standing in the president's compartment glanced at one another with raised eyebrows when they heard Brennan's words. They exchanged glances. They knew this must be serious for Brennan to curse.

The president continued to hear the voice on the red phone. "A man caught with an explosive device has confessed to placing an explosive device on Air Force One. He said if you deviated in any way from your flight plan to land at Atlanta, the bomb would go off. He killed himself, along with an agent, after admitting it."

Brennan's mind went to his wife and daughter back in Washington. At least they remained safe from this madness. Again he focused on the immediate problem and asked, "When did this happen?"

"A few minutes ago at Andrews, but we just got the information. The Secret Service thinks the man is for real. They're notifying your security detachment on board as we speak. The man upgraded the avionics on Air Force One today and placed a worm in the system to detect any deviation from your programmed course."

The president stood up. Color rushed to his face.

The Situation Room's update continued, "If that occurs, the bomb will go off, according to the terrorist. The analyst at Andrews corroborated the existence of the worm in the suspect's test equipment. You must land in Atlanta to prevent the detonation."

"What? How in God's name can this have happened?" He almost threw the red phone across the desk. "I can't believe this. This is Air Force One, for God's sake." The president slammed the red phone into its cradle, then turned to Gary and ordered, "Get the command pilot back here. Now."

He sat down again, pounding the arm of his chair. As he did so he glimpsed his reflection in the airplane's window. Catching the anguish in his eyes, he made an effort to regain his composure. His usually slow Virginia drawl now came out in a rapid-fire manner as he told his closest advisers what he had learned. Disbelief registered on their faces and they each took a seat opposite the president.

Brennan spoke into the phone he had continually held during this entire event. "Matt, I can't order us back to Washington, as you may have heard, so I'm relying on you. If there's an atomic weapon in Atlanta, you must find it before we land in less than twenty minutes." He ended the call. If Matt succeeded, the only remaining danger affected his plane and all on board. At least the citizens of Atlanta would not be at risk.

He clasped his hands behind his head. "How in the hell did we get into this situation?"

2

ON BOARD CONTAINER SHIP SEA PEARL – ATLANTIC OCEAN

Before dawn, Yuri Borisov stood on the deck of the container vessel and stared at the distant horizon as the ocean miles passed by. He felt the warm sea breeze move his hair around as he recalled with photographic clarity the events leading up to the killings he had performed and the trail that had led them to be on this ship.

He let his mind wander back over what had happened in the last few days, he and Basam al-Hanbali had fled south, away from the scene of an atomic device's detonation. His device had worked as he had designed it. Then they raced along a Saudi Arabian highway in a stolen Land Rover headed for the border with Yemen. When they stopped, he felt his sweat-soaked clothes sticking to his body after the all-day high-speed drive across open desert. They had only paused for refueling. Occasionally he took a large swig of vodka to help get the grains of lingering sand out of his mouth, and he preferred using the alcohol instead of water to quench his thirst before he took his turn driving. After they switched seats, he pulled back onto what he thought was the highway — at least what passed for one, always covered with a light covering of gritty desert particles. Basam, his Saudi friend, turned on the radio.

"We need to hear what the news is reporting on what happened yesterday," Basam said. "It's strange, you know, we haven't seen any increased security on the roads."

They listened to the radio for news of the events they had planned and implemented less than twenty-four hours before. The third item reported:

"Yesterday, an American helicopter crashed in the desert fifteen kilometers south of Ras Tanura. All on board died. The area around the site is being sealed off for fear of explosions from the ordnance the aircraft carried. American military personnel, in cooperation with the Royal Saudi Army, are recovering the bodies. Now for the latest soccer scores."

Basam switched off the radio. Yuri understood enough Arabic to get the gist of the news, while remaining focused on driving.

"What did they say?" Yuri asked in English, since both possessed fluency in that language. Basam gave him a recap, ending with "those infidel Americans are liars."

Yuri drove in silence for a half hour. He knew the Americans had interrupted them before they could fully carry out their mission. With each mile, they distanced themselves from that disaster. Military action had foiled their attempt to destroy the Saudi Arabian oil reserves with contaminated radioactive material. They had also initially planned to obliterate the seaport from which nearly all the Saudi Arabian oil flowed to Europe and Asia, as well as the United States.

One weapon, placed in a deep underground cavern where the reserves were located, had detonated, but an American had killed Tewfik al-Hanbali, the terrorist leader and Basam's brother. The other atomic bomb, targeted to destroy Saudi Arabia's oil export city of Ras Tanura and its tanker and refinery facilities, must be in the hands of the Americans since it had failed to explode.

"Can you believe they covered up an underground atomic explosion?" Yuri broke his silence while lighting a cigarette from the one he had almost finished.

"Come on. They aren't going to tell the world that some terrorists detonated an atomic bomb, are they?" After a few minutes of quiet,

Basam continued in his British-accented English, "Yuri, as the nuclear engineer...you built the bombs that we used." Basam shifted and adjusted himself to face Yuri. "What went wrong? Why didn't it go off?"

Yuri pounded the steering wheel. "Damnit, I don't know. The one in the well detonated, but we had to run before I could see the damage. The one in the city...shit, I don't have any idea." He tried to stop himself, but he blurted out, "Maybe your brother didn't dial the cell phone number before the American killed him."

Yuri lit another cigarette. He continued to chain-smoke for another two hours.

"I'm not saying...ahh...that it's your fault personally," Basam said, rotating back to stare out the side window at the desert landscape flying by. "But you received a lot of money to do this job. One of the bombs went off, but the other one . . . my brother paid you ten million American dollars to build the weapons." Basam switched topics and said, "We've got to get out of this country. The authorities will figure out that I'm involved when they identify my brother's body."

"After we can get to the port city in Yemen," said Yuri, "we'll be able to secure passage on something. We will get the hell out of this area of the world."

"Nobody knows what we have with us, do they?"

Yuri noticed the hint of fear in Basam's voice and decided to calm him down. "No. How could they? I'm sure they think it's all over. They killed everyone but us, and they don't know we were part of that attack. But we have to act like they might. We can't take a chance."

Basam waited a few seconds and said, "You know it's safe in the case. We'll use it to punish the ones who attacked my brother."

Yuri took a sideways glance while on a straight stretch of road and reminded himself that Basam did indeed resemble his brother in appearance. The man possessed the sharp, long nose characteristic of many Saudis, and a small beard with a mustache that formed an oval around his chin. His eyes glared with the same cold, intense blackness of his older sibling's. All Yuri wanted was to get away and hide for a few days to let things settle down. He would then gain some time to think. Building the weapons had caused him enough trouble. Now that it was over, he wanted to enjoy his money. Alas, he wished Basam wouldn't keep talking about the device, but that didn't happen.

"Can you tell me now how much damage such a weapon can do? Just in general."

"Well, this one, the one with us, is the smallest of the three I put together. It's a fifteen-kiloton atomic weapon. It could destroy everything within eight kilometers of ground zero and most everything out to about twenty. That's my best guess, anyway." Yuri betrayed his irritation at having to keep discussing the weapons.

"Thankfully you built it small." Basam glanced over his shoulder. The brown leather case mirrored the size of a large overweight bag checked at an airport. By tying it down on the rear seat with bungee cords, he kept it from shifting.

"It's small," said Yuri, "but it can go off up to twelve hours after you set the timer. Real simple. However, right now our priority should be to get on a ship and distance ourselves from this area. I will also need a computer."

"No problem. I always keep fifty thousand American dollars in cash. When we buy a laptop, I can transfer more money to an account we can withdraw from if needed. Then the currency will be safe since no one will be able to trace it to me under the false name I created."

"Great, I wish I could get another bottle of vodka," Yuri whined as he pitched the empty out the window "Now why don't you get some sleep, so you can drive when we cross the border? We'll change places before then. You are much better at talking to the guards than I."

Basam glanced at Yuri and nodded his approval. Yuri's blond hair, worn long in the back, topped a pudgy round face with striking blue eyes. He carried too much weight, compared with Basam's underweight physique. Basam surely assigned Yuri's condition to his use of vodka and cigarettes. Basam again snuck a sideways glimpse at Yuri Marchanovich Borisov, the thirty-nine-year-old Moscow-born Russian nuclear scientist with whom Basam had spent twenty-four hours a day over the past three weeks. He curled up, pulled his feet up, rested his head on the top of the seat, and went to sleep.

They crossed the border separating Saudi Arabia from Yemen, and then put hundreds of kilometers of open desert behind them. They arrived in the port city of Aden, on the Gulf of Aden near the entrance to the Red Sea. Yuri again drove and he observed many ships were at anchor in the harbor. At a slow speed, he steered past shops, looking into the windows, where he noticed the latest gadgets in telecommunication and electronics displayed, but otherwise everything else looked old. He guessed not much had changed since their first Independence Day following the collapse of the Ottoman Empire in 1918. This place was an outhouse of civilization.

Yuri stopped at a computer and electronics store near the harbor and bought a new Sony Vaio. He purchased the latest satellite card so he could have Internet access from just about anywhere in the world. He wouldn't need cables or telephone lines.

"We now have a way of finding out what the international news and reporting is on the events in Ras Tanura. But first, Basam, let's find a ship to get us out of here."

"There." Basam pointed. "I see a shipping office down the street."

Yuri parked the Land Rover in a spot about fifty feet from the entrance with a sign that read Transoceanic Shipping Company, LTD. The whitewashed building, with gray doors and shutters in desperate need of paint, appeared deserted, but they decided to check it out anyway.

They entered what they took to be a ticket agency. The interior gloom contrasted markedly with the glaring sunlight outside. A ceiling fan rotated at glacial speed, creating a barely perceptible movement of air. A few pictures of cargo vessels adorned the otherwise vacant walls. Both dirty windows on the front of the office were propped open in a futile attempt to allow a nonexistent breeze to circulate.

A diminutive man with combed-over hair inadequately covering his balding head sat behind the only piece of furniture in the room. He conversed with a tall man wearing a crisp white navy-type uniform. The small man supplemented the air movement by fanning himself with a Chinese paper fan. The naval man, standing at the parade rest position in his military dress, stood with his back to them as they entered. His shoulder epaulets showed four gold stripes.

Yuri squinted to adjust his eyes and coughed. The man seated at the desk glanced up at him and said, "I'll be with you shortly."

"We want to book passage out of here," Yuri said in English, but his accent caused the uniformed man to glance at him.

"I'm sorry, sir. This is a freight company. We do not carry passengers. There is a passenger office down the street, and the next ferry is due in a couple of days." The seated man turned back to the sailor.

"No. We need to leave sooner," Yuri shouted.

"Sorry," said the man, who didn't look at Yuri, but continued facing the man standing near the desk.

The man with four stripes looked at Yuri and said in Russian, "Where are you from?"

Yuri opened wide his eyes wide on hearing Russian in this godforsaken place and stood still for a few seconds. He moved to where he could face the questioner. He saw a striking man with an athletic body and a round face sporting a short handlebar mustache. Both his hair and the facial hair were blond. The spotless white uniform gleamed, but the feature that caught Yuri's attention was the man's voluminous nose. Yuri answered, "Moscow."

"If you would wait across the street for a few minutes, I will join you," the man said in Russian.

Yuri nodded to Basam and they went outside. Standing beyond the front entrance, Yuri explained what the sailor had said. They strolled over to their car and waited.

Five minutes later, the uniformed man approached and said in good English, "Where do you want to go?"

"Out of here," Yuri replied.

"Are you criminals running from the law?"

"No. We want to get away from here and are willing to pay."

"Perhaps I can help. I'm the captain of the container ship you see in the harbor. We are sailing in six hours to Cape Town, and then on to the United States. Can you arrange to have fifty thousand US dollars transferred to my account before that time? Then you can get passage on my ship."

"Twenty-five thousand, and no more negotiations. And no questions all the way to America," Basam said.

The captain cranked his head back and rolled his eyes. Starting to walk away, he said over his shoulder, "Okay." He returned to where they stood, took a piece of paper from his pocket, wrote down his account information and gave it to Basam.

"I'm Captain Grigori Orloff. Be at that embarkation point, over by that kiosk, at seventeen hundred hours." They could see the small building and nodded their understanding. "That is the last shuttle boat before we sail. When you get on board, one of my seamen will escort you to your cabins. I'll check to make sure the money is deposited before you show up." He marched away.

"Well, Basam, we now have a way to get the atomic weapon to a safe hiding place where no one is looking for it, or for us," Yuri said as a smile spread over his face, including his eyes.

Basam beamed. "No, my friend. Now we have a way to get the bomb to where we can use it."

3

EIGHT DAYS BEFORE THE PRESIDENTIAL FLIGHT TO ATLANTA

DALLAS, TEXAS

MATT HIGGINS AND BRIDGET DONAVAN SERVED AS THE PRESIDENT'S personal covert operations team, tasked by the president with handling certain types of emergencies as needed. They now concentrated on the first job for the new company they had created for a cover. After landing at Dallas International, they took a taxi to the manufacturing plant of Solar Tech Industries, situated in an area outside Grapevine, Texas.

"Isn't it super that we're finally able to start legitimate operations to make money for us and our covert careers?" Bridget said.

She glanced over at Matt for a response. His lanky six-foot-one-inch frame clearly didn't fit well in his suit, but then, on his salary, there weren't likely to be any pinstriped Giorgio Armani pinstriped suits in his closet. Things might change if they could get a few more contracts.

At the same time, Matt glimpsed at his image in a car's window. He viewed his dark suntanned face, the result of the last mission to the Middle East, and then ran his fingers through his thick black hair.

"Review for me exactly how we got this contract, as I'm still not sure I understand the family connection," said Matt. He knew the agreement specified conducting a physical security evaluation and recommending to the company steps to ensure no dangerous breach could occur at the plant. He glanced sideways at Bridget, noticing again that she exhibited all the characteristic of a beautiful young woman. She stood about five foot eight inches, with a slim build and ample endowments, and she possessed piercing golden-brown eyes and flaming red hair.

"Ozman Pasha is my father's friend. He left Turkey soon after what the government called 'bandits' killed his Armenian grandparents. My father gave him a job to get started. He and my father have been friends for as long as I can remember."

"But how did he get into this solar business?"

"He's the financial backer for a group of developers in the solar energy field. If this project succeeds, it will mean millions of dollars in profits. He wants to make sure the plant is secure from any physical intrusion. You know, to prevent industrial espionage. They moved into this location this week, and Dad says the place still looks like a warehouse."

Matt observed the scenery as the Texas countryside whizzed by. He asked, "What do they make?"

"I'm not sure, but when I called Mr. Pasha, he said he'll take us on a tour of the facility as soon as we get there. He warned me that it isn't operational and they're just starting to convert the old warehouse into a production plant for making solar panels for industrial use."

The taxi pulled up to the address Bridget had given the driver at the airport. Matt paid and got out. They were in the middle of nowhere with no other structure in the vicinity. "We'll find a place to stay and a rental car as soon as we get a handle on how long this will take. I'm sure they'll take us to a motel or hotel."

The one-story oblong brick building possessed no aesthetic value whatsoever. Two large windows decorated the front on each side of a sliding door that extended from the roof to the concrete floor in the center. The larger door contained a smaller portal for people. A man waited for them at the small entrance.

"That's Mr. Pasha," Bridget said. "I recognize him from pictures Dad has. We said we'd be here at two p.m., and we're here on the dot."

They approached Mr. Pasha, a medium-sized man with a full head of white hair, who wore an open-collar white shirt and brown slacks. As they introduced themselves, Matt noticed Pasha's height equaled Bridget's. He also sported a ruddy complexion, thick black-rimmed glasses, and piercing gray eyes.

"I'm glad you could come. Please follow me. I'll give you a cursory tour of the plant, and then I presume you'll want to do your own investigative work."

"That would be precisely what we need," Matt replied. He instantly liked Mr. Pasha, sensing the man's intelligence from his appearance and no-nonsense manner.

As they entered the building, they heard two more cars arrive. As they continued into the structure, Matt assumed the new arrivals were some of the workers at the plant returning after lunch.

The structure did resemble a warehouse and reminded Matt of a federal records center. On each side of the main aisle, stacks of old desks and boxes were piled one on top of another. The main passageway led straight to a glass wall at the rear.

"We have positioned the laboratory for the solar tech items behind the glass panels," Mr. Pasha said.

Matt noticed how a small space appeared to exist next to the walls on each side of the building, probably only wide enough to walk through. Mr. Pasha stopped in the middle of the aisle, halfway to the glass divider.

"I'm sorry. I remember you were in a taxi for most of an hour to get here. Would you like to freshen up? The restroom is near the front door."

"I'm fine," Matt said.

"I'll take you up on it," Bridget said. She headed back to the restroom and disappeared into it. Matt started to ask Mr. Pasha the details about the land surrounding the building when they heard what sounded like gunfire outside.

He swung back toward the main entrance and saw a rifle barrel protrude through the front door. Without hesitation, he grabbed Mr. Pasha and pushed him under one of the desks on the side of the aisle, and then he fell flat on the floor and rolled under another desk.

Glass shattered as bullets hit the laboratory windows. Matt recognized the weapons as automatics from their rate of fire. The intruders fired wildly as they ran down the aisle. From the sounds of the pounding feet, he estimated maybe four men. Then he saw four pairs of legs running toward the laboratory. Damn. He had no weapon. Nothing.

His hand swung around under the desk. Something. Spiders. God, he hated spiders. He forced himself to continue searching, flipping his hand over and over to avoid having a spider get on it. Then something. It felt like a round metal paperweight. Not exactly something with which to engage four armed men. He now racked the inner reaches of his mind to figure out how to protect this location. He needed to start protecting it or in the future no one would give them any new business. But to do that he needed to immediately protect himself and get this situation under control.

As the last man ran past, Matt swung his foot out. The man tripped and went down. The others fired their rifles at the laboratory, failing to notice him. Matt rolled out from under the desk, one hand slamming the paperweight into the man's head and the other grabbing for his weapon, an M-16 rifle.

He aimed at the back of one of the men running down the aisle and fired a three-round burst. He went down. Matt had inhaled rapidly before shooting and this caused him some difficulty in aiming on his second target with accuracy. He fired and missed. *Slow down*, he chided himself, *take aim, and squeeze the trigger*.

The two remaining attackers whipped around. They swiveled their weapons toward him and fired, but turned back and continued running. One of their bullets sliced through the outer side of his right upper arm. Damn, it burned. He took a little air into his lungs, then released half of his breath and took aim. He squeezed the trigger this time, like he had been taught in basic training, and saw another man fall. These couldn't be professional soldiers, or even well trained attackers—perhaps fanatics. He hoped not terrorists. His hatred for those types exceeded that for spiders, and he couldn't fathom why they would be attacking a solar energy manufacturing plant in the middle of Texas. It made no sense.

The last man ran around the end of the stacked desks, trying to make his way along the narrow space next to the wall to get back to the exit. Matt sprinted toward the glass lab, taking out a handkerchief from his rear pocket and pressing it on his wound. Blood soaked the right sleeve of his shirt. He stopped at the corner to be sure he wouldn't pass the wall and be in the man's rifle sight. He eased around. No shots came at him. As he moved along the wall, Matt heard the man's footsteps and realized he needed to stop him before he reached the exit. He wanted to question him. Matt moved back to the main aisle, aiming the rifle at the door to nail him when he tried to leave.

The man now moved along the back wall, attempting to gain the exit. The door to the restroom opened right in front of him. He slammed into it. The rifle fell and slid sideways on the floor. The man moved backwards as he staggered, endeavoring to keep his balance.

Bridget stepped out of the restroom, the stunned attacker tried to swing at her with his right fist. She rolled into him, grabbed his arm, and started to throw him over her shoulder, using his momentum against him. He went halfway over her upper back, and with great effort he rolled off. As his feet came to ground, he pulled a blade from his belt with his left hand. A Ka-Bar knife with a six-inch blade swung at Bridget, but the attacker remained off balance. She ducked beneath the swish of the weapon as it passed over her head, coming up under his arm and twisting it back behind him while he tried not to fall forward. She ripped the knife out of his hand, rotated it around to have the blade facing out, and with all her strength plunged it into his neck. Then she twisted it. Blood shot out and covered her hand and arm. She pushed the dead man away. The corpse fell to the floor. Bridget went over and picked up his rifle.

Not the first time this counterterrorist and hand-to-hand combat specialist had killed. Just a month ago in the Saudi Arabian desert, she had witnessed a man approach the prone body of Matt and start to raise a pistol to fire into his supine torso. Bridget had leaped forward to land in a firing position with the M-4 rifle, taken careful aim at the terrorist's head, assuming he might be wearing body armor, and fired. That act had saved Matt's life.

"Matt, I took one out. Are you okay?" she shouted.

"Yes. I'll rescue Mr. Pasha. He's in the center aisle under a desk."

They both approached the supine form of the man Matt had knocked out with the paperweight.

"Who the hell is he? Why attack this place?" Matt asked.

The man on the floor attempted to sit up but fell back. He tried to talk, but only mumbled, "You will pay for this, you and your president. Soon Yuri will see to it."

Matt reached down and grabbed him by his shirt collar. He appeared to be a Middle Eastern youth, dark skin, black hair, and hatred spitting from his mouth. "Yuri who?"

"Yuri the bomb maker. He will get you and your family."

"Who are you?" Matt shook the young man.

"You and your family will pay for this," he repeated.

"When will it happen, and where is this Yuri?"

The youth laughed and rolled onto his side away from them, trying to rise. Bridget's eyes caught the glimmer from the knife whipping out. She raised the butt of the rifle taken from the man she had killed and slammed it into the man's skull. The thud echoed in the building as the rifle butt drove into his brains.

"A little mad, are you?" Matt asked looking into her eyes. "We need to check if there were any more outside."

Bridget followed. "You bet your ass I'm pissed. Those bastards were here to kill everybody." They both held weapons now, and Mr. Pasha followed them to the front door.

"Who were those people?" Pasha asked. "What were they after?"

Bridget examined the man as he was definitely on the verge of shock from the recent events. She grabbed him under the arm to support him as they headed to the exit. The old man was trembling to where she could feel it.

"Where in the hell are all the employees?" said Bridget. "More important, why attack a non-operational solar factory with weapons? Matt, these guys are terrorists. You heard Yuri's name...you know what that means."

Matt looked up at the clear Texas sky. He knew what that meant, but he said, "He talked about my family. How in hell did he know me? What's going on?" He remembered what the president had told them earlier about a Russian named Yuri who had escaped from Saudi and somehow seemed directly linked to the atomic bombs Matt and his team had intercepted at Ras Tanura weeks ago. If Yuri surfaced with an atomic weapon, or some other weapon of mass destruction, there could be hell to pay.

"I don't know," responded Bridget.

"We need to talk to Mr. Pasha, and afterwards I'll call the president," Matt said.

They went back inside. Adrenaline ran high. They stopped and faced each other, giving half smiles as they began to relax, releasing the tension from their necks and shoulders. What had just happened? The fast-paced event had lasted less than two minutes. Both showed some slight shaking in their hands. Matt took her hand. "Damn, I'm glad we're still human. You still want to do this?" Matt asked.

"Oh, yes. We're in this now. Something is going on and we need to figure it out. That threat wasn't an idle boast, was it?"

"No, I don't think so. I think some of the ones who got away in Saudi Arabia may be in on this."

In the building, they searched for IDs on the dead men. Found nothing, and went to Mr. Pasha, who remained standing at the front door.

"Where are your employees?" asked Bridget.

"We're lucky. They all went to Dallas to do a supply run, and I thought they would be here before you arrived. Something must have delayed them. They don't know how fortunate they are."

"Okay. Okay." Matt said. "Why would terrorists want to attack this little plant? Four men are dead, and we need to find out the reason. A real good motive. What is it?"

"They probably came to stop the development of our new solar technology," Mr. Pasha said. He looked around obviously still stunned by the violence of the last few minutes. He seemed to be regaining his composure after seeing the dead bodies in his plant.

"Why?" Bridget asked.

"Because if we succeed, and we are nearly there, we could replace over sixty percent of all imports of oil."

"But solar doesn't work everywhere," Matt said.

"That's a popular misconception, fostered by the early efforts to harness the sun's power and further promulgated by the oil companies." Mr. Pasha unconsciously slipped into the professorial role in which he appeared to be comfortable.

"Today, with the technology we are developing here with new wafer and printing grid embedment, the efficiency will be high. Even in areas that have only forty percent sunshine, ninety-five- percent efficiency will be achieved. Our new design for our photovoltaic systems will need only light, not necessarily direct sunlight, or even sunlight at all to achieve maximum results."

"That's big," Bridget said.

"Yes it is. Provided we achieve our goal, the dependency on Middle East oil will be a thing of the past," said Mr. Pasha. "A field two hundred by two hundred miles could deliver all the power needed in the United States until the end of time."

"Now that would provide excellent homeland security! That would be a super thing," said Matt. "The cash flow to the Middle East would dry up, their influence would dissipate, and there would be nothing to fund terrorism. I believe that if there's no money, there will be little interest in jihad. Maybe they were here to stop this advancement in technology?"

"Yes. I don't see any other reason for such an attack. I want to thank you for what you did. I must call the police now," said Pasha.

"I see a higher hand in this. Don't contact the cops until I talk to Washington. Bridget, can you take care of finishing our security contract here?" asked Matt.

"Sure."

"I'll make the call to get the bodies out of here now that we know they're most likely terrorists. Maybe they can identify these guys. We'll take care of this, Mr. Pasha. Bridget, you take Mr. Pasha inside, and make sure no one enters until the military gets here."

"Matt, come in here and let me treat your wound. I want to make sure we stopped the bleeding. You've got blood all over your shirt." Bridget took him by the undamaged arm and led him to a chair.

"You need a new blouse," Matt said seeing the effect of her knife work on her top.

A few minutes later, after Bridget bandaged his wound, Matt went outside and made two phone calls on his cell. The first concerned taking care of cleaning up this facility to learn as much as they could from the attack. The second went to the President.

"Hello," came the tired Virginia drawl of the President.

"Mr. President, Matt Higgins here. We have a problem, which concerns our Russian friend. I need to brief you as soon as possible."

4

EIGHT DAYS AGO — WASHINGTON, D.C

Matt deplaned from the Air Force aircraft the president had sent to retrieve him from Dallas. A medical technician accompanied the flight and attended to Matt's wound. He arrived at the White House five hours after the confrontation in Texas.

Bridget called him on the ride in from Andrews Joint Base in Maryland. She informed him that all had gone well at Solar Tech Industries. "The military cleaned up all traces of the gunfight. They fingerprinted the bodies and ID'd three. They were on student visas at a nearby college. Two came from Yemen, one from Iran. The fourth is unknown but presumed to be an white American male." She went on to say that she thought the soldiers seemed overeager and on edge about something, but they didn't say what. She thought something else must be happening.

On his arrival at the White House, a Secret Service agent led Matt to the Situation Room. On entering, Matt saw the president in a huddle of people, looking at a map of the United States.

The president said, "Hello, Matt. Come in and give us an account of what happened in Texas. I believe you know Secretary of Defense James Carter, and Secretary of Homeland Security, Eduardo Sanchez, also Admiral Kidd from the NSA, and General Mary Jean Bergermeyer from the Defense Intelligence Agency. And this is the deputy director of the FBI, Mike Anthony. My friend Dick Avery, the national security adviser, is on another mission for me."

Matt shook hands with each. "There's not much to relate about the events that transpired in Texas a few hours ago."

"Go ahead," the president said. "I want you to know that Matt and his partner Bridget have done some exclusive work for me in the past. Now tell us what happened, as I believe it relates to why we're here."

Matt took five minutes to describe in detail what had occurred. He failed to mention his shoulder wound, hidden by his blue blazer.

"Thank you for that detailed account. We can see the resolve and determination we're up against," President Brennan said, "I believe we have to bring you up to date on other, obviously related, events. You were not the only one to experience a terrorist attack today. In Oakland, an army arsenal was destroyed, in Annapolis, a navy supply building was demolished by a bomb with two dead. And at the Training Center in Norfolk, Virginia a sniper shot two seamen."

The president walked to the other side of the map and pointed to the tip of Florida. "A few minutes ago, we received word that the U.S. Coast Guard station in Miami was partly destroyed by an explosion. Seems they filled a motorboat with explosives and rammed it into a Coast Guard cutter. Still waiting to hear on any casualties."

At the president's suggestion, they all moved to take seats around the conference table. The secretary of Homeland Security, a middle-aged Hispanic man wearing gold-rimmed glassed that contrasted with his thick black hair, spoke.

"I see this as a major threat—a deliberate and coordinated terrorist attack on our country. Multiple targets, synchronized timing of the attacks. I believe this warrants a major increase to the threat level against America."

"I'm inclined to agree," the president said.

Admiral Kidd, director of the National Security Agency, wearing a gray pinstriped suit that fit him with the same smartness as his admiral's uniform, gestured with his hand. "We've noticed an increase in the encrypted traffic in the last week. Something was brewing, but we weren't able to pinpoint it. Now we can go back and see if we can crack their codes and possibly use them to our advantage in the future. The increase continued up to the time I came here. I think it's possible that they're planning more attacks."

Then the president got up and addressed the entire group. "These attacks today may be an opening volley in a new front against us. Every federal agency is to go on the highest alert and follow any lead to chase down these terrorists on our soil. As far as I'm concerned, extreme force is authorized. It's time the gloves come off."

With bags under his eyes, the president yawned and pushed his fingers through his wiry gray hair. He continued in his Virginian accent, "Y'all are going to be busy in the normal channels to do this. That's why I'm giving Matt a presidential assignment to get this Yuri fellow. If he calls for help, I want it rendered without delay. Any questions?"

The president went over and stood behind Matt. He put his hand on his shoulder.

"Most of you know what Matt did to stop the terrorists in Saudi Arabia a couple of weeks ago," the president said, "and I want him to follow up on all leads concerning this Yuri. We know he's the maker of the atomic weapons used over there and is therefore extremely dangerous. We have no information on any existing weapons and I hope he doesn't have one now. We don't think he does, but at present I'm not so sure. Matt has the experience dealing with this cell of terrorists. I want him to go after this guy, wherever he is." Brennan patted Matt on the shoulder. "Stop him, Matt."

"Mr. President, is the national alert level to be red?" asked the SecDef.

"Eduardo, what's homeland's recommendation?" the president said.

"I think we can keep the current orange and not increase it. The public tires of the vicissitudes shown by these changes without ever seeing any results, even though they don't realize that we've thwarted many terrorist attempts. We face what's known as the fallacy of being right. We're right to raise the alert because we get good intel that something is going to happen, and then we interdict or terminate the fanatics and consequently nothing happens. We were right, but all they see is that nothing happened after the security level was heightened—so we were wrong—a cry of wolf with nothing to back it up."

The deputy director of the FBI, a strikingly handsome man in his early forties, sitting in for the ailing director, asked, "Aren't we being too careful here? The public will know from the media there are terrorists actively hitting us on our soil, and the threat is real. No longer is it imaginary. They soon forgot 9/11, but these attacks today will cause panic in some people. To raise the alert level would seem prudent to show the public we are reacting in some manner and to keep people on alert for suspicious activity."

"I agree," the SecDef said.

Matt watched the president point to the secretary of Homeland Security with his finger in a gesture of "make it happen."

"I want everyone to put maximum effort into learning why these events took place today and who's responsible for them," concluded the president. As he passed Matt on the way out he placed his hand on Matt's elbow, signaling for him to follow.

In a small room off the main conference room, the president gestured for Matt to enter. He waved at General Bergermeyer, the head of the DIA covert operations directorate and Admiral Kidd the director of the NSA, to join him. The light blue walls held photos of scenes around the District of Columbia: the Washington Monument, the Jefferson Memorial, and tombstone of the Unknown Soldier in Arlington National Cemetery. In the center of the room stood a round wood table surrounded by six chairs.

"I noticed you didn't mention that someone wounded you today," President Brennan said.

"It's nothing serious."

General Mary Jean Bergermeyer, United States Army, in her uniform, looked like a model instead of a general with her beautiful red hair and slim-toned body. She gazed with obvious anxiety at Matt. "Were you hit?"

"A little scratch," he said, pointing to his right shoulder.

"I didn't know you Army types had so much modesty," said Admiral Kidd with a smile. Matt gave the admiral a half grin and glanced momentarily at the floor.

"Just wanted to see y'all for a few minutes. I don't know if this Yuri fellow is anywhere in our country or, for that matter, where he is. He did, however, set off an atomic weapon once before. I have to assume he might have another one. I know assumptions are bad, but I sure as hell hope he doesn't. Matt has dealt with that particular cell of terrorists before. So . . .," The president scratched his head and roughed up his hair. He continued in a slower cadence, "That's why I want you going after that man. The whole government is now going to focus on what has happened today, trying to make sense of these attacks, and what might happen in the near future. I want you to concentrate on that one man."

"Mr. President," Matt said, "last month that bastard killed a member of my team, plus the men in the helicopter. I lost a good man to that cell of terrorists. You bet I want him, and I'll do everything and go anywhere to get him."

The president answered, "I understand your motivation and your drive to pay them back for what happened to you on 9/11. I know it's personal, but I have seen you perform and I'm not worried about emotions getting in your way. Mary Jean, you take care of the paperwork for the contract for Matt to do this."

"I'll get on my people to see if we can use the notebook computer Matt found during that operation in Saudi to try to trace this Yuri," Admiral Kidd said.

"Good." The president started toward the door.

"Matt, I'll come to visit you tomorrow to get a full debriefing," General Bergermeyer said, "but now you need to get some rest. Take care of that wound."

"Okay," the president said, stopping at the doorway, "you three, plus Bridget, make up my special operations team. Let's find this Yuri. I'll keep a fire under everyone else to get those who attacked us today and to try to find out how they did it in such a coordinated manner. Let's get to work."

Mary Jean Bergermeyer stopped the president before everyone started to walk out. "Mr. President, I wonder if there's more to it. All the targets were military, except where Matt and Bridget were. That strikes me as strange. I think I'll take a closer look at that."

"Do it," said the president.

5

NEXT MORNING — LEESBURG, VIRGINIA

"Where in the hell do these files go?" Julia Morrison asked putting her hands on her hips. She and Matt stood in the new office space of the company Matt and Bridget formed.

"Up yours, squawk," responded Gandalf, a foul-mouthed seven-year-old scarlet macaw parrot.

"Stop that," Julia ordered.

Bridget's cat sat close to where Gandalf perched, staring at the bird.

"Stop fucking cat, squawk, squawk." With its partly clipped wings, the bird could fly just enough to get away from the cat, but he had to move fast. A week ago, Julia had called Bridget's cat, Rambo, "a fucking cat." The bird had heard her.

"I never had it this bad when I was a 'working girl.'" Julia put air quotes on the last words. "Whatever possessed me to get that bird?" she asked herself out loud. She always projected an award-winning smile on her rather striking face, and dressed to accentuate her buxomness with an open-collar blue shirt unbuttoned too far down, with the sleeves rolled up, and jeans. Her top, soaked with sweat from bending and lifting to put the few files from two boxes into a filing cabinet, clung to her contours. As she bent over the white roots betrayed her brown hair. In reality, there were few folders since the office was only getting started, but Julia, a tad bit out of shape, huffed and puffed. No, correct that, Matt thought, she was way out of shape.

Matt smiled and chugged his Diet Coke. His eyes scanned the new space. Not exactly plush. The desks were all IKEA products, with computer chairs from Staples. Their location occupied the second floor of a small complex with a single glass entry door that opened outward. The walls waited for the hanging of the pictures stacked on the floor beneath the projected points of display. On each desk sat the most expensive items in the office, twenty-four-inch Apple iMac computers. There were no cables as the wireless Apple Airport system connected them all together and to the laser printer at the back of the office, next to the filing cabinet, the focus of Julia's attention.

Matt believed that Julia's question had been rhetorical, but he responded, "You never had it so good as a working girl, did you?"

"Listen here, young man. I worked as what some might call a lady of the evening, many years ago in Fayetteville. You know, the home of the 82nd Airborne Division. Me, I got lucky, met me a man and we were happily married for many years before he died in Afghanistan. I've been straight for years. So, you watch your mouth, now, you hear?"

"No offense meant. My wife's sister recommended you to be our secretary. You seem to have become fast friends after you moved in near her. She probably knows all about you and besides I trust her judgment, since she keeps my daughter. Besides, I hear you get along with my Laura."

"Your daughter looks just like your wife. I've seen her picture. That child adores you. It must have been hard for you after her mother perished on 9/11."

Matt stepped away from her since he didn't want to go there. Why had she said that? The memory was not as intense now, but it was still part of him.

In 2001, Lieutenant Matt Higgins and his wife, Susan, had traveled to Washington on vacation. It was to be the first real vacation they had taken in two years. Alone and with no one to interrupt them, they intended to spend the week in the nation's capital to see all the sights. Matt took Susan to the Pentagon to see his old Professor of Military Science, Colonel John Forsman. After a short visit to his office, the colonel had offered to take Matt to see some of the classified areas that concerned Army matters. He'd suggested that the petite, blond-haired Susan would find it boring to listen to all the military jargon and topics, and she might like to view the artwork in the outer ring of the Pentagon instead of going with them. They would join her in about fifteen minutes. Matt gave Susan a hug and a light kiss, and she departed.

Susan strolled the halls of the outer ring, viewing the military artwork that depicted various scenes from the far-flung battlefields the American soldier had fought and died on. She sauntered through the halls on the east part of the outer ring of the Pentagon when her cell phone rang. She saw the call came from Matt.

"Hi, hon, sorry we ran over on time. The colonel is showing me some interesting places. Could you meet me at the east exit, say at nine forty-five? We'll be there in a few minutes, and then we can go on over to the Smithsonian."

"Don't worry, I'll meander over to the exit now. I'll be there by the time you are," Susan said. She started walking toward the exit to meet him. It was 9:42 in the morning.

At that moment, American Airlines flight 77, a Boeing 757, smashed into the Pentagon less than twenty feet from where she stood. Susan died instantly in the catastrophic explosion that engulfed the corridor on the outer ring of the building on September 11, 2001.

Matt walked with Colonel Forsman as they made their way through the long corridors toward the east exit. They were two corridors away when the explosion shook the building. Matt broke into a run toward the exit where Susan had planned to meet him. He reached the end of the corridor, turned to his right into the outer ring of the Pentagon, and continued to plow ahead. The horrific scene filled his vision. There he took in all the devastation, smoke, debris, and smell of jet fuel, as well as the roar of the inferno of the flames and the blistering heat.

For a seemingly endless time, but in reality only a few seconds, Matt was dazed, his senses numbed, unable to think or move. He needed to find Susan. At last, getting hold of himself, he ran forward, looking for her, calling her name, and stumbling as far into the devastation as he could. There was no sign of her. He continued his desperate search, but the needs of others were overwhelming, many requiring immediate help. He led some burn victims to the Emergency Medical Aid station. The Pentagon medical unit had set it up in record time. Then he returned to the area to guide other injured men and women, both civilian and military, to the aid station.

Daylight had all but disappeared in the western sky when Matt went back to the hotel room where he and Susan had spent the previous night. The realization that he would never see her again overwhelmed him as he opened the door of their room. He sat on the bed, trying to control his misery and his anger. His head dropped, and he lay facedown. Despite the soft elevator music floating through the room from a preprogrammed station, Matt's head heard over and over the explosive, horrific crash of the 757 as it thundered into the Pentagon.

The sound ricocheted endlessly through his entire being, decimating all feeling. If only he had not delayed. If only he had met with her a few minutes earlier. Maybe. How could he tell their daughter, Laura? She was staying with her aunt so he and Susan could take a vacation alone. No answer came. Hatred for the terrorists built inside his soul. How could God allow this to happen to him? The full impact of his loss finally hit him as he released some of the self-control that sustained him all day. He started sobbing uncontrollably.

BRIDGET PUSHED OPEN THE FRONT DOOR OF THE OFFICE, A BUZZER announcing her entry. "Good morning, all. You too, Gandalf."

That jolted Matt back to the here and now. He nodded to Bridget, and Julia gave her a bright smile. Bridget wore a pair of cutoff jeans and a light yellow T-shirt sporting a stenciled slogan on the back: "If you can read this, the bastard fell off." Her bright red hair, pulled back and twisted into a bun, allowed the clean beauty of her skin to glow in the light. Matt noticed, not for the first time, that she displayed a sensual attractiveness. They'd worked together on their last operation in the Army, but that had entailed military duty, and personal feelings had remained out of his mind. They'd had a mission—they'd focused only on that. Now, he wasn't sure how, but somehow, something had changed.

Julia said, "Hey, guys, time for a break. I've been at this too long, and besides, I'm almost finished setting up the files. Matt, you want another Coke?" she said, trying to get him to focus on her instead of Bridget.

"Oh . . . yeah."

"Bridget, you?" Julia asked as she headed for the small refrigerator they had installed against the back wall behind a small screen. It kept the area from direct view of anyone coming into the office. It also hid the coffeemaker and assorted paraphernalia. Bridget nodded.

"Here you guys are," Julia said. She handed each a Diet Coke. "Since I've only been here for two days, could you take time to indulge me and take the time to tell me how you started this business, or will you have to kill me if you do?"

"We would have to," Bridget said with a smile.

She then related the story of how, at the end of their last assignment, they went to meet the president. They had been granted this meeting as a result of their actions in preventing a disastrous detonation of an atomic bomb in a Saudi Arabian city. She didn't mention the one that detonated, as that event remained highly classified. They had thought all the terrorists had died, but at the White House the president told them at least one, a Russian named Yuri, had escaped. He might also have a surviving partner from the terrorist cell.

The president relieved them of their military duties and directed them to set up a company that dealt in security operations. He wanted them to be at his personal beck and call for assignments.

Matt added that he remembered the president saying, "You will resign as officers, be removed from all active duty lists, and will appear as if you are no longer in the service." He'd also informed them their pay and privileges would continue to accrue, and any promotions would be on time. They would only report to the two officers then in the room, or to him. The offer would be valid as long as Brennan remained president, and it might carry over to his successor depending on the new president's wishes.

Bridget looked at Matt for him to continue the story. Matt took a big gulp from his diet coke, waited, and took another one before he decided to continue.

"Get set up," the president had said, "and perform as any other private organization." He went on to tell them to do business as that entity unless they received a contract from one of them to carry out a mission. Then they'd have all the government's equipment, technology, and communications required for the new venture at their disposal. For Matt and Bridget this offer provided the best of both worlds—they continued to serve their country while engaging in their specialty fields as private citizens. Bridget had promised to work until the end of her enlistment, as she wanted to attend college to get an archeology degree.

Matt finished giving Julia this short, sanitized version of the events leading to their setting up the office. He told her the NSA had conducted a security check on her but performed no detailed background investigation, and that she had received an interim secret security clearance. Matt and Bridget had organized and incorporated their company in the state of Virginia using the name SPAT, Inc. that they'd devised from Security, Protection, and Training. Their new organization assessed physical security for companies as well as selling and installing electronic security measures.

"So we do super-secret tasks for the president?" Julia surmised. "I thought your sister-in-law told me you guys didn't do anything like that."

"This is serious, Matt said. "Never tell anyone, or even let anyone guess that."

"You got it," Julia said. "At least we're up and running, and I'm glad to be here. Mums the word."

"Not only have we had our first contract, but we just got our first paycheck from our visit to Texas," Matt replied.

"You mean I might get paid," Julia said. She went over and resumed her work, plopping another file into the cabinet. She picked up the empty cardboard box from the floor and went out the back steps down to the trash dumpster.

"Bridget, something's bothering me. Mary Jean hinted at it too. Why did those guys hit that plant at the exact time we were there when every other assault was against a military target? They knew we were there. I think there's something rotten somewhere."

"What are you saying?" Bridget queried.

"There has to be a specific reason we were there when the attack occurred. Let's say for a moment the plant was not the objective, as we've been thinking." Matt stopped for a second as he thought through the events.

"Do you suppose we were the targets?" Bridget said.

6

CONTAINER SHIP — YEMEN ISLAMIC REPUBLIC

Yuri grabbed Basam by the arm, moving him along to make sure they arrived on time at the pier. They needed to catch the last shuttle to the container ship. He assured Basam that he had already transferred the money the captain had demanded for their passage using his newly acquired computer. It required only a few keystrokes once he'd accessed his ten-million-dollar account. That was sum he'd received for the weapons he'd assembled for Basam's brother.

As they approached to the rear of the vessel in the shuttle boat, Yuri saw the Panamanian flag. The letters on the back of the ship displayed in barely readable white faded white letters the name *Sea Pearl* and its port of registry, Panama City. Yuri stared in amazement at the size of the vessel. The closer they came, the more immense the ship appeared. The shuttlecraft came alongside the *Sea Pearl* and they climbed a metal gangplank to the top and alighted onto the deck. A crewmember wearing blue dungarees, a blue open-collar shirt, and tennis shoes with no socks, approached, and in broken English muttered, "Follow me." He sported a clean-shaven face with a full head of dark hair and a ruddy complexion.

"Hey, what's your native language?" Basam asked in English.

"Spanish."

"Where are you from?"

"Colombia." They followed the sailor up one deck. The man pointed to a door, and Basam opened it. Yuri looked in to see a small room that held all the necessary items for a comfortable living area. A double bed, two nightstands with small lamps, a single chair, a TV with a VCR, and a clock radio on the nightstand made up the comforts in the small room. A door led to a small bathroom with a little round porthole for some natural light.

Basam entered and placed the case and his small bag on the bed. The sailor touched Yuri on the shoulder and used his hand to give the "follow me" signal. They went down one deck and arrived at Yuri's cabin. It mirrored Basam's. He tossed his small duffel on the bed and closed the door. He felt at ease for the first time in days. Safe. At least for a little while, then came a knock on the door.

"Hello." Nothing. Yuri opened the door, and a sailor stood there with an outstretched hand that offered him a note. He took it, shut the door, and opened the folded piece of paper. The cursive Cyrillic script contained an invitation to dine with the captain at seven.

Before dinner, Yuri decided to explore the vessel. He walked along the outside walkway and then back to the tower at the rear of the massive vessel, about eight stories above the deck. He didn't know then how big the container ship was or how much cargo it could carry. As he took his unguided tour, he saw the sailor from Colombia and approached him.

"Can you show me the way to the dining area where the captain eats?"

"*Si*, follow me."

They went up two flights above the open deck level and entered an area that, from the obvious cooking aromas filling the air and the way several tables were arranged served as a dining space. The yellow-painted steel walls contained no decorations, but a view of the ocean out of a long oblong Plexiglas window allowed natural light into the space. Yuri thanked his guide and returned to his cabin.

At seven, Yuri joined Captain Grigori Orloff, who sat at a small table in the corner of the dining area—the captain's table. Yuri looked around for Basam but didn't see him.

"Your friend will not be joining us," the captain said as Yuri took a seat. "I invited him but he declined. He agreed to pay a man to deliver his meals. Is he sick or something?"

"No. Not that I know of. I'll speak with him. By the way, this is a big ship." Yuri gestured with his hands, spreading them apart. "I couldn't believe the size. From shore it seemed large, but it's really huge."

"I'll be glad to tell you about my ship, but first let's get our food." The captain nodded to the cook and their meal started to arrive—crispy Greek salad, followed by fresh lamb and potatoes.

The two men ate. After they finished, the captain said, "We have a great chef on board."

"Yes, it is tasty, the best I've had in days," Yuri said. The captain sat back, signaled for coffee, and took out a cigar. He offered one to Yuri, who declined and took out his cigarettes. After clipping the end off the Havana, the captain licked the entire length of the curled tobacco before touching it with the flame of his lighter.

"This ship was built in Korea by Hyundai Heavy Industries in 1995 and bought by the company in 1996. She is what they call a post-Suezmax vessel. That's why we're going around the cape in South Africa since the ship will not transit the Suez Canal. We're too large. With a length of nine hundred sixty-four feet, and forty-four point five feet below the waterline when she's full, it's not possible for us to go through that canal. If you're interested, I'll have Mr. Martinez, my first mate, show you around the ship and give you more technical information. He speaks perfect English."

"I would appreciate that, Captain. Could you have him knock on my door tomorrow morning when he's free? I'll wait for him," Yuri said. "Is it okay if we speak Russian when you and I are together?"

"Of course, Mr. Borisov."

"My name is Yuri," he said.

"Grigori. Tell me, Yuri, where are you going?"

"To America, with you." Yuri laughed at his attempt to be humorous.

"I could see that you were in an awful hurry to get out of Yemen. Did you have a problem there?" The captain raised one eyebrow.

"No. No problem there."

"Good. I'm glad to hear that. I don't want to get a signal from some Yemeni police that you're a fugitive."

"I can assure you that will not happen. Where are you headed with all the containers on deck?"

"We came out of Kuwait, and we're going to the United States. We'll be there in about two weeks if we keep on schedule. First to Savannah, Georgia, for one day, then to Baltimore, Maryland, to deliver the rest of our current cargo. We'll be there for a few days, since we need some minor repairs."

Grigori took a big puff from his cigar, exhaled the blue smoke away from Yuri, and tapped the ashes into his saucer under the coffee cup. "After that, I assume we'll head back across to somewhere in Europe to deliver the goods we'll pick up in the States. I won't get specifics until the repairs are completed. These ships can't sit idle with cargo on board. It'd cost the owners too much. A computer program will determine the most efficient use of this vessel's capacity, and where we'll go for a pickup after our maintenance, and then we'll deliver it wherever they specify. Sorry for going on a bit."

"No, no. Not at all. Grigori, will there be any problem when we get to the United States?" Yuri took a few drags on his cigarette followed by a sip of his coffee.

Before answering, the captain blew a smoke ring, allowing it to drift toward Yuri. "There could be. I can do some talking with the port authority to avert attention from your debarkation . . . ahh, but the price would be high. Add another thirty thousand to my account. Additionally, you have no papers to get out of the port area."

"Fine, but no questions about us, where we were or what we do." Yuri mentally calculated the interest that would accrue on his ten million while they steamed at sea. It would almost cover the thirty thousand.

"For that price, I lose my curiosity and you gain my silence while on board," the captain admitted.

Yuri stubbed out his cigarette, got up and extended his hand to the captain. He would work on solving the paperwork problem later. He walked out of the dining area to visit Basam. When he knocked on his door, he heard, "Come In."

He opened the door and found Basam lying on his bunk, watching a video on the television. From the glimpse Yuri got of the screen before Basam shut it off, a man's hands were fondling two large breasts. Basam got up quickly and looked at his visitor.

"What's going on?"

"Well, I got us a ride all the way to the States," Yuri said and related the conversation with the captain. "I will solve the papers problem before we arrive in Savannah. But you. Why are you staying in here instead of coming to dinner?"

"Yuri, I'm going to deliver this bomb to a target in America. You've gotten us a ride there, and we'll get instructions on what to do. I'll not leave this room and our weapon alone while we're on this ship. I saw how a few of the men looked at the case. I'm sure they want to know what we have, since we were in dirty clothes and everything else was in duffel bags, except for a clean, large size case. I think they assume we're smugglers or something."

"Come on, Basam. You can't live in this room for weeks. And I'm not going to babysit it every minute. Why don't we ask the captain to lock it up for us?"

"No. Absolutely not. He'll look inside it. That would be disastrous. Believe me, they want to know what we have. I'll guard it."

"I think you're being paranoid. We'll be in America in two weeks. You intend to stay in this room all that time?"

"Yes. I have plenty of videos that were in the room, and I have books. You can get me more."

"Basam, you have to get some air, exercise, or something."

"No, I have decided. I'll give you the codes so you can contact the people who sanctioned our operation in Saudi Arabia, and I'm sure they'll have specific instructions for me. We can't wait until we dock to get in touch. I mean it, Yuri. I'll avenge my brother's death. They have to pay for what they did."

"I hear you," Yuri said.

"Yuri, my brother never gave me much background on you, other than you two were together in Moscow at the university. Could you take a few minutes, now that we aren't running for our lives, to tell me about yourself?" asked Basam. He went back and sat on the bed, putting the remote controller on the stand.

"There's not a lot to tell," Yuri went and plopped into the single chair in the room. "I spent my youth at a seminary outside Kiev, preparing for the Orthodox priesthood. In those days, the Soviets made it difficult for my family when I went to the seminary. They were not in favor of any type of religious activity. During my time there, I became rather good in academics. I relished and loved various languages and multiple fields in mathematics. In the end, we lost our farm because of Soviet pressure, and my father died cursing the reds for destroying his livelihood and persecuting our religion."

He did not mention his secret determination to get the farm back with the money he'd received from his construction of the weapons, or his desire to go back to his village as a rich and powerful man. He did tell Basam that he possessed a natural gift for picking up languages, including the old languages used in the Bible. Yuri had become proficient, even to the point of being able to read the ancient koine Greek, Hebrew, and Aramaic without a dictionary. However, his real fascination centered on mathematics, and in that, he'd excelled.

"One morning in July, during the morning prayers at the seminary, I decided the religious life wasn't for me. There should be something more to life, and I wasn't finding it there. So I went back to my little cell, packed up my few meager belongings and walked out, leaving nothing, saying nothing to anyone." He took out a cigarette and lit it.

"What about your family?" Basam queried.

Yuri took out the small flask and chugged a gulp of vodka the captain gave him after dinner, but he did not want to answer that question, and so he picked up the story where he thought best.

"Didn't say a thing to anyone and eventually ended up at the Moscow State University, studying math, physics, and engineering. Before I'd completed my doctorate at the university, the military approached me to work as a nuclear design engineer.

"In those days, the defense departments system took care of the people it needed to maintain its lethal arsenal. I lived in a comfortable apartment in Moscow and received a personal computer as part of the job." He put the cigarette to his mouth, and inhaled.

"Where did you meet my brother?"

"We were taking the same economics class. Somehow we started talking during breaks and became friends." He took a few puffs on his cigarette.

Yuri passed over the fact that he'd loved to play with the encryption and other mathematical software programs that abounded in that arena of this emerging technology. He had mastered how to copy what seemed like vast quantities of information onto the small disks and discovered that he could copy music on this new media, as well as projects he worked on both at home and at work. He enjoyed playing with his computer more than spending time in the company of women. That instrument became his real love in life. The little machine understood languages, mathematics, physics, music, encryption, and any combination of them that he arranged.

"I have never been to Moscow. I wish I could speak Russian as well as my brother did."

"Your English is excellent. Where did you learn it?" Yuri asked.

"My father sent me to study at the London School of Economics. There I learned how interdependent the world's economies are, and how oil is such a major component of that structure. That's what got my brother, Tewfik, going on the idea of destroying its flow to the infidels. We almost got it accomplished. But, please, continue with your story."

"I lived a wonderful life until the demise of funding for the military. Paying jobs dried up for a nuclear scientist. I became unemployed, without income, without any way to leave Russia, and without any personal contacts to help get away or get a job. Your brother came to visit and offered me ten million dollars. He made it tempting. So I took it."

Ten million dollars had tempted him enough that it allayed the moral and the few legal scruples that he'd quickly considered. He'd lived through what the Chechen terrorists did to his country, and the thought of working for a terrorist seemed almost unthinkable—but for that much money he had no choice.

"All right. Enough for tonight. I'll get on the Internet tomorrow and see what they have to tell us. Get some sleep," Yuri said. He left and went to his own quarters. Basam might hole up in his room, but he did not intend to spend his time on the ship in that manner. If Basam wanted to babysit the case, that was his decision, but Yuri wanted to explore the vessel and find out how it operated. Before they got to Savannah, he wanted to know as much as possible about the ship and how it worked—their safety might depend on it.

After he returned to his cabin, he thought about his current situation. He had made millions from building the weapons of mass destruction, but he did not consider himself a terrorist. The devices might change the course of history for some, and perhaps in the beginning he had done it out of fear that Tewfik al-Hanbali would kill him if he didn't construct them. They'd paid him to do a job, and he soon realized these men needed him to be alive to build another WMD. He would never be poor again.

As he lay in his bunk, he imagined that when the weapon went off, if he did it right, the world would blame Russia because of the technology he'd employed to build it. He might even start World War III, but before then, maybe his country would get rid of its new "dictator" and try to be a real democracy. Did that make him a terrorist? No. He did it for money—not for an ideal, a country, or a god.

In the moments before he dozed off to sleep, in the back of his mind, he knew that someday soon, they would have to set off his atomic bomb. When and where currently remained unknown. At the moment, he felt safe for the first time since he'd left Moscow to take on the job of building the weapons. He swore that whatever he ended up doing in the future would make him more money.

Tomorrow he would contact the men who controlled Basam's operation. At present, Yuri relaxed in the comfort and security of his bunk, safe from any pursuers.

7

SEVEN DAYS AGO — LEESBURG, VIRGINIA

MATT AND BRIDGET PREPARED TO GO HOME FOR THE NIGHT. They cleared off their desktops, locked the safe, and made sure they'd secured everything before leaving. Matt walked over to stand in front of Bridget.

"It's been a nerve-racking forty-eight hours, including killing four terrorists, briefing the president, hearing the name Yuri, and receiving a mission to go after that terrorist we thought had been eliminated in Saudi Arabia. If that didn't deserve a drink, what would?"

"You have such a succinct way of putting things. You left out getting shot."

"Right," Matt said. "What do you say we go out for a little celebration libation? We've had an exciting two days and completed our first contract in our new business. Let's go. I'm buying."

"Two seconds while I do a security sweep of the place."

A car pulled into the parking lot. Matt looked out the window and saw a woman get out of the vehicle and she headed for their office. Her red hair became visible in the outside light, and Matt knew it must be Brigadier General Mary Jean Bergermeyer, director of the Center for Organizations and Operations at the Defense Intelligence

Agency. That meant she directed DIA's counterterrorist efforts, oversaw the training of the teams that conducted the operations, and made the tough decisions that no one else even wanted to know about. She'd served as their boss when they were on active duty.

The general walked up the steps and knocked on the locked door, and Matt went to open it. They all exchanged greetings. Matt said, "Okay, General, I'm sure this isn't a social call."

"Actually, you're only half correct. It's a social slash business call. But first, let's discuss the reason for my visit."

Bridget offered, "Ma'am, we're just going out to get a drink to celebrate our first completed contract. Would you care to join us?"

"No, thank you. I'll only take a few minutes of your time."

"Take all the time you need," Matt said. "Remember, we work for you now that the president has put us on Yuri's tail. We don't have a starting point yet. Does NSA or do you have anything on that?"

"On that, no. NSA is working on tracking the Russian, hoping he'll use the Internet or check his email. You have my satellite phone number and I have yours. I'll keep you posted on any intel I get on that topic. Actually, I wanted to discuss the trip to Dallas and the attack at the solar factory. On second thought, would it be all right if I changed my mind about a drink? I'll have one."

"Diet Coke, Diet Cherry Coke, chilled water, or Gatorade? Limited menu," Bridget said.

"Diet Coke, please." Mary Jean went over and sat down at the vacant desk that Julia occupied during normal working day, but they were two hours beyond that now.

"Matt, did you or Bridget talk about your contract to anyone else before going to Texas?"

"I talked to my father in New York," Bridget volunteered.

"General, the only other person on our side who knew when we were going was Julia, our secretary, and we only told her that morning. Anyhow, she's cleared," Matt said.

"Something is bothering me about the whole thing. It wasn't an attack on a military or military-industrial facility like all the others yesterday. In case you don't know, there have been two more attacks today. Limited press on it so far. The resources of the government are stretched thin in the homeland security arena, and the FBI is working overtime on these attacks."

"So what's bothering you?" Bridget asked.

"The president asked about you at a reception the night before you left, and I told him you were going to a solar factory in Dallas the next afternoon. You talked to me that morning, and you'd signed a contract to start your legitimate business as he directed. The president appeared pleased to see you up and running so fast. Two staff members were present when I told him. Now this is where it gets dicey. Neither of them knew you do off-the-books operations that are very closely held. Maybe it's nothing, but my gut tells me that one of them told someone else. I don't know why, and I may be tilting at windmills."

"Why would they say anything if they didn't know we were a private team for the president?" Bridget asked.

"I don't know. Sometimes politicians talk to hear their own voices or to show off. It strikes me as more than a coincidence that you two were at that location at the exact time the terrorists hit."

"Funny, Matt speculated that perhaps the plant wasn't the target, but we were," Bridget said.

"For your information, I think I'll follow up on this," Mary Jean said, getting up from the desk with the Coke in her hand. "I've taken enough of your time. I do have one little favor to ask. My niece is coming to stay with me for the weekend to let my brother and his wife get away for some private time. She's a seven-year-old bundle of energy. I remember your daughter is about that same age. I wonder if your little girl might be free to come over to my place and keep her company. I'll admit my motherly instincts are not my forte, and I thought that two girls ... well, maybe they could entertain themselves."

"No problem. I think that's doable," Matt said.

"Good. I can pick her up here tomorrow after work?"

"Okay, I'll have our secretary pick her up and she'll be here at six."

After the general left, Matt said, "Well, how about that drink? Now we have another thing to talk about."

"We need to celebrate a little," Bridget said as she grabbed her windbreaker and headed for the door. "We done good, if I do say so myself, so let's go."

MARY JEAN LEFT THE OFFICE OF SPAT, INC. AND DROVE TO THE GIO restaurant in Georgetown. She discovered from a casual conversation with a secretary in the White House that one of the two men who had heard her give the president Matt and Bridget's Dallas itinerary, often dined there. She didn't know exactly what to expect, but it resembled what she called "playing a hunch." She started with Avery for no particular reason, because she knew where that man would be tonight. She would have to check on Gary Fazio as well. Her people could do this, but sometimes the boss needed to get her hands wet.

Mary Jean believed that someone had talked, leaking information willingly or unwillingly running his or her mouth off. She suspected a leak had motivated the attack in Dallas, but no concrete evidence existed. If a disclosure had occurred, it must be one of the two men who'd heard her tell the president, as no one else besides her knew about their mission.

Otherwise, the events in Dallas were simply a pure coincidence. Mary Jean believed in some coincidences—one in every three hundred million, just not in this case. She remembered not wanting to say anything at the time, but President Brennan had asked her about Matt and how he was doing. She gave him a brief update in front of Gary Fazio, the press secretary, and Dean Avery, the national security adviser. It shouldn't have meant anything to either one of those men, since they weren't in the meeting where the president had set up the black operations team of Matt and Bridget.

Something bugged her. She couldn't put her finger on it, but something smelled rotten. So, she decided to examine each man's movements. Tonight she would start with Avery. She wore large fake glasses and a dark scarf to cover her hair in an attempt to create a "wouldn't be noticed" disguise. She chose a spot in an alcove of the restaurant and was enjoying a shrimp cocktail when Dean Avery entered and sat down against the far wall. He remained alone. After viewing the menu for only a second, he opened a newspaper and started reading. Mary Jean's research told her he had been a lifelong bachelor. He had served the president as an adviser since their days together at graduate school in political science at the University of Virginia in Charlottesville.

After Avery ordered a drink, he put the newspaper aside and again looked at the menu, but this time he stared at it for a long time. After a few minutes, Mary Jean could see his mouth moving, but she didn't observe anyone sitting at a table with whom he could be talking. She let her eyes wander to survey the rest of the tables. She noticed another man at the table behind Avery. He was alone, too, and also seemed to move his mouth from time to time. She thought they might be speaking to one another. Weird.

She reached into her purse and got her cell phone. She managed to open it under the table, quickly brought it up to eye level, pushed the photo button and hoped the light proved enough to get a picture. Not of Avery, but of the man at the table next to him, who sat on a thirty or forty-degree angle from her. A good side shot provided it took without using the flash. She hit the camera image twice and put her phone back in her purse, left a twenty on the table and exited the restaurant without passing near their tables.

What the hell was that all about, she wondered. The national security advisor had talked to someone surreptitiously. She knew they definitely had talked and held high confidence in her conclusion. What were they saying? This evening had indeed proved fortunate, to find something out of the ordinary on her first night on the investigation, but sometimes she got lucky. Luck must reside in her genes.

This might be their regular meeting place, a public restaurant with no one seeing them together. Someone might recognize the national security adviser, but he would appear to be having a solitary meal, relaxing by himself to take a break from the rigors of the office. He had never married, didn't like to cook, and eating out was always his norm.

She remained certain he'd talked to the other man. She would do some planning, and the next time she'd have a way to hear what they said. Somehow this might involve Matt and Bridget. She would get Admiral Kidd to render some assistance. He controlled the means at the National Security Agency to listen to phone conversations. For clandestine operations, he must know of a way to listen in on two people talking in a restaurant. She felt sure he did. Tomorrow she would take care of that little detail and come up with a solution before the next evening.

The other major problem centered on uncovering the identity of the unknown man, and she knew exactly where to go to find out. One of her former comrades-in-arms worked at the FBI. They had served as second lieutenants together and remained close friends for many years. He would help, and as a deputy director of the FBI, he knew how to keep his mouth shut.

8

SEVEN DAYS AGO — ATLANTA, GEORGIA

MARILYN'S ESTRANGED HUSBAND STORMED INTO THE LAW OFFICES OF Hunter, Boyd and Clark on Peachtree Street, not far from the Georgia state capital. She sat in a conference room with her lawyer when he made his thunderous entrance. He looked at Marilyn, but she presented a stone-cold face and displayed dagger-sharp eyes.

"Marilyn, why are you trying to ruin me?" he said in a loudly, walking over to stand in front of her.

"Ruin you? You slimeball," she shrieked. "Cheating on me with the next-door neighbor! I told my lawyer to get me justice. I hope it hurts you like you hurt me." She put her head down and hoped he wouldn't say anything else.

The overweight husband, dressed in an expensive blue three-piece suit with Bally black shoes and sporting a small mustache, did not wince, since the woman next door had fixed his guilt by telling his wife everything. The neighbor, with whom he'd enjoyed countless sex adventures, had caught him with another woman in a bar. Marilyn assumed he had forgotten which woman he'd intended to meet, and somehow they'd both shown up at the same time. The neighbor had rushed to tell Marilyn everything to inflict maximum damage for her betrayal.

Marilyn felt deep in her heart that she could only demand money, since her lawyer insisted that remuneration remained the only justice she was likely to get. She was glad that there were no children. They owned an expensive house in Buckhead, a well-to-do suburb of Atlanta, and his job brought in over $700,000 a year. She loved her position as an air traffic controller at the Atlanta Hartsfield International Airport, but she earned substantially less pay than her cheating husband.

Larry Boyd, their attorney, entered the reception area. He looked twice at Marilyn, who wore a black pantsuit with a white blouse, stunningly simple but exquisitely beautiful on her gorgeous frame. "Would you follow me? This should only take a few minutes."

In a small room with a four-person table, the attorney sat between the two onetime lovers, now enemies.

"I know this may be difficult, but you both agreed to use me as your attorney and I have discussed this settlement with each of you in private. This meeting is to sign the separation agreement, and for her to formally file for a divorce."

"I only want to sign and get out of this room," Marilyn stated.

"Come on. We have to get on with our lives," the husband said.

"Get on," she shouted. "You ruined our life. Couldn't keep your pecker in your pants and you want to go get on?"

"You're getting the house, and a god-awful amount of money from me. So yeah—get on. Go on and sign it. Then get the hell out of here, so I don't have to look at a sniveling money-hungry bitch."

Marilyn picked up the pen and signed on the lines where the yellow tabs stuck out of the multipage document. She used to go ballistic at times like this. *Hold it in, girl.* With all the documents notarized by the attorney, she stood up.

"Thank you, Mr. Boyd, for your help." She retrieved her purse and left without even acknowledging her estranged husband. She headed for the Capital Grille, where she planned to meet her friend Honey Jo for lunch before they went on duty at three in the afternoon. Her evening shift had provided her husband five nights a week to play while Marilyn worked.

Honey Jo sat in a booth waiting for her. She wore a red blouse accentuated by a gold brooch of some modern design that complimented her gold necklace. Her hair was slicked back into a bun, and her black face, although thin, shone with simple beauty. She raised her head, took in Marilyn, and said, "Girl, you look like shit. How did it go?"

"Just as bad as I thought it would." Marilyn shook her head from side to side, sat down, and placed her purse on the seat next to her.

"Did you get all you wanted?"

"I didn't get to cut his pecker off, if that's what you mean, but yeah, I got most of what I wanted," said Marilyn. "Now, I'm determined to start a new life."

"Well, honey, at least you won't be broke."

"After ten years. The bastard. Banging the neighbor. No brains."

"He possessed brains, honey, but they was just all in his lower regions," Honey Jo giggled. "You need to find you a new man so you can quit this nerve-racking job we do."

"I got the supervisor to approve my leave starting tomorrow. I'm going to Savannah to spend at least one day on the beach at Tybee. I love it there. I'll only be gone for three days, but it'll be a welcome getaway after the scene in the lawyer's office today. Anyhow, we have two hours for lunch before we go on shift, so let's do it on my new money."

She and Honey Jo arrived at the airport and parked in the FAA employee-parking garage, took the elevator up to the top level and walked to the base of the control tower. They swiped their ID cards to gain entry to the tower and took the elevator up to the top, some two hundred feet above the ground elevation.

On entering the airport control center, a group of Girl Scouts getting a tour surprised them. Not a normal thing, but someone had pulled some strings to get this exceptional treatment for the scouts. Kevin, the supervisor, was explaining which equipment in the tower allowed the controllers to talk to the airplanes. He saw Marilyn enter and motioned her to come over.

"Girls, this is Marilyn. She will finish telling you how a control tower works in a busy airport. She's one of the best controllers we have here," he said. "Marilyn, they're all yours."

He smiled at Marilyn, who winked at him in understanding. It seemed to Marilyn that he wanted away from these little munchkins as fast as possible and had given only a short presentation while waiting for her to arrive. He quickly exited on the elevator.

Marilyn picked up the commentary about the control tower. "This airport is the busiest airport in the United States. We have over two thousand flights a day, sometimes over a hundred planes an hour, and one of the three people in the tower gives the pilots permission to land on one of our runways. Of course, in a few days, we'll get busier when the new runway opens." She walked over to the window, which offered a panoramic view of the airfield, and pointed. "You can see it from here. It's the one without any planes on it. They're putting on the final touches to get it ready for the dedication ceremony in a few days."

She waited for all the scouts to look out at the new runway, then continued. "Now I'll show you how we get planes to land safely here. This control tower has many functions, but the area you're in now is where we control the airplanes after the Atlanta center directs the planes to get ready to land at Atlanta Hartsfield International. Look out these windows and you can see the planes landing and taking off on different runways all at the same time." She pointed to the runways on both sides of the control tower. "Our duty here is to coordinate that movement. We tell the airplanes when they have permission to land and when they can take off. We don't move the aircraft to or from the passenger gates to the taxiways. Ground control does that, and they're located below us. Once it has them on the taxiway, we get the planes into position for takeoff by directing them to where they can line up on the runway."

One of the young girls asked, "How do they know where to go when they take off?"

"Very good question. Move over here, let's listen and you'll hear this controller"—she pointed at Honey Jo—"as she talks to that Delta airliner you see moving onto the runway." Marilyn pointed out the window to the aircraft taxiing into position.

"Delta 97 Heavy, taxi into position and hold," Honey Jo said. "He's going to Chicago," she said to the scouts. "It's on his flight plan."

"See how the plane is now going out onto the runway? But it doesn't have permission to take off yet," Marilyn said.

"Delta 97 Heavy, clear to take off, runway heading. Contact departure on 122.3." They could not hear the pilot repeat the transmission in the controller's earpiece.

"Look out there." Marilyn pointed to a plane out in the distance. "That aircraft has now been handed over from the person in approach control. Approach control lines up the planes for the landing sequence. Then they pass them to someone in this control tower. Honey Jo here will soon give it permission to land. Let's listen."

"Continental 2132, clear to land, runway nine west, winds zero seven zero at six," Honey Jo said.

"That's the last transmission to the aircraft before it lands," Marilyn explained. "The plane is still a few miles out, but no further transmissions will come from the tower unless some emergency occurs. Any questions?"

"Yes," said one of the scouts. "Why was one a heavy and the other plane wasn't?"

"We have to call them heavy when the gross weight of the aircraft is over three hundred thousand pounds. It's information for other aircraft, so they'll know that a heavy will cause air turbulence if they're following one. Okay, young ladies, I'll escort you back down to ground level, and that concludes your tour."

God, I'm so looking forward to the day on the beach, she almost said aloud.

WASHINGTON, D.C.

Ricky felt Clare Ann Rawlings as she snuggled up to him on a cold morning. They'd met in a bar in Old Town Alexandria a month before. He'd had a successful climax and lay on his back exhausted.

"When are you going to be ready again?" she said, groping him to see if any life remained. She flaunted her supersized breasts, which Ricky knew were her weapons of choice.

"Not now. Three times in one night is all I can do. Give me a little rest. Tell me what happened at the White House."

Clare, a White House intern, moved her head quickly to flip her long black hair away from her face. She possessed a dainty body, but the large breasts attracted involuntary stares from many men. Her face appeared like an exact replica of an angel's, cherubic in appearance. "Not much. We did have some soldier come over to get decorated by the president for what he did in Saudi Arabia, . . .he . . . uhh . . .stopped some bomb or something. The chief of staff wasn't in the meeting, and he had a hissy fit outside. That's why I know about it. He asked his aide what was going on and why wasn't he included and she told him about the soldier."

"Who was this man?" Ricky asked as she continued to fondle him.

"I think she said Captain Matt Higgins, or Hestings. Something like that. Anyhow, the interesting thing happened when the First Dog got loose and peed on the rug in the Oval Office. You'd think the world had ended. The boss threw a shit fit." Her continuous massaging of his lower region started to produce results. "You have such lovely green eyes. I've never had a man with green eyes. I need a green-eyed man right now."

Ricky rolled over onto her.

After Clare left, Ricky took a shower and then got on his computer and sent the information gleaned from Clare to an email address. He didn't know exactly where it went, but they were the control element for his cell.

After he had converted to Islam a few years ago, he'd adopted the Fundamentalist philosophy of the imam at his nearby mosque. After taking the name al-Banna, he'd joined and now provided the leadership for the local jihadist cell of al-Qaeda. He worked as the supervisor of an equipment service unit for aviation electronics and navigation systems.

Ricky headed a five-member team, all dedicated to the same goals as himself, each having a specialty. He recruited his cell members from those who believed the world must be converted to Islam by any means. There were another two men, not from his service unit, but available to him because of their same dedication to the jihadist's calling, who worked as computer programmers with a major software company.

From Ricky's reports submitted by emails, the worldwide terrorist control network called Fatimah received the information on Matt and sent an order to act on it once the target's exact location became known.

A clear message would be delivered to any individual or group who thwarted the will of Allah, or the will of Fatimah.

# 9

SIX DAYS AGO — BEFORE DOCKING IN SAVANNAH

Yuri confronted the captain and attempted to obtain papers to go ashore in Savannah. The captain balked and refused to provide them. Yuri left the man's cabin and went to ponder his situation. His mission now centered on getting the captain to realize that he must fulfill Yuri's demands.

The eerie glow of soft red and yellow lights vaguely brightened the distant shoreline. The ship would reach the Port of Savannah in the early morning hours.

Twenty minutes after exiting the captain's cabin, Yuri Borisov hung his head over the side rail of the vessel. His stomach contracted, did it again, and he lost all its contents—not from seasickness, but from what he had done. Everything had happened so fast. He sweated and took in large gulps of air. A mere twenty days ago, the disaster at Ras Tanura had occurred, and now the aftermath had forced him to kill.

He knew the crew used this door to go back and forth between the deck and the sleeping area, so he had hidden in a passageway off the entrance to the deck and waited until the unsuspecting victims passed him before attacking them from behind with a steel rod. Yuri bent down and stripped the IDs from the corpses of the two men he had pummeled to death. With great effort, he tossed the bodies overboard and returned to Basam's cabin with the documents from the murdered crewmen.

He discovered Basam on the bed. The place smelled like the inside of an old jockstrap. Yuri hadn't seen him for three days but now his skin appeared ashen white, and the man looked ten pounds lighter. Basam had remained in his cabin for the entire passage, and Yuri hadn't impinged on his privacy. Now, however, the time had come to get their final plan in order and prepare to leave the ship.

"Yuri, have you responded to the latest query from Fatimah?" asked Basam as soon as Yuri sat on the only chair in the room.

"Not yet. Let's go over what we have so far and see where we want to go and what we want to do." Yuri took out a cigarette and lit it. He did not offer one to Basam. "You look awful. Are you sick?"

"No. It's nothing, only some vomiting. Some sort of flu."

"Okay." But Yuri didn't believe him. "Remember, we got our first communication from Fatimah as we rounded the cape off South Africa. They told us to wait. It took them by complete surprise when I told them we were alive and had the atomic weapon." He gave a small laugh and stood up to go over to the porthole, opening it for air. Yuri knew about Fatimah from his dealing with Basam's dead brother. That organization, or group of jihadists, or Islamic fundamentalists, or whatever they called themselves, ran a worldwide network of terrorists.

Fatimah's headquarters, located in Iran, continually provided overall direction for operations on a global level and had done so for decades. They conducted operations through the entities known as al-Qaeda, Hezbollah, Hamas, Muslim Brotherhood and many more names, and they were funded, given leadership, and ultimately controlled as a worldwide terrorist network by Fatimah.

"That was about the same time we saw on the news the president of Iran called for eliminating the U.S. president. The press was also talking up the new 'Axis of Evil' between Tehran and other states," Basam said.

"Yes," Yuri said. "That's why I think they gave us Atlanta as our target. They told us the president would be going there. They stated they would have the date before we got to Savannah." Yuri came back and sat in the chair, trying to get comfortable. "In the latest email, they say they're going to punish the man who murdered your brother."

"Do you think something happened to cause that?" Basam asked as he tried not to cough.

"Must have. Somehow they found out who attacked us in Saudi Arabia. I think they went to eliminate him. The email didn't tell us how, only that another attack would be made on him soon. They said the first attempt failed and he killed all their people."

Basam jumped up from his bed and ran to the bathroom. Yuri heard him throwing up.

"Basam, come outside by the rail to get some real air. We'll stay by the door next to the barrier. We won't go far from the door. You haven't been out of this room for two weeks. In the morning, we get to America and will stay in Savannah until they tell us to move. We now have a job to do there, and only a few days to get it done. I hope Fatimah gives us enough lead time."

"I'll go out, but just for a few minutes. How do you think they found out who attacked us?" Basam asked.

"Don't know. Come on, I'll help you." Yuri could see he would have to help Basam to walk. He walked like a frail old man.

"Did they find out who killed my brother?"

"Don't know." Yuri couldn't even guess how Fatimah had discovered the identity of the man who had thwarted their attempt to destroy the lifeblood of oil supply from Saudi Arabia.

Yuri helped Basam to stand by the outside rail. The man appeared so weak when he took steps that Yuri wondered if he would drop dead right here.

"How are we going to get off the boat without papers?"

"I left our dear captain a few minutes ago. I told him that we had brought automatic weapons on board, and that we would kill everyone and jump overboard if he didn't go along with my plan. I told him I killed two of his crew and had their papers to get us ashore. If he sounded the alarm, or if there was any interference with us on arrival, he would be the first to die."

"You didn't."

"Yes, I did. How do you think we could pull this off if he doesn't help and keep quiet till we're gone? If he does, then he'll report two crewmembers missing when he leaves Savannah. The authorities will presume they have jumped ship. His hands are clean, and he will have reported it. He also won't lose his job for aiding us."

"Do you think it will work?" Basam whispered, barely audible, sounding even weaker than Yuri had suspected.

"The last communiqué from Fatimah approved the fee of five million for doing this job. Not as generous as your brother." Yuri scanned around to see if anyone could hear them. He saw no one.

"I didn't tell you that I got an email from the Americans."

"What? How?"

"I think they found that laptop we lost following the detonation of the underground atomic bomb. My email address, likely discovered on it, could be the reason. They're trying to get me to surrender the weapon and receive immunity if I do. I don't trust them to keep their word."

They both continued to stare over the side of the ship. The coastal lights appeared closer. The sky reflected a yellowish glow in the clouds from the electric illumination along the Georgia coastline.

"I didn't answer them, so they don't know we exist."

"Why?"

"I think it was a shot in the dark to see if I'd bite. They don't even know if we're alive, and they couldn't know we have an atomic weapon," Yuri concluded.

"I'm tired. Let's go back inside," Basam said as he tried to walk. Yuri grabbed his arm, but Basam twirled back and threw up over the side of the ship. He turned back, and his face caught the light. Yuri couldn't believe this same Basam had accompanied him on the ride across the desert two weeks ago. What had happened? Then Yuri helped him to his cabin.

As a nuclear engineer, Yuri started to suspect radiation poison might be the problem with Basam, but if Basam wanted to stay in the confined room and kill himself due to a small leak in the cylinders holding the radioactive material, what did he care? He was in this for the money.

TAKING HIS EVENING STROLL ON THE DECK, THE CAPTAIN ROUNDED A corner just as Yuri turned his head in the opposite direction and searched to see if anyone approached. The captain stopped and backed up. Cautiously, he peered around the corner. He could hear bits of the conversation. Basam turned back from vomiting, providing a clear look at the man. Horror filled the captain at what he saw. He knew what afflicted the man. At least, he was nearly certain he knew.

After the two went into Basam's cabin, the captain retreated to his quarters. That Russian, Yuri, had killed two of his crew and threatened all the others, including himself. He knew what he would do, but it would have to be after he played along with their scheme, because he wanted them off his ship as the first priority. The second step demanded that he get the information to an old friend and former comrade-in-arms.

There could be only one way that Basam had arrived at his current condition under the present circumstances. He remained absolutely sure. Many years ago in the small town of Chernobyl, where his parents lived when he served in the Red Army, he had seen the same sickness with the same symptoms when he'd returned home to take care of them in their final days. It had only taken a few weeks for them to die, but in the end it was not pretty. There were no medicines to help. Just pain.

Yes, he knew what caused the Arab's suffering. There had to be a leaking uranium source in the enclosed steel cabin the man occupied, and it must belong to him, as it was not part of the ship. They might possess an atomic device of some type, or weapons-grade material.

He needed to let someone know about it.

10

SIX DAYS AGO — LATE EVENING — LEESBURG, VIRGINIA

"Why don't you leave your car here and we'll just take mine for our drink?" Matt said. They turned off all the lights, locked the doors to the office, and set the alarm before going out. "We're only going a couple of blocks. There's a place at the corner near my new apartment that looks good. Let's try it out."

"Okay by me." Bridget gave him a nod and got into Matt's black two-door 2007 BMW, a 3 Series convertible that his father had given him as a present for getting out of the military. Well, at least that's what he'd led his dad to believe. The old man, a Wall Street hedge fund manager, hated his son serving in the army. His "little" gift was actually a bribe to force Matt to consider joining his firm. So far, that strategy hadn't worked, but Matt did like the car.

Matt drove the five blocks in silence. He searched for a parking spot near the bar but found none, so he parked at his apartment building ten doors away. They got out and walked. On entering, they saw a contemporary décor with a U-shaped bar in the center and chairs and tables around the center area. Nothing as spectacular as the Red Coach Inn, located further down the street in the middle of the historic district, but it was clean and comfortable.

"I don't think champagne is in order, especially since I don't like it," Bridget said.

"I agree. How about an expensive bottle of wine and some steaks here?" Mark said.

"Great," she said.

While eating in the corner with a view of the entrance, they chatted about the mission to Dallas and how pleased they were with the initial setup of the company. Bridget mentioned that she knew some additional prospects for more security opportunities in the near future.

"Where did you get these contacts? Not that I mind, it's awesome to have business coming in, but I've brought us nothing so far."

"Remember I told you at the start that I thought I could get a few contracts to get us started? If we do good, then I believe word of mouth will help us continue."

"Yeah. But where do your contacts come from?"

"Mostly from friends of my father's friend. He was the son of the village elder in Turkey. You know, they're Armenians by ethnicity and Christian by religion. The persecution by the Turkish government got so bad that many left, and so did he after his grandparents were killed." Bridget filled her wineglass and took a sip.

"Somehow, many people from that village arrived in San Francisco. They were merchants by trade and started fresh here. Over the years, they and their children did well. They helped each other the best they could and kept in contact with my father. They have their own church with their language and rituals, which provides a cohesive force in the community."

"So these are the people who are employing us now? Like Mr. Pasha in Texas?"

"Yes," Bridget responded.

"I never understood how you joined the counterterrorist business at DIA. No one seemed to know. I asked General Bergermeyer, and she told me if I wanted to know I would have to ask you. Now seems like a good time to tell me," Matt finished. He stared at Bridget with intense interest and waited for what seemed like a long time before getting an answer.

"I'll give you the shortened version. No details of my youth. I planned to go to college after high school, but 9/11 happened. Mind you, I still want to get my archeology degree and maybe a doctorate at some point."

"Damn. Something happened after 9/11?" Matt reached over and placed his hand on top of Bridget's. She didn't pull back.

"Yes, and that's why I haven't said anything, because it's too similar to your experience. 9/11 devastated me. I withdrew from school and started to drink. At Christmas, my father attacked me as not being true to myself, nor how he had reared me. It took me a week to sober up, then I returned to my studies. In January, I heard the president's State of the Union address and realized that I had to do something to pay these people back."

"So what did you do?" Matt asked as he refilled the glasses.

"I wanted revenge. I tried to think of how to get it. I've always been a strong athlete and in excellent shape."

Matt looked at her. "I can see that."

"I wanted to punish the terrorists and get away from my family. I wanted to show my father that I was a person in my own right. One day, I visited an army recruiter. It never crossed my mind to check out the other services."

"Did you volunteer for airborne training?"

"Yes, and after that I got a call from someone in the DIA to come for a visit. After they told me what they wanted me for, I was in, and delighted. I got my wish, and we did go after the bad guys. We wiped out an entire cell on our last mission. We . . .you and I . . .we worked well together. So that's my story."

Matts separated their hands, picked up his wineglass and toasted Bridget. "Very interesting. Thanks for telling me. So, the old boy network of Armenians is supplying us with work?"

"For starters. And I think we have enough knowledge and drive to make it on our own."

"So do I."

After the meal, Matt said, "Let's get out of here." He put the money for the bill on the table. They got up and walked out.

As they exited the bar, Matt's ingrained senses alerted him to something. Someone must be watching. He scanned the area but saw no one. Then he focused his attention on his partner and forgot about it.

"Before we go back to your car, let's stop by my place and you can see the neat little apartment I got. We have to walk there anyway."

"Sure. But remember, we start work early tomorrow. Maybe they'll have something for us on Yuri. Also, you have to get Laura over to the office so the general can pick her up."

On reaching his place, Matt led her up to the second-floor apartment. His space appeared fixed up beyond the cave-dwelling aspect of his old place in Arlington. The wall held two fake oil paintings by Monet, and a complete set of furniture from Rooms-to-Go adorned the main space, including the lamps and a home entertainment console with a large TV.

"Nice digs," Bridget said on entering.

Matt went over to switch on the lamp. He then walked back to the entrance to escort Bridget in, offering her his hand.

AT 6:30 THE NEXT MORNING, THE ALARM CLOCK WENT OFF. MATT WENT over to the couch where Bridget had fallen asleep last night after they'd talked for what must have been hours. "I don't know about you, but I could use some breakfast."

"Me too," she replied, stretching out her arms and getting up.

"I'll call you when it's ready. Do you want to do a morning run?"

"No, but thank you very much for offering. It's got to be freezing outside," Bridget said with a smile on her face.

Matt returned to his room and took a shower and then went to the kitchen area to make the coffee. He pointed her to his bedroom, where he had put out fresh towels, and in a few minutes he heard Bridget running the water. After she cut it off, he put the toast in the toaster. Rather simple, but he hadn't expected a guest for breakfast.

Bridget came out with her hair wet and wearing the same outfit from last night. "I'll have to get to my place to change before we go to work. Can't wear this again after last night."

Matt got the sense that she didn't care about the clothes. "Coffee?"

"Yes, please. No sugar or cream," she replied.

As they sat around his small two-person table on stools in the breakfast nook of the apartment, Matt again became smitten by Bridget's extraordinary beauty. His thought had not gone to his deceased wife, as he'd expected they might even after spending a night with a woman in his apartment with nothing sexual happening. There remained, however, a sticking point if it did happen. How would any sexual involvement influence their working relationship? What impact would it have on the bond with his daughter? How would it affect him? Why the hell was he pondering this now as Bridget stared at him?

"Is something wrong?" she inquired.

"No. No . . . I was just thinking."

"Of how the murders would affect your daughter," Bridget injected.

"Well, yeah. Sort of," he said as he shook his head. "It was that I'm surprised at my reactions in thinking about the future. All in all, I'm glad we're working together. I am."

"So what's bothering you? You don't like what we're doing?"

"Hell no," Matt said.

"You are something. All I want is for us to be open and honest with each other. You start. What were you thinking just now?" Bridget asked.

"First, I surprised myself that I had no regrets about our renewed relationship. Second, that we'll successfully manage our work association. We're not superior to subordinate, we're equal partners. Lastly, I thought of my daughter. We've started something that I hope is a good thing for both of us. I want it. Does that make sense?"

"Thank you," Bridget said. "That's a lot of honesty. I'll try to be that way with you always, and that way we'll make it work."

Bridget came over and gave him a light kiss on the cheek. "That's for being you. Now it's time to get our butts in gear and go make some money or we'll be on welfare."

"I want to look outside before we go. I don't usually do it here in the States, but last night I had a feeling we were being watched. Just a hunch, but . . ." Matt wiggled on the kitchen stool. "There was no one I could see, so I forgot about it. It might be something to check out, since we *are* in the security business."

Matt went over to the window and, without moving the blind, peeked around both sides to observe the street. He saw the condensation on the pane and knew the temperature had to be near freezing.

He put on his down overcoat and a wool beanie before heading downstairs. At the bottom of the steps, he looked outside but saw no one, and after a quick check of the cars on the street, he decided that his imagination had run wild. Still, he retained a lingering feeling of being watched.

11

SEVEN DAYS AGO — PORTLAND, OREGON

"Nodira, you and I, we've been selected to go on a mission for al-Qaeda," said Ahmad, the cell leader and a graduate student studying engineering. "Fatimah has ordered us to kill a man in Washington, D.C. It seems the guy had interfered with a big plan of theirs, and this is to be a reprisal for his actions."

"When do we have to do this?" Nodira asked.

"The one I report to told me there was an attempt on this man in Texas and it failed. We will not let that happen again." He lit a Turkish cigarette and inhaled deeply. "We're to go tomorrow. On arrival, we'll met a man who'll supply us with the weapons and a picture of the target."

"Not that I don't think we've had the training to carry out the mission, but isn't this a little out of the ordinary for us to conduct such an operation without a long planning time?"

"Yes, but I understand there's another plan to attack the Americans with a huge weapon. I don't know the details. Our mission is our only concern. The tickets and transport are all arranged, and we're going to a student conference in Washington. That'll provide us a legitimate cover for being there."

"Do you know anything about the weapon?" Nodira said.

"No, I don't. Rumor has it there is a Russian involved. I think the team in Texas knew more about it, but we don't have any details. They are trying to limit all information about the Russian, if he exists. That cell's al-Qaeda leaders must've told them about an atomic bomb. Their cell was in Texas and got wiped out by our target. So, this won't be an easy mission, but we will succeed where they failed. We'll have to rely on Allah to guide us. Let us pray now for our success."

While on his knees, Nodira remembered how all this had come about. He could not engage in the required devotional supplication because a vivid memory overpowered his concentration and he couldn't help it. It must be part of Allah's plan for him and it had started a long time ago.

UZBEKISTAN, UNION OF SOVIET SOCIALIST REPUBLICS - 1990 A.D.

Shahri, situated on the Turanian plain, remained as it had been for the past two thousand years. Now it is part of the Xorazm Viloyati district, slightly east of Urganch in the Republic of Uzbekistan. The electrification of some buildings in the small village and the arrival of farm trucks and a few automobiles in this century didn't change the fundamental rural lifestyle of the community. Islam is the religion, and the language leans on Turkish as its base.

Many residents also know how to speak Russian. The flags flying over the land differed over the years from the Imperial banner of the Czars to the red of the Soviets, but the people there cared little for the politics of the far-off leaders. The country, in previous years, remained part of the Soviet bloc. The villagers' world, however, centered around managing their meager assets and ensuring adequate food for everyone.

Muattar and Nodira Karimo, twin brothers, grew up in the village. Their father, Islam Karimo, had worked as a poor wine merchant. Even though alcohol might be less popular than in the West, wines were widely available for a majority Muslim nation like Uzbekistan because, as in Turkey, it is largely a secular state. The twins demonstrated enterprising traits and, on reaching the age of eighteen, concluded that hunting giant lizards for food and eating the noodle-rich cuisine of Uzbekistan, augmented by the rare piece of mutton, wouldn't suffice as the life for them.

"Well, have you decided what you are going to do?" asked Muattar. They were sitting around the kitchen table in the evening near the wood-burning stove that provided the only heat in the dwelling.

"Yesterday, I talked to the head of our school and he is helping me get the money and paperwork to go to a university in the United States," Nodira replied.

"You can't go there," Muattar shouted as he got up from the table and stood with his finger pointing at his brother. "It is the home of Satan. You know what the imam has taught us about those infidels."

"I know, but they have a superlative university system, and I can learn about engineering. When I come home, I can help our people here." Nodira signaled his sibling to sit back down. "I know there is a cell of al-Qaeda in Portland, Oregon. I will contact them when I get there. That way, I will keep my faith strong." He took a sip of what was undoubtedly the most popular beverage in the country, tea. "Brother, what are you thinking of doing?"

"I have decided to enlist in the Red Army. They will provide me enough money to send some back to Papa, and I'll have a better life, as opposed to here, where there is nothing for me. I will also change my name to Ravshan after our grandfather when I join and to sound more Russian and less Muslim in their army."

Muattar had joined as Ravshan, had become a trained sniper in the red army, and served in Chechnya. His kill ratio had exceeded that of all other snipers in his unit. He'd never came back home and had learned from his brother that their father had died recently.

Nodira hadn't taken the trip to the States that year, staying to help his father instead. He'd then gone to Afghanistan in the summer to receive training at an al-Qaeda camp. This had inspired Nodira and solidified his belief in the justice of the jihadists' cause. He'd returned home three months later a changed man. By then, the old USSR no longer existed, after it had suffered defeat in Afghanistan, which proved to the world the mighty superpower was not invincible. Now only the mighty USA remained, and the forces of Islam would rise up against it and destroy it. The West must surrender and the inhabitants convert to Islam or perish. He would fulfill the will of Allah as the almighty's instrument.

He'd returned home and studied the Koran at the local mosque while the other brothers ran the business. Later, he'd received the funding and paperwork to go to America. Last summer he'd reached Portland, Oregon to start his studies.

DULLES INTERNATIONAL AIRPORT — WASHINGTON, D.C.
Six days ago, early morning

AS THEY WALKED OUT INTO THE ARRIVALS HALL, AHMAD SEARCHED THE area for their contact. He spotted him by the Avis rental car counter because the man wore what they expected to find on their contact here, a black windbreaker with the Bendix logo and dark glasses. They approached him, noting his body builder's frame, and when he took off his glasses as they came close, they could see that he possessed brilliant green eyes.

"You must be Ahmad," he said, offering his hand. "My name is al-Banna, but folks around here know me as Ricky. Let's get out of the terminal as quick as we can. I have transport and a driver who will take you wherever you need to go. He'll stay with you at all times until he brings you back here to leave. Those are the orders I received."

"As you wish. We're dependent on you to get us to our objective," Ahmad said. "Interesting name you adopted on your conversion. Al-Banna was the founder of the first modern jihadist organization, the Muslim Brotherhood." Ahmad and Nodira followed Ricky out of the airport terminal to the waiting car.

Ricky introduced them to Claude Moreau, a Frenchman and a devout Muslim. Ricky told them that Claude's mother came from Algeria and grew up a Muslim. Claude had become active in the religion in Washington, where it enjoyed the status of being the fastest growing sect in America. He explained that the greater metropolitan area contained cells of Hamas, Hezbollah, al-Qaeda, al-Fugra and Islamic Jihad. Claude saw the faith as a way to convert the world to Islam in the name of Allah and to destroy the United States, which became the cell's single goal. Their jihadist cell, headed by Ricky, would carry out any order they received to achieve that end.

"I'll take you to attend your conference, and then pick you up at five. You can do your surveillance of the target then," Claude said. "Your flight leaves tomorrow at six. The weapons you asked for are in the trunk—two assault rifles, AK-47, and two Berretta 9mm Px4, type F."

"Do you have the picture of our man?" Nodira asked.

"Yes. His name is Matt Higgins and he has a partner called Bridget." He handed over a piece of paper with the image. "Here is a photo and the address of his office. Don't worry, I've already checked out how to get there, and I can take you anywhere you want to go."

After they attended the student conference, Claude picked them up and headed towards Leesburg. Ahmad asked, "I suppose you are along to report on all we do?"

Claude didn't answer.

They arrived at the SPAT, Inc. office as Matt and Bridget were getting into Matt's BMW. Claude pulled into an empty space and waited to see which way they were going when they drove off.

"Don't worry, I'll keep up with them."

He followed and watched as Matt searched for a parking place, but eventually had to park near a building almost a block away. The subjects walked to the bar on the corner.

"What are you guys planning on doing? I just want to know to plan our route of escape."

Ahmad responded, "We will wait till he is away from the girl, and then we will kill him. Is it always this cold here? I'm freezing."

Claude turned on the heater. He moved the car down the street to keep Matt's car under observation. After about an hour, his two passengers began to get out to go on foot to explore inside the bar. At that moment, Matt and Bridget appeared and started to walk towards his car. Ahmad expected that Matt would take the young woman home, and they would kill him when he got back.

"What are they doing?" Claude said.

"Looks like they're going into the building. I thought you had his address in Arlington, Virginia," Nodira said.

"We do. That's what is in the phone book. Maybe he moved," Claude surmised.

"Now what? It seems like this is a badly planned operation," Nodira said. "You don't even know if this could be the girl's place."

Ahmad said, "Now we wait to see."

12

FIVE DAYS AGO — ARLINGTON, VIRGINIA

THE TEMPERATURE HOVERED AROUND FREEZING. THE THREE TERRORISTS in the car fogged the windows of the vehicle with their exhales onto the frozen glass. They scrunched and wiggled in a vain attempt to keep warm, assuming they would be moving at any moment when the target appeared. Time passed as silence reigned in the car. Claude fell asleep and snored. Ahmad clucked his tongue from time to time. Nodira stayed focused on the apartment building, hoping their prey would emerge.

"They've got to come out," Nodira said. "We could accomplish our mission before daybreak and be on the next plane." They waited in vain for Matt to reappear, not wanting to try and take him in his own dwelling after they learned what had happened to the team in Dallas. At seven in the morning, the door opened and Matt and Bridget appeared. The men decided to follow until Matt was alone.

Matt emerged from the apartment building bundled in a heavy anorak and a navy beanie. Bridget came into view in only a windbreaker and ran for Matt's car. The men followed Matt's car to what they now took as the woman's place and then on to the offices of SPAT, Inc. No opportunity presented itself for them to carry out the hit at her place. At the office location, they took up a position across the street to keep the office under surveillance. They took turns walking to the local McDonalds for food and to use the facilities.

"Good morning, you two," Julia chirped when they entered the office. She continued to feed something to Gandalf.

"Stop cat, stop fucking cat, squawk," was their greeting from the bird.

"Let me take care of Rambo," Bridget said and went off to check on the litter box and his food.

"Julia, I have a favor to ask," Matt said.

"What can I do?" replied Julia.

"I need you to go pick up my daughter and bring her here. General Bergermeyer stopped by last night. Her niece is coming to visit, and she asked if Laura could come over and play. I think it's to get her some relief from her non maternal disposition," Matt said with a smile.

"No problem. When?"

"She'll be here after five. You know how the Friday afternoon traffic is. She may decide to come early to pick her up, so I guess you should get her after school. I'd go, but we have a meeting with a prospective client at four, and we're waiting on some information on our new assignment from the president."

"Okay. I'll leave about two. Please be sure to be back here in time," Julia said.

"Here are the keys to my car. Use my gas, not yours. Here's a fifty to fill it. Please remember to do so, as it's nearly empty." He handed her the money.

The phone rang, and Julia moved to answer it. The office day began.

At two o'clock, Julia prepared to leave. "Matt, it's very cold outside and I don't have my down coat. Could I borrow yours?"

"Of course, go ahead," Matt responded without looking up from the computer screen.

"Okay, see you later." Julia put on Matt's heavy coat and his hat, went out, and left in the BMW to pick up Laura. She drove straight to where Matt's daughter lived with his deceased wife's sister and her husband. She knew the neighborhood and enjoyed seeing the full-grown trees instead of the shrubs prevalent in the new subdivisions going in all over the area. Their house dated from the days when Herndon was out in the country—a long way from the District of Columbia—but today it functioned as a bedroom community. Julia couldn't believe the elevated prices of property in the area. After ten years the homeowners found the current value of their dwellings mind-boggling.

Julia pulled up in the drive of an average red brick ranch house as the car's engine sputtered and died. "Shit, I forgot to stop and get gas. The damn traffic. Damnit," she said aloud.

Going up to the house, she pondered what to say and how to get fuel for Matt's car. Susan's sister, Sherry, greeted her friend at the door.

"Matt called to tell us you were coming. Take your things off and have a cup for coffee. Jim just flew in this morning, and is asleep in the bedroom, so we'll go into the kitchen."

"That would be a delight. It's as cold as a well digger's ass out there," Julia said.

They went into the kitchen and after small talk and a few sips from her cup, Julia asked, "May I borrow your car? I must admit that I ran out of gas when I got here. Matt told me to fill it, but in the traffic, I forgot."

"Sure. Take our car. It's in the garage and it's warm since I recently used it to go to the store. There's a gas can you can take on the far side by the door."

Laura ran into the room. "Julia, Julia." She threw her arms around her and gave her a kiss.

"Hi, Pumpkin. Your dad'll be glad to see you. You're going to stay with the general for the weekend."

"He told me. It should be fun," Laura said.

"I have to go and get some gas for the car. I'll be back in a few."

"Let me go with you, please, please."

"All right, get your coat."

Laura came back holding a lightweight red jacket.

"Here, Julia, you take Sherry's coat. You won't need Dad's heavy coat in the car since we just got back. Come on, let's go. I want to see Daddy before the general gets there." Julia put on the red windbreaker.

Julia took Laura by the hand and walked to the garage. They drove off a minute later, heading for the local gas station.

THE THREE WATCHED AS THE FIGURE IN THE DOWN ANORAK AND NAVY beanie got into the BMW and left the SPAT office. They easily trailed the car, as the vehicle in front of them didn't seem to take any precautions against surveillance.

"Not much of a pro, is he?" Claude said. "Doesn't take any action to see if he's being followed. I thought this guy was some super counterterrorist man. Maybe he feels completely safe in America."

They reached the house with the BMW parked in the driveway and continued past it. They stopped at the corner.

"How do you want to handle this?" Nodira inquired.

"We have him in a house in a suburban area. It's too cold for anyone to be out walking, so we'll drive right up to the house, break down the door, and kill him in the house. That way we know we have the target. We know he's in the house now. If someone else is there, just shoot first. Let's go around the block, come back, and do it," said Ahmad.

The driver didn't obey the instructions, but instead executed a U-turn to stay in sight of the house. As he positioned the car to go toward the house, they saw a car pulling out of the driveway with a woman and a child in it. The BMW remained in the driveway.

"Great, he's still in the house," Ahmad said.

They waited until the departing car turned the corner and disappeared from sight. Claude rolled the car up into the driveway beside

Matt's BMW, and the two attackers jumped out, ran to the front door and smashed it open.

As they entered the house, a woman came around the corner into the entrance hall and Ahmad fired his pistol into her chest. The man was supposed to be alone, she had taken him by surprise and he fired without thinking. The woman's body flew backwards and banged against a hallway table, toppling it. A loud shattering noise occurred when the lamp careened from the table onto the floor. Her body landed on top of a photograph that portrayed a happy couple on the beach.

Sounds of movement came from another room. They rushed forward and scanned down the hallway to their left. A man stuck his head around the corner. They only saw the top of his head as he pulled back when he saw them. He disappeared into the room after slamming the door behind him as they opened fire.

They ran down the hall to the door and kicked it open. They entered and saw a man in his shorts attempting to escape through the window. He dove toward the window he'd flung open, but his leg snagged on the sill. He twisted around in an attempt to free himself and to fall forward out of the room. They fired rounds into the man and emptied their magazines at the target. Blood splattered all over the windowsill, bullets shattered the glass, and the body, with the foot still caught on the sill, toppled toward the ground.

"Come on. Let's go. He's dead," Ahmad said.

They ran back and got into the car. Claude reversed out of the driveway and headed for the airport. "Did you get him?"

"Yes. He's dead," Nodira said.

"Did you check to see that it was the target?" Claude said.

"He took two magazines of bullets, no one survives that," Ahmad offered assuming that would satisfy the question.

"Okay, leave the guns in the car when I drop you at the airport. You'll be on your plane to Seattle in less than two hours. Good work. Allah akbar!"

In unison they all shouted, "Allah akbar."

13

SIX DAYS AGO —EARLY MORNING — SAVANNAH, GA

No one looked closely at their stolen papers when Yuri and Basam presented them to immigration and customs. Yuri took a deep breath and tried to relax after they made it ashore at the Port of Savannah without incident. He guessed that getting out of a port was easier than getting back in, since all the seamen arriving were getting off ships. At most ports, the custom existed to allow seamen to have passes to go ashore. They would all be back in time to sail on their respective ships.

The port authorities hardly ever experienced any trouble from crewmen trying to stay in Savannah. Maybe one a year. In general, the overstaying resulted from drunkenness, and the local police handled it. Whenever the wayward seaman turned up, he was sent to rejoin the ship at the company's expense.

"We have to find a place to rest," said Basam. They walked to the road at the port exit, with Yuri occasionally having to assist Basam.

"I'll get us a taxi," Yuri said, and he went off to hail one.

Basam walked at a turtle's pace, rolling the case beside him until he reached the corner. Yuri put their duffle bags and the case in the taxi and helped Basam get in.

"I told the driver to take us to an area where we can rent a small house or a duplex. He says he knows a place. I told him we wanted to be close to downtown."

"Good, there will be a pharmacy somewhere nearby," Basam said.

"I think you look awful. Maybe we should find a doctor for you."

"No. As soon as I get some medicine, I'll be fine," Basam insisted.

The taxi arrived at the Custom House complex, made up of individual small houses for rent. Yuri negotiated the rental and the owner led them to the house. Inside, they found the place to be a small two-bedroom dwelling of only nine hundred square feet. Basam rolled the case in and Yuri got the two duffle bags, and then went out and paid the taxi driver. After the landlord and the taxi departed, Yuri walked to the corner convenience store where he used an ATM and bought some supplies and some medicine for Basam.

At that moment, on board the container ship, Captain Grigori Orloff dialed his triband phone, calling an old friend who served at the Russian embassy in Washington.

"Andrei Andrei, it's a delight to hear your voice. Too long, my friend," Grigori said.

"Yes. We must get together, if you ever get off that ship of yours. Whatever happened to the Spetznaz-trained killer I worked with in Afghanistan? You were something else then, my friend."

"That was a long time ago. I'm calling you because I believe there is a real danger that you must know about. I think a Russian and an Arab have an atomic device and have brought it into the United States."

"You're kidding," Andrei said, raising his voice.

"No, my friend. Two weeks ago they got on my ship at Yemen and the one stayed in his cabin the entire trip. He was healthy when he got on board, but now I know, almost for sure, that he has radiation sickness. Believe me, I know what it is and how one looks if one has it, as I watched my parents die of it in Chernobyl. The weapon must have a small leak and the steel of the cabin kept him in its deadly focus for the entire voyage. He never left his space. I have faith from his looks that he could have gotten a lethal dose."

"Okay. I believe you would know. Go ahead."

Grigori relayed to Major General Marshankin the story of the Russian, Yuri, and his pal, Basam, ending with, "I'll have more on them for you when my first officer gets back. I sent him to trail them and learn where they were going."

"As always, you remember your training. You should have never left the army. You would be a general by now."

"I am the admiral of my ship and very happy about it. But those two, Andrei, are trouble for the Americans and maybe for us."

"Thank you again and I hope to see you soon. Call me with additional information from your first officer."

Grigori disconnected and waited for his man to return.

14

SIX DAYS AGO — RUSSIAN EMBASSY — WASHINGTON, D.C

Major General Andrei Marshankin, a decorated combat veteran, put the phone back in the cradle and ran his hand over his receding salt-and-pepper hairline. He paced his office, as he liked physical exercise and this was all the workout he would likely get today. His slim body and muscular shoulders attested to his devotion to constant workouts.

His mind raced with the information he'd received. It held major significance to his post in Washington. It also fit in with the intelligence on the atomic attack in Saudi Arabia he'd recently shared with the director of operations and organizations at the DIA, Brigadier General Mary Jean Bergermeyer.

He decided on his immediate course of action. First, he called the director of counterterrorism in Moscow. In that conversation, he told him what he knew, relaying the information over a secure line. Second, he requested approval to speak to the Americans. After talking to Moscow, he received approval to inform his counterpart at the DIA.

"Hello," he said when he heard Mary Jean's voice on the phone.

"Good morning, General. To what do I owe the pleasure of this call?"

"I was feeling a little peckish," he said in perfect unaccented English, "and wondered if you were up to a midmorning pastry?"

"I think you read my mind. I thought about having a coffee. It would be a pleasure," she said as the game continued.

"Could you make it to the top of the Marriott at, let's say, a ten thirty?"

"I'll be delighted. See you there." She waited for him to hang up before putting the phone back in the cradle.

Mary Jean sat back and wondered what the hell the Russian was up to. In a few meetings over the last month, they'd occasionally exchanged data concerning the atomic explosion in Saudi Arabia, and she'd revealed that the American intelligence community thought a Russian could be involved. A call out of the blue for a quick meeting meant that something important must have occurred. She went to her closet, where she kept a change of civilian clothes, and changed out of her uniform. She completed her transformation, did a cursory check of her makeup in the mirror, and finally checked her watch to ensure she would be there on time.

In the car, Mary Jean dialed Admiral Kidd at the NSA. He had played an instrumental role in stopping the bomb in Saudi by using some of the sophisticated interception devices available to that agency. Recently she'd learned that he'd managed to disrupt cell phone usage in the area for a specific period, preventing the detonation of the atomic device by the terrorists. He controlled that unique equipment plus many other super-secret intelligence collection means at his disposal as the director of the agency.

"Good morning," she heard the admiral's booming voice over her cell phone.

"Morning, sir. Just got a call from the Russian attaché. Going to meet him now. Thought I'd ask if you have any increased activity in my area of concern."

"Wait a minute." She listened as the admiral gave an order. "I'll see," he said when he came back.

"I'll keep you posted on what the rendezvous is about. He gave no indication over the phone," Mary Jean said.

"To answer your question, yes. There has been some in the ministry that you are concerned with. Hopefully, the Russian will tell you what's going on."

"Thanks, Admiral. We'll talk later," she said as he hung up.

Mary Jean arrived at 10:30 and saw Andrei Marshankin sitting at a table overlooking the Potomac. He put on glasses but Mary Jean suspected only to read the menu. The general rose as she approached, placing the specs in the pocket of his starched white shirt. He stood five feet eleven and possessed a handsome face, with striking blue eyes and a full head of salt and pepper hair. He wore an expensive tailor-made dark blue single-breasted suit.

"It's always a pleasure to see you, General."

"And you, General."

"Please, in this informal situation, call me Andrei."

"I'm Mary Jean."

"I took the opportunity to order coffee and a few sweets. I hope you don't mind."

"I shouldn't be eating those things, but I'm addicted to sweets," she said.

"I'm glad I'm not the only one, because at home, my wife forbids sweets. So I indulge whenever I'm out." He held the chair for her and then sat, opening the button on his suit.

The coffee and a tray of croissants and cinnamon rolls arrived. The waiter filled their cups and they waited for him to depart. Andrei leaned forward a little and spoke in a soft voice. "I have something to tell you. I learned it this morning."

"I'm anxious to hear it," Mary Jean said in a lowered voice and quickly did a clearance check of their immediate surroundings by turning and observing around them. Then she nodded to Andrei to continue.

Andrei relayed the story from the ship's captain. "In addition to all that, I have an old picture of a Russian nuclear engineer who is no longer in Russia. He left the country a few months ago and we don't know where he is. His name is Yuri Borisov. I will get you the biographical data as soon as Moscow sends it to me. There is a good possibility, according to my people, that he may be the same man I am telling you about."

He passed the picture over to her. Mary Jean viewed the face of a young man on it and realized that she would have to have something to trade for this information. Even in the counterterrorist business nothing came for free.

"Andrei, I will get you the intel we have on what is going on in Savannah as soon as we have anything. If your captain friend tells you any more, or any specific details on the two suspects, we'll act on it immediately. In the meantime, I have to get this to the right people." She grabbed her handbag and stood up.

"Thank you," she said sincerely. "I owe you one."

"Please forgive me for not escorting you out, but these cinnamon rolls are still calling me," Andrei said, giving her a wide smile.

Mary Jean headed for the White House and made some phone calls to alert the appropriate people. She learned they would all be present in the Situation Room when she arrived. On entering the room, she showed no surprise on seeing the President already seated.

"Well, Mary Jean, what have you got for us?" President Brennan asked.

"We have a problem."

15

FIVE DAYS AGO — AFTERNOON

Office of the Director of Security Operations, Moscow

NIKOLAI VASILEV, THE DIRECTOR OF SECURITY OPERATIONS, SWORE OUT loud to no one in his empty office. His day resembled an airplane crash for him. The initiation of this current state of mind had begun first thing that morning, with a call from his mistress to say she would be gone for a few days to visit her mother. Then, to compound his problems, his wife had informed him that they had accepted a dinner invitation with her society group that night. He would be bored to death, and besides, he had forgotten about that social arrangement, hoping something would come up to save him from it.

Now came the call from Andrei Marshankin. He replaced the receiver in the cradle afterward. At last, redemption, as the information from the attaché in Washington would suffice to get him out of the dreadful evening with boring people. Perhaps the day wouldn't be a complete loss.

He picked up the phone that connected him by direct line with the minister of defense. "I'm sorry to disturb you, Minister. There is a situation that I think you need to know about."

"Damnit, Nikolai, can't it wait till morning? I'm already late for the state dinner with the Chinese."

"No, Minister. You remember the recent incident with the atomic detonation in Saudi Arabia. The one the world doesn't know about."

Nikolai fidgeted in his seat as he waited to ensure the minister remembered.

"Yes, of course. So what?"

Nikolai clenched the phone tightly. "Well, we may have another incident brewing from the same source. The Russian who got away is apparently in the United States with an atomic devise."

"*Gavno!*" (*shit*, in Russian) was all the minister uttered. There followed a moment of silence before the man said, "Tell me what you have, Director," addressing Nikolai by his title to put whatever followed on a formal level.

After relating the information provided by the attaché in Washington, Nikolai went on to remind the minister of the shared intelligence with the Americans following the incident in Saudi Arabia. Then he concluded with, "The methodology to construct the weapon was definitely Russian, and the device is now on American soil. We must assume the Russian also constructed this weapon."

"I'll have to go to President Grinko on this. I'll get back to you shortly." The minister hung up.

Nikolai figured the politician would without doubt order him to do something, but what? He needed to think. To help in this difficult task, he went to the sideboard, got out his private vodka, and poured himself a large shot. In one quick motion, he gulped it down. There, much better. Now he could think.

What would he do if he were in charge? Of course . . . he would need to stop that Russian. *We can't allow an atomic explosion in America with a Russian-made weapon.* Not good. He needed to get a team together to prevent this, and he knew of only one man he could trust to act in time. If the thing ever reached America, it would be used soon or risk being discovered. So he must act fast and be ahead of his masters in the Kremlin.

"Tasya," he called to his secretary. A plump elderly woman

dressed in solid black entered his office. "Get me Colonel Anton Petrovich Ivanov."

"Yes, Director," she said over her shoulder as she exited the room.

No wonder I need a mistress before going home to my wife. He put up with that fat old bitch of a secretary all day every day. *Why can't I get a beautiful young thing?* He knew the answer—the bureaucracy of tenure. *You can't make them work and you can't fire them. I bet it's the same all over the world,* he thought.

His direct line to the minister rang as he refilled his glass with a second shot of vodka. He slammed it down on the sideboard, splashing most of the vodka out of the glass, and rushed to pick up the phone. "Yes, Minister."

"The president is extremely worried about this development. He has directed that you are to do everything possible so that Russia will not be blamed or implicated for any event that happens on American soil with a weapon built with Russian technology. The West, or maybe the entire world could blame us for this attack. They might see it as a Russian plot to get back in as a major superpower by crippling America with an atomic explosion on their territory. Am I making this clear?"

Does the asshole think I am deaf? "Of course, Minister. Perfectly." Nikolai wished he still held that glass of vodka in his hand.

"The president," the minister continued, "doesn't want us to be blamed for supporting the terrorist attempts against America. If possible, he wants the weapon retrieved without the Americans having knowledge of our actions. Do you understand his order?"

No, minister, why don't you tell me again since you seem to like the sound of your own voice? thought Nikolai, but he said, "Clearly. I'll handle it."

"See that you do. Keep me informed, and tell me when you have succeeded."

Nikolai heard the buzz of the telephone line.

Well, at least he had correctly anticipated their actions, and he'd already initiated his own plan to accomplish it. His secretary let him know that Colonel Ivanov had arrived.

On entering the director's office, the colonel presented himself at attention. His frame towered over the director as he looked at Nikolai with his bulldog face. The director took the man in and saw the picture of someone you would not want to piss off on a bright sunny day in the open, never mind a dark alley at night.

"Colonel, I have an assignment for you. First, however, I do want to go over a few details, as it has been some time since I last saw you. It was right after you had returned from Chechnya, if I am not mistaken."

"Correct, Director." Not even a muscle of Colonel Ivanov's toned body flinched as he stood at attention.

"Relax, Colonel. You accomplished a very difficult and dangerous mission for this office. You were able to take out the command and control structure of a large group of rebels with only a small force, and then you were in charge of the soldiers who killed the terrorists at that school and rescued the children. So I think you have what it takes to accomplish the mission I am now assigning you."

Anton moved from the attention position to a more comfortable stance. His uniform bore the insignia of a colonel of infantry, with numerous decorations for bravery, and he sported the badge of the elite paratroopers.

"Have you ever been to the United States?"

"Yes. I went on an exchange visit for three weeks last year."

"How is your English?"

"Not so good. I can understand a lot better than I can speak."

"Before I go on, would you join me in a drink?"

"Of course, Minister."

Nikolai went over to the sideboard and poured two hefty shots. He presented one to the colonel and toasted to his health. They both downed the liquid.

The director continued, "For this mission I will get a translator to go with you. He will be fluent in the North American English and will be able to help in that area. Do you have someone who you would like to take with you?"

"Well, Director, that depends on what you want me to do," replied Anton.

"I want you to go to America, retrieve an atomic weapon and either kill or capture a renegade Russian scientist."

"In that case, I do have a soldier I would like to take with me. He served in Afghanistan as a sniper and was with me in the same capacity in Chechnya. He's the best marksman in the army, and if I need to engage the target at a distance, he's the man for the job. At close range, I can handle any situation."

"By my authority, you can take him and get any specific equipment you deem necessary for the mission. If the weapon is used in America, the president fears we may be blamed for aiding the terrorists since the technology is Russian. We would prefer to get it back without the Americans ever getting hold of it. In any case, you must stop this man, this Yuri Borisov."

"I will provide your office with a list for our embassy in Washington. They will need to prepare certain items to be ready on our arrival. When do you want us to go?"

"I will arrange for the three of you to be on Air France flight 2045 tomorrow morning. It arrives in Washington at three fifty-five tomorrow afternoon. Someone will meet you and provide the equipment you request, and they will give you an update on any changes in the situation. At that time, they will inform you of the target, give you a picture and any current information on his whereabouts. We also believe he's working with a Middle Eastern terrorist group. You don't need any of those details, pictures, etc., and you can't carry it with you on the flight."

"What authority do I have?"

"Your orders come directly from the president. You will have a written order that will give you blanket authority to get this mission accomplished. Do you have any questions?"

"No, Director. I'll get it done."

"I'm counting on you, Colonel. I also relay the president's desire not to have a trial for this man. Do I make myself clear?"

16

FIVE DAYS AGO — AFTERNOON — WASHINGTON D.C

Mary Jean wanted to unravel the mystery of the man in the photograph taken in the Georgetown restaurant. As a first step in finding out the identity of the man, she arranged to meet with Michael Anthony, deputy director of the FBI and her longtime friend, at the Starbucks at Thirteenth and Pennsylvania Avenue. She ordered a skinny double latte and was sitting down at a small two-person table when she saw Mike enter.

Mary Jean smiled at him and he returned it. He wore a lightweight raincoat over a dark suit to help protect him from the blustery wind. She saw some gray starting to appear near his temples.

"Hi. Sorry I'm a little late. You said it was important, so I got here as quick as I could."

"Thanks, Mike. I had to call on you on short notice. I thought you might be the only one who could help in this, or more precisely, the only one I could trust to keep his mouth shut outside of my agency."

"Sounds clandestine," he said, smiling, "but then again, you have nothing to do with covert activity according to your job title. Do you?"

"You know damn good and well what I do."

"Let me get a cup of joe and I'll be right back to hear what you have to say."

He returned with his coffee and reclined in the chair, getting comfortable. "I'm all ears."

Mary Jean relayed to him how she had briefed the president on the movement of two operatives in the presence of Avery and Fazio. Subsequently, the named individuals had withstood an attack at the location she'd provided. Then she related what she'd witnessed at the restaurant, with Avery and another man apparently talking in a covert manner, and how she had taken a picture of the man in the restaurant. Mike sat back and said nothing for a long time.

"Do you have the photo?"

"I had my people make a print of it." She passed the small four-by-four print to Mike. He glanced at it for only a second.

"Well, I know who this is."

"You do. Out of all the people in the world, you know this man?"

"Yep. He's the third secretary at the Iranian embassy here in Washington. You know the FBI is responsible for monitoring diplomatic personnel on US soil. This guy has come up before. He gets around and talks to all kinds of Islamic groups all over the country. We suspect he carries instructions for some of the operatives here, but we don't have definite proof. At least, not enough to declare him PNG. Mary Jean, I'm getting tired of all this, so I put in for retirement. Not real soon but within a year. A guy named Rose is most likely to replace me. Good man, you'll get along with him."

"I'm sorry to hear that, but I know that when someone decides it's time, it's generally the right thing to do. I'll miss you." She stopped, her train of thought broken by his announcement. After a moment, she refocused and continued. "Can't you tag him as persona non grata without evidence?"

"Yes, but not without causing an allegation in the Islamic community that the FBI is profiling Muslims and that we're harassing the Iranian embassy. Besides, you didn't see him talking with Avery directly."

"That's true, but it sure seemed like it from where I was sitting."

"I can get someone I trust to check into Avery a little more. You know, you could be opening up a can of worms. He's the president's oldest friend." Mike took a sip from his coffee, put it back on the table, and then looked at Mary Jean.

"I don't like it, but there appears to be something going on, or else my instincts have gone south. Since both Avery and Fazio were there when I told the president about where . . . hell, you know who they are, since Matt briefed you on the attack in Texas."

"I figured they were the ones you were talking about."

"Could you check up on both Avery and Fazio? You guys can operate legally in the States, the CIA can't. We can but don't really have the assets to do it properly. You do," Mary Jean concluded.

"You always know when you should listen to that sixth sense. That's how you saved my ass in the Gulf. You've said enough to convince me that there's something here, especially with your spotting the Iranian. I'll do some checking. What about anyone else who knew they were going to Texas?"

"Only the secretary at their office, SPAT, Inc. in Leesburg," Mary Jean said.

"I'll get back to you in a day or two."

"Thanks, Mike."

"Can you tell me what's going on with the operatives you mentioned? I assume they're your assets and there's something like a black op going on if the president asked about them."

"Mike, can you just trust me on this? If it gets to the point that you have to know more, I'll get it to you, but right now you don't want to know. I can tell you that the recent attacks on the military installations seem to have a direct bearing on this. Your agency is balls to the wall and overextended on trying to solve those occurrences, as is the military. What if another set of assaults happens in the next few days? Could you handle more?"

"I didn't say this—no. Hell, we're getting nowhere on the attacks of the last few days with no real leads. They all appear to have been planned for a long time. They were executed with precision, and the attackers have disappeared. The only connection that we've seen, and it might be coincidence, is that all the attacks happened at installations near universities."

"Well, all I can say now is that those operatives are involved in trying to solve a problem related to the attacks." Mary Jean's cell rang, and after seeing the caller, she ignored it. "Your office might get a call from Matt or Bridget in the near future for assistance in their efforts. If you do, I'll give you more then. Sorry I can't tell you more now, but it's over my head."

"No problem, since I know the president's involved. Let me see what we can come up with on those two. It's odd, but the national security adviser doesn't get a detailed background check, nor does the press secretary. They're given the clearances because the president puts them in the jobs and he trusts them. I'll admit it's not a perfect system. We'd like all people who get high-level security clearances to be checked out in detail, but that doesn't happen on all presidential appointments."

Mary Jean finished her coffee. "Thanks for coming. Say hello to Katie and the kids for me. I hope you enjoy your upcoming retirement."

"I'll be in touch, hang in there," he said, then got up and departed. Mary Jean waited a few minutes, lost in her thoughts about what they had experienced in the Gulf War. She hadn't thought of it in a long time. But now was not the time to reminisce. Now was the time to get the men who possessed the bomb.

She stood up, walked out of the coffee shop, and headed to SPAT, Inc. to give Matt and Bridget the president's orders.

17

FIVE DAYS AGO — 5 P.M. — LEESBURG, VIRGINIA

MATT WATCHED MARY JEAN'S CAR PULL UP IN FRONT OF THE BUILDING. He saw her retrieve her briefcase and walk toward the office. Her earlier phone call had alerted him to be prepared to move. He'd told Bridget and they'd gathered their to-go gear. They both checked their ever-ready suitcases that contained the necessary items for at least a week. The carry-on kit included the weapon they'd selected after many tests, an HK USP .45 Tactical with extended barrel, threaded for sound suppression with a suppressor, an ankle holster with a Kel-Tec 380, a KA-BAR knife, a Maglite flashlight, bottled water and high-energy snacks plus clothes.

Mary Jean's red hair flailed about in the breeze as she pushed open the office door. She'd arrived earlier than Matt had expected, and it would be more than another hour before Julia came back with Laura. Julia should be getting to Sherry's house about now. The general had stated that she carried orders for them from the president. Something must have come up, and they were prepared to go wherever she would send them. At least Mary Jean would care for Laura and get her back to Sherry's house after the weekend.

"Hello, General. Something must be up."

"Yes. We have reason to believe that the terrorist Yuri and his accomplice are in Savannah, Georgia," Mary Jean said. "After I brief you here, you are to go to Quantico Marine Corps base for a ride to Savannah in an Osprey 22."

"So what are we to do?" Bridget asked. She went over to the refrigerator and got out Diet cokes for all. She also unwrapped a cigar, but didn't light it.

Mary Jean sat down at a desk and nodded at the parrot.

"Don't worry, he won't repeat anything you say," Bridget joked. Matt grinned and Mary Jean went along with the humor as she shed her jacket and hung it over the back of a chair.

"Okay. Here's what we have." She relayed the conversation with the Russian attaché.

"It's time for us to get to Savannah. Julia will be back any minute. Can you wait for her?" Matt asked.

"Of course. By the way, I borrowed this little gadget for you. It's brand-new from the tech boys, and they say it can detect the presence of uranium up to a mile, and the residual radiation for a short time after an atomic device is moved from a location. If there is a weapon, you should hear it beep. The sound increases as you get closer to a source. As you can see, it's only the size of a pack of cigarettes. Now, I must make some calls. If I receive any info on the exact location of our terrorists, I'll get it to you and arrange for the local FBI to assist you in their apprehension. Capture him if you can but take no unnecessary risk. We know why he's here, and there's some information to be gained by interrogation, but not that much. Clear?"

"Yes, ma'am," Bridget said with enthusiasm, then picked up her backpack and the atomic detector, and headed for the door.

"Be careful," Mary Jean said.

Matt got up to get his things and the phone rang.

JULIA PULLED INTO THE DRIVEWAY AND PARKED BESIDE MATT'S CAR SO that Laura could get into it while Julia parked Sherry's car in the garage. She needed to return the keys and jacket. Laura got out on the passenger side, went around the BMW, and got in. Julia clicked on the remote to open the garage door. At that moment, she noticed the front door slightly ajar. Weird, she thought. A sixth sense kicked in, perhaps women's intuition, but she felt something not right. The door would not be left ajar with this cold weather.

"Laura, you wait here." She got out of the car, went to the front door, and pushed it open with her arm.

"Oh! Shit!" came out at the sight of the body of Sherry on the floor. *Run*, she told herself. No, she needed to find out if Sherry was alive. She rushed to the prone figure and felt for a pulse but found none. She shouted for Sherry's husband. No response.

Julia looked to her left and saw what were without doubt bullet holes in the hallway. Swiftly for her size, she moved along the hall. When she reached the bedroom door, she peered inside. The shattered glass, the bloodstains by the window, and a foot caught on the sill were taken in at a glance. No shoe, only a bare foot. She figured it was useless to go outside to check on him with the number of bullet holes everywhere, but to be certain, she tiptoed to the window and stared at the bullet-ridden body.

"My God. What happened here?" Her heart pounded and her mouth became dry as her hands trembled. She tried to walk but found it difficult. She almost stopped breathing, and her mind raced ahead to what this might mean to Laura and to Matt. *OMG*, she thought, *this is unbelievable. Holy shit. I didn't think anyone would do this.*

She deliberately touched nothing except to press on Sherry's neck to find a pulse. She must call the police. *No. Not a smart idea. Get hold of Matt. Have to get my ass in gear and get out of here before Laura gets fidgety and comes into the house*, she thought. *Must go.*

Julia carefully moved down the hall way and out the door without closing it for fear of leaving fingerprints. On the way in, she only pushed the door with her elbow. She walked, telling herself not to run, to the car.

"Is everything okay?" Laura asked.

"Sure, sweetie. It's all okay. We're going to your daddy's now. Let me drive Sherry's car into the garage." She did this and wiped the steering wheel clean, then the door handle as she got out. She went inside and took the overnight bag Sherry had prepared earlier for Laura. Then she decided to go into the little girl's bedroom, packed more clothes, put them into another suitcase, and left the house.

She stepped outside and walked to the BMW, put the gas into it, and drove out of the neighborhood at normal speed. Three minutes later, she pulled into a CVS store and told Laura she needed to buy something and to wait in the car. She entered the drugstore, tugged out her cell, and called SPAT, Inc.

Answer the damn phone, come on, she thought. Then she heard Matt on the line.

"I want you to listen. Don't talk till I'm through," she said at breakneck speed, hoping Matt would get the meaning.

"Okay."

"Your sister-in-law has been murdered, along with her husband."

"What?" said Matt. "Where's Laura? Is she all right?"

"Listen, damnit. Listen to me." Julia stopped for a second to compose herself. "Sorry, but this is bad, so I need to tell you everything before you ask questions."

"Go on."

Julia tried her best to relate all that had transpired in as much detail as she could. She stopped to take a breath and then asked, "What do you want me to do?"

"Hang on, I've got to talk to the general and Bridget. Get in the car and come here. I'll speak to you after I confer with them. Try to make sure no one is following you."

"Okay. Call me back soon."

MATT FELT HIS FACE DRAIN OF ALL COLOR WHEN HE TURNED TO FACE Bridget and Mary Jean. Both had heard his end of the conversation and knew something was up. He took a long swig from the Coke.

"We've got a real problem," he said.

Mary Jean pulled out her cell as soon as Matt finished relaying what Julia had told him. "Wait till I get some people moving on this. What's the address?" Matt gave it to her, and she moved away as she spoke into the phone. Matt walked over to where Bridget stood, and she grabbed his hands. "Laura is safe. This must be aimed at you some way, somehow."

"Yeah . . . possibly. But why, and how?"

"Remember that asshole's threat to you in Texas?"

Matt took a few seconds before he nodded. He was attempting to think. How could this have happened?

"We'll get through this, but there is a terrorist with an atomic bomb in Savannah. That's our priority. The general will keep Laura, I'm sure," Bridget said.

"No. I think we should leave her with Julia. She knows her, and they've been together before. I'll ask her to take care of her until we get back. I'll take the time to figure out what will happen then. Right now, you're right. First thing is Savannah, and that's what we have to do at this moment."

"Matt," Mary Jean said, "I'll have the house looked after and see what we can learn. Then the police will come and find what looks like a simple home invasion gone wrong. Julia will be briefed on how to handle the questions and told that you and your daughter are on a winter cruise in the Caribbean. I'll be glad to take Laura for the time you're away."

"Thank you, but I'll ask Julia if she could keep her. You're going to be very busy over the next few days as we go after these guys."

"You're right, and I'll have to cancel my niece again. One of these days we might find time to get the kids to play together," Mary Jean said.

"Let's hope." Matt picked up his suitcase and headed for the door, following Bridget out to her car.

"I'll call Julia when we're on the way to Quantico and tell her what to do and what's going to happen."

Mary Jean's phone rang. She indicated for Matt to wait. She

answered it and handed it to Matt a few seconds later, saying, "I made two calls while you and Bridget were talking."

Matt took the phone. "Hello?"

The president conveyed his condolences and assured him everything would be done to catch the killers of his sister-in-law and her husband.

18

FOUR DAYS AGO — SAVANNAH, GEORGIA

Marilyn reclined on the sand, thinking of the events in her life over the last six months. She stretched out her arms and legs to their full extent as she enjoyed her five hours on the beach at Tybee. God, she still couldn't believe her husband had cheated on her with the next-door neighbor. That bitch wasn't anything exceptional—a little plump, small tits, and a crooked smile. Why? What had possessed him?

She rose, stretched, and walked to the water's edge. She dipped her foot in and felt the chilly ocean saltwater. Too cold for her to go in, but it felt right for a refreshing walk on the beach.

After ten minutes, Marilyn returned to her spot and decided to give her back a few more rays. She couldn't stay on her stomach long as the silicone implants in her breasts made it uncomfortable to lie in that position. Eventually she rolled over onto her side and picked up the book she'd brought along. The pages started with a steamy sex encounter.

She put the paperback down and laid her head on the extra towel she used as a pillow. Now the memory of her first time came back. They weren't married yet, and she was a virgin. They went back to his place and drank more wine after planning the wedding guest list.

One thing led to another, and she ended up on his bed. She remembered being a little woozy from the wine, but she went along with it. They were going to be hitched in a month, so what did it matter?

The next time proved not so traumatic and he showed more consideration. He helped her get comfortable, and she came to enjoy it. She thought she'd always provided him with all the sex he could use or need. Obviously, she hadn't. The bastard had gone and dipped his wick in every hole he could find.

Well, she was rid of him now and a free woman again. Checking her watch, she realized that the time really did fly at the beach. Four o'clock—enough sunbathing for one day. Gathering her things, she headed for the hotel to indulge in a gourmet dinner.

The drive back along US-80 to downtown Savannah took twenty minutes. She was staying at the Inn on Bay Street in the heart of the old historic district. This city, so different from the throngs of people and cars in Atlanta—she loved this place. The feeling of peace emanated from the streets of old Savannah. The traditions of the Old South remained alive and well here. Life seemed to progress at a slower pace, more livable, more enjoyable instead of the more dangerous existence in Atlanta. She planned to move to this lovely city after the divorce came through. An air traffic controller position at the Savannah–Hilton Head International Airport had opened last week. She decided to apply. At the least, it would give her a start in her new life.

Marilyn arrived at the hotel, showered, and dressed for dinner. She went out onto Bay Street and took the steps down to River Street. This street stretched along the river for blocks and offered bars, restaurants, specialty shops, cookie stores, bike paraphernalia shops, and many more ways to separate one from one's money. She enjoyed the feeling that it was alive, exciting, and bustling with pedestrians, with little motor traffic. Old stones from sailing ship ballast made up the bumpy pavement of some streets. What had once been rails for a trolley, at present unused, lay embedded in the middle of the street.

As she strolled along River Street, a monstrous ocean-going vessel passed only a few yards from the sidewalk. Its size gave the impression that it was barely moving from where Marilyn stood. The ship towered at least a hundred feet over her head. Where else could a large cargo vessel pass you by on a city street full of people, mostly tourists, and not cause even the slightest interruption? Amazing, thought Marilyn.

She decided to stop at Kevin Barry's for a beer. The Irish pub bustled with people having a late afternoon drink. After ordering a Guinness, she found a table near the door to watch the human parade moving on the street. From her vantage point, she stared in amazement at an open-topped hearse passing by, advertising ghost tours. *Later I might do that*, she thought.

She looked around and sensed a man watching her. The inside of the pub was too dark to make out his features, but he held a lighted cigarette. No one else in the place smoked. Somehow she knew his sideways glances examined her. She could feel it. Time to move on. She finished her drink and went out to inquire about the ghost tour. She would take it. What the hell, she intended to enjoy her short vacation, and going back to her room alone held no attraction.

She walked to the Hyatt hotel and took the outside elevator up to the Bay Street level, crossed the street and proceeded toward Congress Street and the open market area.

After the American Revolution, the city had changed the names of the streets from King, Queen, etc., to President, Congress, State, etc. Savannah exhibited all the characteristics of a colonial city. She had read in an information booklet at the hotel that the city had been founded in 1733. Marilyn wanted to learn more about the history of the place. If nothing else, it would enhance the charm and pre-Revolutionary character of the city for her. Where did the ghosts come from? She decided to find out.

She arrived at the old market, where a small sales office advertised GHOST TOURS on its little board. She paid and planned to return at the start time. She had an hour to kill and decided to get a light snack. On Congress Street, she found Garibaldi's restaurant and went in. A warm décor greeted her, and the long bar to the right of the entrance beckoned.

"Can I get a glass of wine and order an appetizer here at the bar?"

"You certainly can," replied the barman, taking a good look at her in the light blue low-cut blouse that displayed her boobs at their best. Her blond hair was combed out from the bun she had worn it in on the beach, and it lightly touched her shoulders. The tight jeans showed off another of her physical assets.

After eating a dish of delicious calamari and having a glass of chardonnay, she headed out to start the ghost tour.

19

FOUR DAYS AGO — SAVANNAH, GEORGIA

Yuri returned to the rental house with some over-the-counter medicines and a few snacks from the convenience store. At least they would have something to eat until he got some sleep. Exhaustion now plagued him after being up all night. He regretted the death of the two seamen, but his and Basam's survival came first.

He worried about Basam's condition. Something wasn't right there, but he couldn't fathom why the man rejected going to a doctor. He stressed to Basam that they were safely ashore in America and no one pursued them. Now there existed an opportunity to get medical attention. Basam refused again, so he gave him the Tylenol and the aspirin, along with some Pepto Bismol to settle his stomach. Now he needed sleep, but he wanted to try one more time.

"Basam, you look awful. We should take you to see a doctor."

"No. I'm okay. I'll be fine now that we're here. What's the latest from Fatimah?"

"I'll send them an update on our location and ask for their instructions. Then I'm going to get a few hours' sleep."

"We have to get ready to carry out the mission," Basam insisted.

"Not now. Now I sleep," Yuri said with emphasis.

Yuri thought Basam looked at him with hatred, something like when his brother had spat out "infidel" at the pursuing Americans in Saudi Arabia. He didn't need this now.

"Basam, we'll take care of it and do the mission, but we need to be rested to get it done, and now I must rest."

"Okay," Basam replied, and Yuri could see that he softened.

"Take the medicine and get better. We both need to be up for this. I'll send the message and get up in four hours."

"I'm going to hide the weapon. While you were out, I discovered the bathtub can be moved, and the panel behind it contains what looks like the plumbing connections. There's enough room to conceal it inside there and slide the tub back into position. No one would search there."

"Okay. See you later." Yuri went into the bedroom and fell on the bed, asleep in less than a minute.

Basam went into the bathroom, pulled the old bathtub aside, and opened the panel behind it, exposing pipes and insulation. He wedged the case behind the pipes and covered it with the insulation. Then he replaced the wood cover and slid the tub back into position.

Three hours later, Yuri woke in a sweat. He got out of bed and wobbled on his feet. He still hadn't gotten his land legs after the two-week sea voyage. Sometimes the floor seemed to sway, and then he steadied itself. Bizarre feeling. He checked the email but found no new messages, so he sent an update to the Fatimah people, hoping for a quick response.

He went out to find Basam asleep on the couch. Going back to the bedroom, he emptied Basam's duffle bag. It contained a pair of jeans, two shirts, underwear, toilet items, a 9mm Glock, two magazines, a box of ammo, and a flashlight.

He put on clean clothes and placed his pistol at the small of his back. No reason, as no pursued him, but it made him feel comfortable. In the living room, he placed Basam's weapon on the table near the couch where the Arab slept. He shook him awake.

"I'm going out for a while. Will you be all right?"

"Sure. Did we get a message yet?"

"No. See you later," Yuri said.

"Where are you going?"

"Out to do some looking around."

"Don't go until we get our instructions," Basam said.

"I'll be back in time to do whatever they order," Yuri promised. "I'll leave your pistol here and take mine, and the computer is in my backpack. That way I'll get the message as soon as possible and then come back to get you."

"Okay." Basam started to doze off again.

Yuri left, walked to the main road, and headed toward downtown. After thirty minutes of walking around the open market area, he ended up on River Street, went into Kevin Barry's, and ordered a vodka.

"What would you like with it, tonic or a vodka martini?" asked the barman.

"Just vodka and some ice."

"You got it," replied the barman in a poor imitation of Irish.

Yuri took his drink and moved to a vacant table. He saw the Wi-Fi sign, took out his computer, and opened his email account. A response arrived.

"The target will be going to Atlanta in a few days. Exact time will be provided in next message. Meet him on landing at airport to give your present. Details will follow within twenty-four hours."

Yuri knew what that meant. Take out the president when he lands in Atlanta. He considered what he would do, but first he wanted his money.

"Will meet plane in Atlanta once money for expenses arrives in agreed amount into account. Will check account before meeting man."

That should achieve the desired result. They hadn't deposited his five million as yet, and they understood that if they wanted him to move on the target, the money had to be there. He felt certain they would comply.

He ordered another vodka, as he could afford just about anything now, and he would be smart enough not to flash his wealth and attract attention. He signaled for the barman when something caught his eye. A woman had seated herself near the window, and her silhouetted shape captured his gaze. She had a beautiful figure. On that thought, he lit a cigarette.

Stop it, Yuri, he ordered himself. *This is no time to think of women. You've had no interest in them for years, and now that you have lots of money, you start to think about getting laid. Dumb ass.* But he continued to glance at the woman. She apparently noticed his attentions, or someone else's gawking. Observing the woman as she glanced in his direction, he concluded that she possessed inordinate beauty. She picked up her purse and headed out the door. As she exited, he got a good look at her. She opened a desire in him that he hadn't experienced before. He believed in fate. In this case, she couldn't see him in the back of the dimly lit bar, so why not?

He paid his bill and after a minute set off in the direction the woman had gone. He thought it odd, both of them going in the general direction of his place. As he walked, Yuri realized he couldn't abandon Basam. He broke off his trail on the woman and headed back to their rental house. There, he would attempt to solidify his intention of forgetting that woman.

He passed a grocery store and bought cigarettes and food to last a couple of days with money he took from an ATM. For a second time, he used the card that Basam's brother had given him in Moscow at the start of all this.

When he entered the house, Basam gave intermittent snores from the couch. Yuri put the supplies away before he heard Basam stirring.

"How are you?" Yuri questioned.

"I'm fine. Did we get instructions yet?"

"Not really, only some details regarding the target, who will be in Atlanta in a few days. We will go there when they give us more instructions. I replied and gave an update on our situation. They said to wait for further information. You sure you're okay?"

"I'm all right. The medicine seemed to help, but I can't stop the runs."

"Can I get you something to eat? I brought in some supplies for a few days."

"No. I don't feel like eating."

Yuri didn't want to stay here and watch Basam—a depressing thought. The image of the woman flashed into his mind again.

"Look, Basam, I'm going to go for a walk around town. Here's sixty dollars if you decide to go out anywhere. You all right?"

"Sure. We're safe here, so don't you get into trouble. Come back as soon as you get the order to move. Okay?"

"Will do." Yuri picked up his knapsack containing the computer and gun. He headed for town. No, he'd proceeded toward the last place he glimpsed the woman.

20

FOUR DAYS AGO — 4 P.M. — WASHINGTON, D.C

Major General Marshankin, the Russian defense attaché in America, picked out Colonel Anton Ivanov as he exited the customs area at Dulles International Airport in the Virginia suburbs outside Washington, D.C. He recognized him from the digital picture Moscow had sent him along with the list of requested items the colonel wanted on his arrival.

After a brief introduction, the general said, "If you will follow me, I have your equipment. There is only one thing missing. I couldn't get my hands on the radiation detector you asked for. I have arranged for a private aircraft to take you to Savannah. It's over at Signature Fixed Base Operations and is prepared to depart in one hour. The items you requested are already loaded on the aircraft. We'll transport you over to the plane in my vehicles."

"Thank you, General. Is there any new information on our target?"

They got into the general's car, and the other two men accompanying the colonel got into another sedan with their luggage. The two vehicles headed for the FBO.

"I wanted to wait until we were in the car to relay that there has been new information. I believe we have the exact location of Yuri Borisov. An old friend of mine, who is the captain of the ship that brought them to the States, called me back a few hours ago and gave me the address where the men went after they left his vessel." He handed Anton a map taken from an Internet search engine, and it contained the target's location.

"My friend," General Marshankin continued, "said that they were there as of early this morning. He can't assist further as he has now departed Savannah."

"It's nice to have such a good friend," Anton said, "and I bet there's more to the friendship than you're letting on."

"Perhaps you're right, Colonel. It's enjoyable to have old comrades-in-arms."

They arrived at the Signature FBO.

"I leave you here. I'll have to share this information on the location with the Americans, but I can wait until morning. You should complete your task by then, and I can maintain the appearance of cooperation." He handed him a card with phone numbers. "When you call, I'll arrange for the same plane to pick you up. Enjoy success in your mission. When you're finished, I'll book your transportation back to Moscow."

"Thank you, General. I'll be calling you soon."

Marshankin departed. Anton and his two assistants went out to the airplane. The jet, a blue-and-white Cessna Citation V, the largest member of the straight-wing Cessna fleet, possessed sufficient fuel to travel to Savannah.

Anton met the pilots and asked if he could check on the bags delivered on the plane. After retrieving them, the pilot went forward to prepare for departure. Two suitcases, one containing communications gear to enable inter-team voice and audio transmissions, plus three pistols, all Glock 17s with fixed sights and seventeen-round magazines—one extra magazine for each weapon. No additional ammo, since this mission wasn't envisioned to include a firefight. The other suitcase contained a Russian SAKO TRG-22, a 7.62mm sniper rifle, broken down into component parts.

"Ravshan, what do you think?" he asked the brother of Nodira from the Republic of Uzbekistan.

"It's an old model, Colonel, but I employed it in Afghanistan, and it's reliable. They've included a high-power scope. We have no time to zero the rifle, but I'll enter the settings I used then and that should put me within acceptable tolerance of four centimeters up to five hundred meters."

"Okay, we'll distribute this when we get to Savannah and rent a car. Igor, you'll do the talking to get the car, since you're here to take care of things in English."

Igor Belofsky nodded as he wrinkled his brow. His sandy hair, egg-shaped head and thick glasses gave him the appearance of an old college professor, and indeed he was, in a sense. For many years he had taught English at the army language school after his return from four years of study in America.

The flight to Savannah took only an hour and a half. The plane deposited them at the Signature FBO on the cargo side of the field, where the Georgia Air National Guard facilities stood diagonally across from the Signature building. The Gulfstream aircraft factory, where multimillion-dollar executive jets were assembled, occupied a large space on the airport.

The copilot deplaned first, helped them off, and placed their luggage on the ground near the steps of the plane. They picked up their bags and headed for the inside lounge. The pilot started the engines and taxied away.

On the flight, the pilot had radioed before they landed and asked for a rental to be available, and Igor attended to the details while the other two moved the gear to the car. Anton opened the suitcase with the pistols and distributed one to each out of sight of any prying eyes.

"Now it's time to get this done," he said.

"Colonel, you know I'm not field-trained and am only here to help with the language." The short, stocky man didn't look at Anton.

"Yes, Igor, but you are under my command here, and you will do as you are told. Understand?"

"Yes," Igor said, lowering his eyes and hunching his shoulders. He moved to get into the back of the car.

"I hope," Anton said, "that it won't be necessary to use the rifle now that we know exactly where he is. It's only here in case we need to do the job from a distance."

"Inside a house, the pistols will be better," Ravshan replied.

"Agreed." With everyone in the car, Ravshan drove away from the passenger terminal out onto Dean Forest Road and headed for the city. The clock on the car's dashboard read 8:35 p.m. as they sped along I-16.

21

FOUR DAYS AGO — SAVANNAH, GEORGIA

Air National Guard Terminal - 8:30 p.m.

Matt and Bridget deplaned from the Marine Corps Osprey minutes after the Russian team exited the airport in their rental car. An airman waited to take them over to the civilian passenger terminal on the other side of the field, where Matt arranged for a car. He drove out the long exit road to I-95 and addressed Bridget. "I'll book us into separate rooms."

"Sounds good to me." Bridget took out a map of the area she picked up at the rental office. "Where do we start looking? We don't have a clue as to his exact location. If we do find it, we should get the FBI to handle it, don't you think?"

"We might need help, and the general told us to give her a call and she'd get the cavalry to come to our aid in no time."

"If we find him," Bridget said in a deadpan tone, "clarify for me. Do we try to take him alive, or just shoot first and ask questions later?"

"I'm in favor of shooting first, but I realize there's substantial value in getting this guy alive," Matt stated as he merged onto I-16 and headed for downtown. They checked into the Comfort Suites on Bay Street and went to their rooms.

Matt bought two Diet Cokes in the hall machine and gave one to Bridget. They went to his room to check on the gear.

"Let's put on our commo in case we're separated, and get the weapons ready," Matt said.

They accomplished both tasks. The communication gear allowed them to talk to one another through almost invisible microphones on their shirt collars and an embedded receiver in the ear that was much smaller than the average hearing aid. The power pack slipped easily onto the belt or could be hidden under some clothing. They both chambered a round in the weapons and put on the safety. The army training proved difficult to overcome. A weapon without a bullet in the chamber when you are going into battle is nothing more than a club. In the two seconds it takes to chamber a round, you could already be one second dead.

"What now?" Bridget queried.

"Let's sit and play this out," Matt said as he chugalugged the Coke.

"What about some food?"

"Sure, let's go out and find a restaurant." Matt stood up and headed for the door.

They exited the hotel and walked toward the sound of music they heard in the distance. In a few minutes, they arrived at the market area of old Savannah, where a band performed on the stage in the opening between two rows of buildings. They strolled the two blocks of the market area to the end of the plaza and picked one of the open-air restaurants. After they ordered a large pizza and two Guinness beers, they settled back to listen to the band that played somewhere out of sight.

"Okay," Bridget said, "this is the way I see it. They're here in Savannah. Why? Because, after getting off the boat, they would want to rest for a day or so and make sure no one was on to them."

"Sounds reasonable," Matt said.

"They would also need to get some supplies, since they wouldn't carry any from the container ship the general said they arrived on. It wasn't like a cruise liner with all the amenities of home. What would you do if you landed here without much and carried an atomic weapon with you?"

Matt took some time to think. He sipped on his beer and said, "I'd find a place to hide. Not a hotel. Too many questions, and there is room service that might find my bomb, and I couldn't put it in the safe."

"So where?"

"A short-term rental, maybe—"

"There are too many to check," Bridget interrupted, "and we don't yet have a picture of the man to pass out. The general said we might get one by tomorrow if the Russians provide it. If it's old and he's now using some kind of disguise—at best, it's probably a long shot."

Matt took time to search Bridget's eyes. He saw those beautiful browns, flaked with a glittering of gold, and he smiled. She was something, but at present he concentrated on the task at hand—find the terrorists with the atomic bomb.

"What would you do if you were them?" Matt asked.

"I'd need some time to get my land legs back. We don't know if they have a target and a timeframe at this point. Assume they don't, because if they do, we're already in deep shit and won't be able to stop them without some outside help and a lot of luck if they act within the next twenty-four hours."

"Let's assume you're correct and they're still here waiting for instructions. I'd want to go out and see the place. They have time on their hands until they receive orders, and nothing to do in a strange city. I'm guessing, but it's probably the first time they've been in America."

Bridget got up and headed for the restroom. Matt tried to think what he would do. It seemed logical to stay out of trouble, not to drink too much to arouse suspicion, not to be together. Right. It would attract too many looks to have a Russian and an Arab hanging out together. *I'd split up and explore on my own, not going with someone people would glare at with distrust.*

On her return, he told Bridget his thoughts. "Do you think they're horny after being on the boat for a few weeks? Might seek some companionship?" she queried.

"Yes," said Matt, "but I believe at this stage they've already obtained money, probably acquired from some ATM with cards we don't know about. Maybe they'll hit the nightlife here in the city to get some action. I bet they would be afraid of our hookers here. Besides, the Saudi might not touch an infidel woman. But then again ... maybe the Russian will go out to find some entertainment around town."

"If he has money, he can hang out in the nice places. Maybe we should take a look at the upmarket establishments," Bridget suggested.

"Before we do anything, I'll call Julia and see how things are." Matt took out his cell and dialed. Julia answered on the third ring.

"Julia, it's Matt. How are things?" He could hear Gandalf in the background, saying, "Pretty Laura, pretty Laura, squawk."

"Everything is fine. Where are you?"

"In Savannah. We're about to go chasing the bad guys and I just wanted to check on Laura."

"She's doing wonderful, considering the trauma of the day. You know I switch off the phone at midnight and we go to bed. So please don't try to get me after that until six in the morning."

"May I speak with her?" He waited.

"Hi, Daddy. Are you and Bridget in Savannah? Is it warm there?"

"Yes, sweets, we're here and it's hot. Are you all right?"

"Sure. When are you coming home? I need to talk because Julia told me some things, but what is going to happen to me."

"We will talk as soon as I finish this job. It's very important that I complete it and then we'll settle everything for the future."

"Okay. I have to go to bed now. Good night, Daddy."

"Good night, little one." The phone call ended.

Bridget waited for Matt to say something. He could tell she wanted to hear his thoughts on the Laura situation.

"I don't know how to solve Laura's future right now. I'll have to do more planning and thinking, but that'll have to wait. Let's get out and see if we can figure out where we might find the Russian. We eliminated the Saudi from doing the nightlife, but that may be a false conclusion, since I've seen many of them go bonkers in a Western city, away from the restraints of Islam."

"We have to start somewhere, but for now we have nothing to go on until the general gets us more information."

IN JULIA'S HOUSE IN RESTON, VIRGINIA, LAURA FINISHED FEEDING THE parrot and learned how to cover the cage for the night. Julia led her to the guest bedroom in her small condominium and got her tucked in for the night. She stayed until Laura slept and then turned off the light and closed the door.

Julia went to her closet and put on an outfit she would wear for a regular meeting she attended every week on the same day. She slipped out of the apartment at 9:15 without a sound.

22

FOUR DAYS AGO — DISTRICT OF COLUMBIA

AFTER MATT LEFT FOR QUANTICO, MARY JEAN HEADED BACK TO THE White House for a briefing. The president had asked her to come and tell him everything about the hit at the kid's house. Mary Jean arrived at 8:30 p.m.

The room contained representatives from the NSA, DIA, FBI and Homeland Security. The president opened the meeting with a summary of the report Mary Jean had given him earlier. They now assumed that a terrorist had landed on US soil with a weapon of mass destruction. As of a few hours ago, they believed it to be in Savannah.

"Anything new?" President Christopher Brennan said, sitting in the largest chair, with the presidential seal imprinted into the leather.

"I've prepared copies for everyone of the picture I received from the Russian attaché." Mary Jean said. "Unfortunately, the photo is over ten years old. It may be a guide, but in that amount of time, things could be drastically different, and we don't know if he has a beard or other disguises."

"I'll have this sent to the office in Savannah immediately," the FBI representative volunteered. He added, "It'll be like looking for the proverbial needle in a haystack, since we have no prints, and the perp has no previous contacts here in the States and no known associates for us to lean on. But it'll give us something to use to ask for assistance from the locals."

"All right," the president said, "do what you would normally do in such a case. I know you're all stretched to the max in trying to find the active terrorists who are continuing to attack our installations, like the firebombing of a barracks in Fort Benning today. I've sent a special team to go to Savannah to hunt for this Russian. That's their sole mission. No protocol or bureaucratic red tape will hamstring them. If General Bergermeyer contacts the FBI with a request for you move on information she passes to you, I want you to consider it a direct order from me. You will act as quickly, and without regard to any obstacle in order to comply. Am I clear on that?"

"Yes, Mr. President," replied the FBI man.

"NSA, do you have anything on this?"

"At present, no. Nevertheless, we'll target the Savannah area. We have some information on the Russian from his laptop, captured by Captain Matt Higgins in Saudi Arabia that he may not be aware of. It's hard for someone to completely change the way they use a computer and how they access the Internet. If he uses the web, there might be a slim chance of picking it up," replied the NSA representative.

The Homeland Security representative said, "There isn't a chance in hell they would try to take the bomb onto an aircraft, but I'll still pass the picture to all our agencies."

"Every agency here is busting a gut trying to stop this rash of terrorist attacks. I know you're doing everything to prevent them, but if we get a handle on this WMD, everything else stops and we go after it." The president stood up, and all followed suit. He headed for the door and indicated for Mary Jean to follow him. They went up to the Oval Office, where he offered her a seat on the couch, then took the single armchair, his usual habit.

"I need a bourbon and water," the president said as he pressed a button on the table for an aide. "What can I get you?"

"A gin and tonic would be great."

He placed the order and looked at Mary Jean. "What do you think is happening? I think this is all too organized. It all started everywhere at the same time—the installations getting attacked, Matt and Bridget at a place where terrorists hit, his daughter or someone connected to Matt attacked in a Virginia house. What do you think? Wait, before you answer, let me get Dean Avery in here."

Mary Jean had no way of forestalling this. Avery was the president's friend from college days, who held the position of the national security adviser to the president, and what they were going to discuss fell under that purview. Just the same, she would be careful of what she said.

"Before he gets here, Mr. President, I need to inform you that I think someone in your office is leaking things, and I'm doing an off-the-record search of various people who have access to certain facts."

"Come on, Mary Jean, you don't suspect Dean?" the president said as he waved his right hand in a circle.

"Sir, I'm investigating what I think is a leak. It may be nothing and a pure fantasy, but I feel that it's in your best interest to know if there is one without going through official channels. Please don't reveal this to anyone, and I'll tell you the results of my investigation." Mary Jean felt like she'd fulfilled her duty in apprising the commander-in-chief of her actions.

"Okay, I guess such draconian measures are necessary in light of the attacks on our country, but I can assure you Dean Avery is not a problem. If you find anyone who is cavorting with these terrorists, you have the team to take care of any situation. So do it. No questions asked."

Dean Avery entered the Oval Office.

"Hi, Dean. How did the speech go at our old alma mater?"

"I had a really splendid time and saw some of our now really aged professors. They're still pounding things into the students' heads. What did I miss?"

"You know Mary Jean Bergermeyer from the DIA?"

"Yes, I've had the pleasure." Avery took a seat on the couch next to her without shaking hands.

"I'll let her bring you up to date on events that happened while you were away. Mary Jean, the floor is yours."

Mary Jean recapped the happenings of the day. After describing the attack on Matt Higgins's sister-in-law and the information received from the Russian defense attaché, she concluded with the fact that she had recently dispatched Matt and Bridget to Savannah to intercept what could be an atomic weapon. She did not want to say anything more, and acted as if the team of Matt and Bridget operated under her orders and not as the president's black ops unit. The president did not correct that impression.

"Boy, see what can happen when you get away from Washington for a few hours. So we're now in a wait-and-see situation?" Avery said.

"Yes," the president said, "and we're hoping the Russians can provide some more information. Thank you, Mary Jean. Keep me informed. Now if you'll excuse us, I have some things to discuss with Dean on the goings-on in Latin America."

"Good night, Mr. President. I'll keep you updated as things occur." She got up and shook hands with the president, nodded at Avery on the couch, and left the White House. The time arrived for her to pick up the listening gear, put on her disguise, and head for Avery's favorite restaurant in Georgetown.

She arrived at 9:45 wearing a curly black wig, a high-necked green turtleneck sweater and black pants. A medium-sized white handbag hung from her arm, and a pair of silver-framed glasses completed her appearance. The altered look was not designed as a total makeover, just enough to prevent instant recognition by someone surveying the restaurant to see if they recognized anyone.

She sat in the same position as the last time and ordered a cup of coffee and an appetizer. In front of her, she noticed the Iranian man now sat beside a woman in a chador, her face completely obscured by the black veil. The two appeared engaged in a whispered conversation.

Mary Jean placed her handbag on the chair opposite, but she could move it with her feet under the table. The large purse contained a unidirectional parabolic antenna, sufficient to capture the sounds from a small space up to one hundred feet.

The antenna needed to be positioned to point directly at the target. She used a new type unidirectional antenna, since the use of an omnidirectional one would result in the capture of all the sounds in the restaurant and then require time to filter out each voice. Mary Jean knew whom she wanted to aim at and placed the small earpiece in her ear. The sound of the man's voice rose to slightly above a whisper and she needed to keep moving the chair with her feet to get the right direction. At last, she picked up a clear voice.

"He'll be here soon. Don't worry. No one knows what we're doing. You have your assignment to get the instructions to al-Banna. Make sure you deliver them."

The woman's response emanated as muted and unintelligible. Before she could move the directional antenna toward the woman, Dean Avery entered and positioned himself at his usual table, with his back to the Iranian and the woman.

A few minutes of silence followed. At last, he tilted his head toward the woman and said, "Let's go. We have work to do." Then the Iranian diplomat, bending in the direction where Avery sat, said, "Don't go with the man to Atlanta, no matter what."

23

FOUR DAYS AGO — LATE EVENING, GEORGETOWN, D.C

Mary Jean watched as the Iranian diplomat got up to leave. He did not help the woman up or show her any civility at all. They both left the restaurant without making eye contact with anyone. Dean Avery remained in his booth and took out a newspaper.

There would be nothing to gain by remaining, so Mary Jean paid and walked out of the restaurant. She scanned and saw the man, but she did not attempt to follow the diplomat, nor the woman, who had already vanished by the time she got outside. How the woman had arrived, by car or taxi, couldn't be determined. The Georgetown street overflowed with heavy evening traffic, and any car that had left over a minute ago would be lost in the maze.

She called Mike Anthony. He might have some new information for her, and she now had some for him. They agreed to meet at the Grill on Sixteenth Street in thirty minutes. At her car, she abandoned the disguise, and with a light combing of the hair and a little makeup applied in the rear view mirror, she returned to her old self as she set off for her rendezvous.

On entering the establishment, Mary Jean spotted him and approached with her hand out in greeting. He took it and gave her a quick peck on the cheek. Mike Anthony wore jeans and a blue denim shirt with the sleeves rolled up, sipping on what looked like a Gibson with three onions.

"Let's go over to a table," he said and led her to an empty spot against the wall. "You called, so you talk first."

"This is getting bizarre. I think I'm sinking in over my head. My hunch seems to be playing out and I don't like it one bit." She waited while he took a sip from his drink and then continued, "They were at the same restaurant tonight and a woman in a chador sat with the Iranian—"

"He's not married," Mike interrupted. "Hey, you want a drink?"

"I could use a gin and tonic. Thanks."

He sat back down after getting her the cocktail. She took a small sip and looked at him. Mike said, "I just got home when you called. I also received information that you aren't going to like, and I don't know how I'm going to handle it either. But, you finish first."

After relating the events she'd witnessed earlier and all she'd heard in the restaurant, she relaxed back and took a long, slow drink. "Okay, your turn. None of what I have is any good in a court, and I didn't ID the woman."

Mike wiggled in his seat to get comfortable and then started. "My God, I don't want to believe all this, but it's starting to add up. He's the national security adviser, for Christ's sake, and what you have is completely circumstantial." He bent over closer and spoke in a softer voice. "However, we are dealing with attacks on American military installations and the possible use of a WMD on our soil. The Patriot Act can only go so far, and then we become compelled to do whatever is necessary to stop these maniacs. So you need to interpret what I'm going to tell you not in any legal sense."

He stopped and looked down at a piece of paper, then continued, "If I know you, it will be in the purview of military intelligence that's collected, then correlated, then a decision is made once all the data is fused into a single conceptual plan. So I present this to you as information, not as a conclusion."

"Come on, Mike, cut the bullshit. What do you have?" Mary Jean asked.

"First of all, there's no record of what I'm going to show you. You asked me to get what I could, so I tasked someone who owes me, and there's no trail to anyone else. It took him two days to track down the only lead he could come up with.

"We don't do security checks on political appointees. Their background is usually only given a cursory glance by the media. In Avery's case, as a close personal friend of the president's since college, they only published the stories of his success in business and how he was a master of mergers and acquisitions and that made him wealthy. So my man went back to his collegiate days." He stopped talking here, leaned back in his chair, and took a drink. "This is going to take a while. Want another round?"

"Sure, I'll get it this time. You want the same?"

He nodded. She went over to the bar and got the drinks. After she got herself seated again, Mike opened a couple of sheets of paper that he'd previously viewed and straightened them on the table.

"These papers do not exist. You can read them here and then destroy them, and I'll forget I ever saw them. What you do with the info is not my business, but I sure as hell don't want to be the one to leak this information. You must understand that it's not fully corroborated, but it won't get any better either." He handed them to Mary Jean.

She opened the folded pages and started to read.

SPECIAL REPORT
FOR: DEPUTY DIRECTOR MICHAEL ANTHONY
FROM: SPECIAL AGENT THOMAS SYLVESTER

In order to do a background check on NSA member Dean Avery, I looked into events prior to his graduation from University of Virginia Law School. I questioned classmates who were specifically identified as friends by others prior to his long-standing association with the current president.

During his undergraduate studies, Avery became involved with a group studying Islamic culture and religion. The nearest major center of Islam in those days was in Washington. An interview with the current imam produced no useful information, since he had only recently arrived. After I searched his registry for the name of Avery from the period in question, he informed me that no one by that name appeared in his books. He suggested I contact Margaret Walsh, a member there for many years.

Ms. Walsh remembered students coming for instruction during the timeframe I asked her about. She remembered Dean Avery as one of the students who came to the Friday call to prayer every week for months and reported that he became a favorite of the imam. Avery went with the imam as part of a group to visit some holy sites in Arabia or Israel. They went for about two months.

The group included Avery's girlfriend, a woman named Johnson. She stayed with him for months. Shortly after returning from the overseas trip, the girlfriend and Avery split up, and she left school and moved to the South—Georgia, North Carolina, or thereabouts. Walsh did not know the reason for the breakup.

After interviewing two other close student friends, I concluded that the romance seemed to be hidden. Both said that Avery did not go out with a girl on a regular basis during his college days. No one remembered the name of any girl he might have dated.

I will attempt to find the Johnson woman and that will conclude the scope of this investigation. Expect a supplemental report in two to three days.

No copy of this report exists. I made it on a typewriter.

Mary Jean handed the paper back to Mike. "Thank you. I imagine it cost a few points to get this report so no one was the wiser."

"What report?" Mike got up, gave Mary Jean a peck on the check, smiled, and left.

24

FOUR DAYS AGO — EARLY MORNING

Andrews Air Force Base, Maryland

CLAUDE MOREAU PREPARED TO EXECUTE A PREVIOUSLY INSTALLED program on the GPS system of Air Force One. He received the call late last night from Ricky, his cell leader, to initiate his part. The planning for this exact moment had taken months. Ricky's company rendered technical support for aviation electronic components to three airlines operating in the Washington area, and he had sent Claude to become a factory-trained repairman on the GPS flight navigation systems of those aircraft he serviced.

This business provided a very lucrative cash flow for the cell that Ricky led, and also gave Claude a noble sense of accomplishment. Today, however, Ricky had received a specific mission from his commander, and Claude could not fail him. As he drove by Andrews Air Force Base, he sent a remote activation code to the receiver in the GPS unit, which he had embedded in the flight following system on the president's plane last time it was serviced. He'd installed it so that the system would fail four days after initiation. Ricky had ordered him to be available at any time to come to the Air Force base to fix the "problem" when they detected it. Maintenance personnel would discover it on the morning of the next presidential trip during normal preflight inspections.

Air Force technicians fell short of the training needed to handle all the complex components on the Boeing 747, which was, after all, a civilian airliner, not a military jet. The maintenance on many subsystems aboard was contracted out to local firms that held factory certification to provide repair services on the equipment.

Claude had visited the president's aircraft a week ago to perform a scheduled inspection on the components he serviced. With a quick connection via a USB cable, he had sent the command to the GPS unit, telling it to fail a certain number of hours after receiving the activation code. He verified the system had accepted the command, then disconnected the cable and exited the aircraft a few minutes later.

He felt elated at having accomplished this part of the mission. Whatever the ultimate purpose of this task, he would carry it out for the good of Islam, and to aid in the destruction of the Great Satan. *God is great*, he mumbled to himself, exiting the front gate of the air base.

He successfully activated the code to have the GPS fail in four days and called Ricky to inform him of the successful completion of his assigned mission.

"Well done, Claude. Come on back here. We have to put together an item for you to use."

"Okay. Be there in an hour."

He arrived in exactly one hour at the office of the Shenandoah Avionics Repair and Maintenance Company in Reston, Virginia. Claude found Ricky in the component repair facility in the back in a closed-off area.

"Claude, well done. Now we have to put this together. I got a thermos. It's all metal, and we can take the time to melt the C-4 into the small opening and then secure the detonator into the top part. We'll have enough room to reattach the silver cap, and it will look like a thermos you would take with your lunch box," Ricky said.

"Do you want me to make a connection to the GPS unit with a

USB cable? The unit can provide the electrical current to set it off if I reconfigure one wire in the tracking unit and have the electronic pulse that would send the data to the cockpit diverted from the connector to the explosives. I also have a handheld method to set it off."

"Get that fixed up, and make sure you can put it in without causing suspicion," Ricky warned.

"No fear. I'll get it done or I'll die to ensure it goes off."

"Don't do anything so drastic."

"If it has to be, then it's the will of Allah."

They worked for two hours to accomplish the task of turning the thermos into a bomb. In the end, they were satisfied that all would work as planned. Claude took the deadly container with him to his maintenance van and departed.

With four days to prepare himself for the chance of planting the bomb on Air Force One, he knew he could do it. He would not fail.

25

FOUR DAYS AGO — RESTON, VA — 10:22 P.M

RICKY JOBIN ANSWERED THE PHONE ON THE FIRST RING.

"They're off. Mission accomplished," he heard.

"Did they take care of the target?"

"Yes, I just dropped them off at the airport. They'll be in Seattle in a few hours. I kept all the equipment they used and will bring it to you tomorrow."

"Excellent. Good job," Ricky said as he closed the phone and smiled. Now his cell had something to be proud of. They carried out Fatimah's orders in completing a mission of the highest priority for that group. He might get some out-of-the-ordinary recognition for his men from the controller.

The woman who gave him the orders was someone he had never met. The call always came in from a cell that showed up as "ID blocked." In the beginning, he'd met the Iranian who had assisted him in setting up his cell and then been told that his orders would come by phone, preceded by the name *al-Banna* so that he would know the order was from him. How long ago was that? Before he got started on a trip down memory lane, reminiscing about his conversion to the one true faith that would soon be the religion of the world and the law of the land in America, the ringing of his phone interrupted him. Opening it, he saw a blocked number and smiled as he said hello.

"Al-Banna, you are a blithering idiot," the female voice said in a loud staccato tone. "You blew it. They got the wrong man. I told you to have them wait until I told you his location. No, you and those morons moved in and killed the wrong man."

"What? What are you talking about?" He threw up his free hand.

"Which word didn't you understand? They didn't get Higgins. They got his sister-in-law and her husband. Why didn't you supervise them? They were to wait for a confirmed location. Instead, those buffoons tried to track him down on their own in a foreign city and eliminate a target they have never seen before. All they had to do was to receive my call about where he would be."

"I'm sorry. I thought they did the job," he said in a soft voice. The fiasco that had occurred at the house in Virginia, caused by the bumbling students from Seattle, was not his responsibility.

"First of all, stop thinking and do as you are instructed. Second, I have an order for you. This time there is no room for mistakes. Do you understand my meaning?"

Ricky clearly understood her implication, and he did not want to end up dead over another mistake. He breathed in deeply and reached for a piece of paper in case he needed to copy part or all of the order she gave.

"Did your avionics man plant the device to make the GPS tracking go out?" she queried.

"Yes." Ricky gradually recovered and sounded stronger.

"He'll be called in to repair it in four days. He will then use the software that we developed. Is the explosive ready to be used?"

"Yes, it is, and it'll be in place, along with the update to the system," said Ricky with a little more confidence in his voice.

"Make sure it is. There's nothing we can do about Higgins at this time. You'll have to handle that later."

"I'll do it myself. There will be no mistakes."

She concluded by mentioning the chapter and verse of a passage that read, "And remember the favor of Allah on you and His covenant with which He bound you firmly, when you said: We have heard and we obey, and be careful of your duty to Allah, surely Allah knows what is in the breasts." The line went dead.

"How does she find all this out so fast?" Ricky al-Banna wondered.

26

THREE DAYS AGO — SAVANNAH, GA

Yuri felt confident about Basam's security in the short-term rental, with food and medicine, so he took a taxi downtown. He arrived in the old open market area of Savannah, which provided the distinct feeling of days gone by. While walking around, he observed the open-air cafés. The wood floors and antique tables that festooned the inside of the restaurants, the horse-drawn carriages making clop-clop sounds as they passed—all combined to create the atmosphere of the "good old days." The appearance of a hearse with the top cut off so that tourists could view the city while being fed tales of ghosts from the various stages of the city's history seemed a little bizarre to Yuri.

A band played on an outside stage in front of Wings restaurant. Yuri sat down at a nearby table where he could hear the music and took out his laptop. He signed in, and after a few seconds he received a new email. The decryption program did its job and the plain text appeared.

"Basam al-Hanbali,

You and the Russian are to proceed to Atlanta in time to arrive there before the target does in three days from the date of this order.

He will land at Hartsfield Airport at 1430 hours local time. Have the weapon detonate five minutes after that time.

Orders have already been sent to cells to cause maximum distraction of law enforcement from our primary target. We will ensure that the plane lands at that time and location.

The transfer of five million to the designated bank account will take place after detonation.

God is great.

Fatimah"

They had failed to send the money that he requested. Yuri sat back and took a drink from the lager he had ordered. It tasted awful. *American beer is so bad. It's weak and taste like water.* He thought for a minute before he typed an encrypted reply.

"Fatimah, Russian will not cooperate without money in account twenty-four hours prior to time you specify. If funds verified, mission will be accomplished.

God is great.

Basam"

Now he must wait. He picked up a tourist magazine he'd noticed on top of the empty table next to him and perused it. The response should come within an hour or so, based on previous communications. He signaled for the waiter, planning on ordering vodka to wash away the taste of the beer. Then he saw her. She walked like a tourist —slowly, turning her head from side to side, taking in all the sights. She was only a few yards away. He left money for the drink, put his computer in his pack, and started to walk in her direction. His own actions were a mystery to him. He should stop and go back and forget this madness.

Never before had he chased a woman. Wasn't that what he was doing now? Maybe, it was because he was in America and he knew things were different here. Maybe the money he now possessed had caused his change in mentality. Maybe he was horny.

The woman walked through the market area and took a left, heading for Bay Street. She arrived at the corner of Jefferson and Bay and turned left again. A short distance from the corner, the entrance of the Churchill Pub came into view. She entered the building, and Yuri followed her, ending at the elevated outside bar. From there he could see out over the entire skyline to the south. The rebuilt city square, a reclamation effort to establish the original plan of the city laid out by Oglethorpe when he had arrived in 1733, appeared below the terrace of the outside drinking area. The woman approached the bar.

Yuri gathered his wits and sauntered over, arriving at the same moment she ordered a vodka. "Excuse me, but I must say, I'm pleased to see a woman drinking our Russian vodka."

Her blond hair swirled away from her shoulders as she rotated to face him. He saw her lips make a small upward curl and her eyes came to focus on him.

"I've always enjoyed vodka, especially in the evening."

"May I be so bold as to buy you this drink?" Yuri said. Without waiting for an answer, he eyed the barman and ordered two vodkas on ice. They were placed on the bar and he faced her, raised his glass and said in Russian, "To your health, madam."

She lifted her glass and touched his. "My name is Marilyn. I suppose that means to our health."

"I am Yuri. Yes, it does." They began the small talk that is ubiquitous with first-time social encounters at a bar. After a second round, Marilyn said she planned to go on the ghost tour.

"That sounds haunting," Yuri said, trying to be humorous. "Since it's already seven, may I invite you to dinner? I saw a tapas restaurant over there." He pointed over the top of the wall that opened out over the city. "Would you care to join me?"

She leaned forward, revealing her ample breasts, and said, "I would indeed. You are an interesting person, and I've never been to dinner with a Russian. I'm starting my life over, and here seems like an excellent place to begin."

"Do you like to dance?"

"I love to."

"I read in a tourist magazine that there is a small jazz bar where we could go to listen to the music."

She nodded approval at his idea. Yuri marveled at his luck in meeting a woman who would talk to him and even agree to go to dinner. America, what a wonderful place. He loved Russia, but this country was something else. He could never do this in the village he intended to return to after this mission. Tonight, he would enjoy himself.

After eating, they went to the Pink House bar and spent an hour listening to the music and drinking. Yuri held her hand in the corner booth and leaned over to kiss her. She moved his hand to her breast. "Why don't you come back to my hotel room and we can get comfortable?"

Yuri forgot waiting on the response from Fatimah, forgot Basam, and forgot everything except his need for this woman.

"I accept," he said.

27

THREE DAYS AGO — SAVANNAH

The three Russians followed the map acquired at the rental car agency during the drive into town from the Savannah airport. The first problem arose when they neared downtown and the map they used didn't show all the little streets. The second glitch occurred when they figured out they hadn't adhered to the written instructions the general had given them in Washington. They were lost. Ravshan stopped the car for Igor to ask directions. The information he received did not take them to the address they sought.

Anton spotted a CVS Pharmacy and ordered Igor to go in and see if they carried a map of the city. In a few minutes he had obtained a detailed street map and they knew where to go. They arrived on the correct street and there found the rental house observed by the first officer from the container ship. Many people walked on the sidewalk and kids were out playing.

Anton, surprised to see people out walking at that time of evening, formed some initial doubts. He could smell the aroma of barbeque in the air and realized people were eating and he would need to delay any action until the activity wound down. He did not want to take the targets out with the whole neighborhood awake on a warm spring night.

"We'll go back to that little convenience store we passed at the corner and get some food. We wait for the neighborhood to go to bed before we move in. From there, we can see anyone who leaves in a car or on foot. Staying in the store's parking lot is less likely to arouse the locals' interest," Anton said.

At one in the morning, they approached the address they'd received from the attaché. The deserted street gave Anton confidence, and no lights shone from the target house.

Anton ordered Ravshan go on foot up and down the street and observe their surroundings while he went behind the building. There he found a high mound, part of the seawall against the Savannah River. No one would be coming from that direction. He returned to the front of the house, where he discovered Ravshan checking his weapon and turning his high-powered flashlight on and off to ensure it functioned.

"Igor, you keep your weapon out, in case they come this way," Anton instructed. "Do not cut off the engine." He signaled Ravshan to return and took him by the shoulder, leading him a few yards away from the car.

"We can't count on Igor during this part of the mission. I doubt if he has fired a weapon in years, and he hasn't ever killed anyone."

"That's obvious, sir," Ravshan said.

"There's a door in the back and one in the front. I would like to avoid the noise of kicking in the door. Let's go to the rear and see if the door can be opened."

They went in darkness to the back of the house. Both men drew their pistols and stood ready to use them. Ravshan carefully tried the handle of the door. Locked. They moved away from the house.

Anton ordered Ravshan to take the trash receptacles that were behind the house and move them in front of the back door.

"Now let's go around front and make our entrance," said Anton. "If he tries to go out the back those trash barrels should cause him trouble, and we'll be on top of him before he can get away."

They rounded the house and quietly approached the front steps.

Ravshan moved up onto the porch. He tried the doorknob and signaled a negative with his head.

Anton raised his pistol into a firing position and stepped onto the porch. The combined weight of the two men caused the wood floor to squeak.

"Yuri, is that you?" came from inside.

Anton nodded, and Ravshan raised his foot and charged the door. A cracking, crunching sound filled the air as the lock ripped the metal keeper out of the wall and the door swung open.

Ravshan's flashlight lit up the interior of the small room. A figure on the couch attempted to reach for a weapon that lay on the table. He grasped it, attempting to raise the weapon, but Anton fired three bullets from his silenced pistol into the man's chest. He hoped the muffled sound remained contained in the room, not knowing that in that area of town, the sounds might not arouse much interest.

Ravshan closed the door and turned on the lights. They left the corpse on the floor where it rolled. Food wrappers littered the couch. The place smelled like the inside of an old tennis shoe.

They each took a bedroom and entered with their weapons at the ready. Both rooms appeared empty. No other presence in the house.

"He's not here," said Anton. "I'm going out to tell Igor to be on watch for someone returning here. You look for the weapon."

After he returned, Anton assisted in the search. They tore the place apart, trying to find the device. After ten minutes, they determined Yuri had probably taken it somewhere else.

"If we had the radiation detector I requested, it would be a simple matter to determine if the weapon had been here. We'll wait here for our man to return," ordered Anton.

"What happens if he has gone to complete their mission?" Ravshan queried.

"If he's not back by dawn, we'll leave and report to Moscow. I'll ask for new instructions. They may have some ideas for us by then. Remember, this guy asked if it was Yuri when we came through the door. He's expecting him back."

"I'll go and tell Igor what we're, and we'll rotate on guard duty outside," Ravshan said.

Anton waited until Ravshan had left and then sat in a chair. Where was that renegade Russian? He couldn't wait here past dawn. People would get suspicious of them staking out the place. The owner might come to investigate a complaint about the noise they'd made, or want to come in to see if the place sustained any damage. They couldn't allow anyone discover them with a corpse.

Anton's revised plan focused on keeping the house under observation from a distance. Operating in a foreign country without much support when things didn't go as planned proved to be a considerable challenge. He would devise some stratagem to apprehend the scientist and obtain the weapon, and he must remain vigilant until he succeeded in his mission.

With absolute confidence, he knew he would catch the renegade scientist and kill him. He felt it in his bones.

28

TWO DAYS AGO — SAVANNAH, GA

Matt woke and decided to order breakfast. He made the call to room service and then showered and dressed before calling Bridget's room.

"Come on, sleepyhead, want some breakfast?"

"We shouldn't have had that last drink," Bridget said.

"I've got the wake-up juice coming from room service. That should fix you up. Come over."

"It'll help, but first the shower."

He heard a knock at the door, and when he turned, he noticed an envelope had been slid under the door. He opened it and pulled out a picture with the name Yuri Borisov printed on it. The general had faxed it to the hotel for delivery to their room. Matt called Bridget, and when she arrived, they studied the image.

"Now we know what he could look like, and it gives us an advantage we didn't have yesterday," Matt said.

The food came and they sat down to eat. Matt wore jeans and a short-sleeved blue-and-red polo shirt, while Bridget had dressed in black shorts and a short-sleeved white pullover.

"The weather is delightful. It's seventy-five here and thirty-six in Washington. Maybe we should move our operations to Savannah.

This is a beautiful city, and the temperature is a hell of a lot better than up north." Bridget took her coffee and walked to the window to gaze out over Bay Street and the Savannah River while talking.

"Hold on, we haven't solved this case yet. After we're finished, we can discuss the future of the business," Matt said.

"I have two points to raise. The first is last night. What did we learn, and where do we go from here?"

"Well, we didn't learn much about our man. But, let's assume he was out on the town last night to spend some of the money they must've paid him for the Saudi job. Today we should have better luck. More chances that someone saw him. Plus we have a photo to show. If this was your first time in Savannah, what would you do?" Matt walked over to the table, picked up a piece of toast, spread strawberry jam on it and took a bite.

"It's my first time, and I want to go on some of the tours and explore the market area and River Street. That's what a tourist would do and let's assume our guys are tourists, or at least pretending to be acting like visitors. If not, they'll stay locked up in a hideout, and we don't have a snowball's chance in hell of getting them." Bridget fixed a piece of toast for herself and went over to gaze out the window.

"I'd like to say I have a better plan," Matt said, "but I don't, so we'll go and do the tourist thing during the day and show his picture to people who might remember. If no luck, tonight we'll do the same in the clubs here. I want to check in with the general this morning and tell her what we are doing."

"Good idea," Bridget said as she came back from the window and sat in a chair. "My second point. Are we all right?"

Matt got up and went toward her, held her chin in his hands and looked straight into her eyes. "Yes, we're all right. And we're going in the right direction. Let's give it some time."

"Okay."

He picked up his cell and called Mary Jean, giving her a succinct report of their activities and what they had planned. "Do you have any more information from the Russians on what our guys might be up to?"

"Not now. I'll call the defense attaché today and let you know. Anything else?"

"No," Matt said.

Mary Jean took a few seconds to gather her thoughts before calling the Russian embassy. She recognized Major General Andrei Marshankin's voice on the phone, but she did not engage in small talk, instead started right in, "Andrei, do you have any more information on the location of the man in Savannah?"

She had no idea who might be listening in on a phone conversation on an open line. She didn't want to give away anything to an eavesdropper.

"Actually, I received a message and planned to call you in a few minutes. I have an address for you in Savannah, where you might find what you're searching for."

He gave her the address. Mary Jean thanked him and hung up. She wondered how long it would have been before she had gotten his information if she hadn't called. She picked up the phone and called Matt. He answered on the third ring.

"Matt, here's the location the Russians gave me. Be careful. Check the meter reading for radiation in the area and let me know if it's high. I can get a team there in an hour from Ft. Stewart for decontamination if needed."

"Wilco. We're on our way. We'll report after getting there. We'll do a little surveillance, and if need be we'll call for help from the feds."

"Would it be all right if I stopped in to visit Julia and Laura since I have to be out there for another reason this afternoon?" Mary Jean inquired, not knowing Matt was already on the way to the address.

"That would be very thoughtful," Matt responded.

"Good luck," Mary Jean concluded and said a little prayer that this would work out and end this threat to her country. People didn't get the real danger presented by these Islamic fascists or Muslim extremists, or radical jihadists or whatever they called themselves, she thought.

She stretched back in her chair, put her hands behind her head, and looked up at the ceiling. It was difficult to believe there were so many people in this country who didn't understand that we were at war with an enemy who had sworn to destroy everything we hold dear—our way of life, our culture, and our very existence as a nation, she thought.

She now began to practice for a speech she planned to give to the Military Officers Association in a few days, pretending to talk to an imaginary audience. She spoke aloud to hear how the words would sound coming off her lips. She opened with, "There are many people who disagree with the president's way of conducting the antiterrorist campaign, but this antiterrorist war is our only chance. Neither side gave any quarter in this ancient fight. Diplomacy will not solve this confrontation. There is no way to achieve a negotiated peace, because the other guys will only use it to strengthen their position and capabilities." She knew a negotiated peace would be the death warrant for the American way of life.

"It amazes me"— Mary Jean actually felt pleased about the tone and tempo she was using—"that our people cannot understand that there are those in this world who would kill you because you are an American. The number of people whose animosity against the USA knows no bounds has dramatically increased in the past decade.

"All I see is our people putting their heads in the sand and not wanting to engage in a conflict where their sons or neighbors or friends might be hurt or killed. Without our ability to battle these terrorists, the radical wing of Islam will invade us. We have no way to effectively combat the suicide bombers, unless we get to them in the planning stages, before they strike, and that can only be accomplished by on-the-ground intelligence operatives. So the real question comes down to, is it better to die on the battlefield, fighting against this, or is it preferable to go to the mosque for prayers after we lose?"

Mary Jean returned her chair to the upright position and put her hands on the desk. That ought to get them talking. She occupied a very difficult post, and nobody else wanted it, because all you did was stick your neck out without any safeguard. She made the decisions, she bore the responsibility, and she could not shift the blame for failure to anyone else.

Her team would get the weapon, regardless of the cost. No second place existed in this contest. The destruction that would be caused by an atomic explosion in one of our cities was unthinkable.

29

TWO DAYS AGO — SAVANNAH — 10:35 AM

Yuri rolled away from Marilyn and found a pad and pen on the nightstand. He wrote a short note saying he would be back in a couple of hours. Basam would be worried about him since he hadn't returned last night.

His head hurt from the amount of alcohol consumed on the previous evening, and he needed a cigarette. He dressed and took the elevator down. At the entrance of the hotel, he took a cab. The ride to the house took only ten minutes.

He arrived in front of the rental and asked the driver to wait. He got out and staggered to the door. Something instantly felt wrong, and he shook his head to clear it. The door stood ajar. This shouldn't be. *Come on, come on, and get a hold of yourself*, he thought. On pushed the door open, and his mouth dropped on seeing the scene in front of him. Basam lay on the floor, filled with bullet holes.

The weapon. Did they get it? He ran into the bathroom. The tub didn't look to have been moved or disturbed, so he pulled it to the side and exposed the panel. He opened it, removed the insulation, it, and viewed the case with the bomb.

Relief swept over him, but only for a moment. Now what to do? He must get out of here with the weapon, because he still needed to carry out the mission to get his money. It was too bad about Basam, but now he would be operating on his own. The hell with their jihadist ideas. He would get the money, then go to Russia and live like a king.

He took the case, gathered all of his belongings, and put them in the duffle bag. After a quick search to make sure nothing of his remained, he took the case and the bag out to the taxi.

The taxi took him back to the hotel. He headed to Marilyn's room. Now he needed to think, because someone did pursue them. Someone knew they possessed the weapon and had attempted to get it. The condition of the house indicated they had unsuccessfully searched for the case. *Stop and think, you idiot.* He didn't believe the Americans had done it. If they had, the police and FBI would have been there, processing it as a crime scene. Fatimah couldn't be involved, since they wanted him to carry out the mission. Couldn't be the Saudis. They didn't know anything about this operation. Who did that leave?

The Russians. The fucking Russians now targeted him. His own government. Damn them.

Now he started to sweat. His hands trembled as he lit a cigarette.

30

TWO DAYS AGO SAVANNAH, GA — MID MORNING

Matt closed his phone and told Bridget they had obtained an address for Yuri. They rushed down to their car and used the GPS to enter it in. They turned off Bay Street and cruised up to the house.

"What's the plan?" Bridget asked.

"We pull into the driveway and get out. We assume we're at the right address. We knock on the door and say that this is the address we have for my uncle Mr. Morgantown, and we've come to visit after not seeing him for years."

"You have an uncle named Morgantown?"

"No. Do you?" he said with a wide grin.

"Weak plan. I guess we'll have to go with it. I'll keep my hand in my purse on my weapon."

"Okay."

Matt drove into the driveway and shut off the engine. "Let's go."

They approached the front door and saw the destroyed doorframe. Both pulled out their weapons, and Matt shoved the door open. He went low on entering and Bridget stayed high, pointing their guns, ready for any target to appear.

"Damn, looks like someone beat us to it," Matt said, observing the body on the floor. He checked it for a pulse, and then searched the rest of the house. "God, this guy looks like he was dead before the bullets got him." On coming back to the main room, he holstered his weapon and observed Bridget as she examined the spread-eagled corpse.

"Three hits to his front in a small pattern. Someone tore this place apart. We aren't the only ones searching for the weapon," Bridget said.

"Who else could know about it? Let's get back to the hotel and we'll see what the general thinks."

"The police haven't been here, so no one heard anything. Silencers on the weapons, I think. This has the smell of a professional hit. Yuri must have escaped, because this isn't the guy in the photo," said Bridget.

"I don't know. Let's brainstorm it with her. We don't want to be here if anyone arrives. Let's get going."

Back at the hotel, Matt called Mary Jean. He gave her a brief summary of what they discovered at the address and ended with. "So who's after them besides us?"

"I don't know for certain, but I might guess the Russians are trying to find the weapon and get it out of here before it's used on American soil. They wouldn't want to be blamed for the attack, since it's Russian technology and one of their citizens who would detonate it. That could be interpreted as state-sponsored and land in the Kremlin's lap."

"We found only one body, so our man Yuri may have already left town. I think our best bet is to continue to search for him here."

"Okay. I'll get in touch with my Russian friend here and see if I can get anything. Did you use the NSA tester for radiation?"

"Damn. Sorry, I didn't. We rushed over when you gave me the address, and I didn't take it. We can go back and do that now. At least that way we can confirm that it had been there," Matt said.

"Call me when you've done that and, if positive, I'll get the team from Fort Stewart there. They can also work with the local police at a murder scene."

After disconnecting, Matt gave Bridget the gist of the conversation and they headed back to test for the presence of radiation.

MARY JEAN MADE A CALL TO THE RUSSIAN DEFENSE ATTACHÉ IN Washington. When came on the phone, she said, "I think you've been holding out on me, General."

"It's a pleasure to hear your voice again, General. What have I been keeping from you? I gave you the information we received from the ship's captain on the whereabouts of the man in Savannah, did I not?"

"Andrei, you did give that to me and my people acted on it. The problem I see is that your people got there first."

"My people?" Major General Andrei Marshankin said with surprise in his voice.

"I thought we agreed not to jerk each other around. That's what you're doing now. You and I knew about that location. So the Arab is shot to death before my team gets there. I eliminate the Islmofascist, the FBI and just about everybody else, and I can logically conclude you had men who did it. Are you with me?"

"Yes, I am. I'm constrained in what I can relay, but in the spirit of cooperation that we have established, I will say that your logic is impeccable. Do you understand?"

"Now, I do. You're trying to prevent the same thing we are. So why send your own team? We would gladly hand him over to you when we get him."

"I think that some in Moscow view this as a point of honor. We need to get the renegade and retrieve the weapon. That's all I feel comfortable saying. I hope you understand, Mary Jean."

"Yes. Thank you. I'll advise my team to be on the lookout for your people. I don't want a shootout between the good guys."

"That's an excellent idea, and if we had anyone here, I would do the same."

"Thank you for your time, Andrei."

"Always a pleasure to speak with you. We must meet again soon, General Bergermeyer. Good-bye."

Mary Jean hung up, knowing for certain that a Russian team currently operated on US soil in a clandestine manner.

Her private phone rang, and the identification showed Matt's name.

"General, there's residual radiation in this house. No doubt about the weapon being there. We'll keep after it," said Matt.

"I have to go to a meeting right now. I'll call you back as soon as possible and give you an update. Keep looking for our man," she said and hung up.

"Anything?" Matt said to Bridget, who had just returned from a search of the outside of the small house.

"No, but I get a feeling we're being watched. Couldn't see anyone, just a sense," she said.

"Let's get back to the hotel. We'll notify the general to have the house put under surveillance in case the man comes back here. Let's start our search around town for Yuri. Who knows? Maybe we'll get lucky."

"Don't you wish, mister? We have work to do, a company to run, bills to pay, a country to save, and I bet we're on a short time fuse with this Yuri now that his partner is dead," she concluded.

They left the house, and headed for the hotel.

Igor wasn't a soldier and shouldn't be on the watch detail. He returned to the car to take up his observation duty on the house after sitting in that restroom for the tenth time. He suffered from diarrhea that had hit him from the spicy chicken at the fast-food joint where they had eaten last night. Why did people eat it? He couldn't stop running to the toilet.

Down the street, Igor watched as two people departed the house. They were not his targets. He called Anton.

"Anton, we have visitors to the house."

"Is it Yuri?"

"No, they're definitely Americans, as best I can tell. Looks like military or cops."

"Did they wait for the cops to come?"

"No."

"Then they're not cops, and my guess is that we have an American team after the weapon and our man. They'll arrange to have the house under surveillance now that they know the Arab is dead. Get back to our location before they're able to spot you."

"I'm leaving now. I didn't see anyone else, but I've been on the toilet a lot," Igor said.

31

TWO DAYS AGO — SAVANNAH, GA

Matt and Bridget returned to the hotel. They contacted Mary Jean, who informed them about the suspected Russian team on Yuri's trail. While Matt conversed on the phone Bridget lit up a cigar and handed him a Diet Coke. She sipped a Red Bull.

"What's with the cigar?"

"I used to smoke them when I was happy. Haven't done it in a long time. I'm enjoying our mission."

They went out for a walk, stopping at the gelato store for a cone and sitting outside in the open market area to watch the world go by.

Matt started the conversation. "We have to pick up on this guy's trail. I feel like we're too late. We have no real clue where he is or what he's doing." He stopped and pushed his hair back from his forehead. Then he pointed at Bridget, "What do you think is our best course of action? You're always good at planning. Let's hear it."

"We're at a dead end here. He's left that house and there's really no chance he'll go back there. If he has a mission with the bomb, he's already on the way, but if he's still in Savannah, we need to concentrate on places he might go." Bridget licked her cone and continued, "After being on the boat, my guess is he's hunting to get laid, unless he's a three-dollar bill or something."

"Maybe. Let's go check out locations a guy might go as a tourist. Someone might remember a Russian. Probably not a lot of Russians in Savannah."

"Let's start with the restaurants. They're open this afternoon, and the evening staff is probably already on duty," Bridget said.

They strolled down Congress Street to Garibaldi's. After looking around the place, Bridget approached a waiter and asked him about a Russian tourist who might have been in last night. She got a negative response. Matt received the same answer from the other waiter. They went back out onto the street.

"Well, we didn't get lucky at the first place. Let's try the other places here. You take the left side and I'll go right."

"Meet you at the end of this long open-air street," said Bridget.

After two hours of searching the restaurants for any sign of a Russian, they regrouped and realized they were not making any progress. Sitting at the outside tables on the rooftop bar of the Churchill pub, they started to reformulate their plan.

"We should shift our focus from eating establishments to bars, like this one and the ones that open later. No one here remembers a Russian, but the evening staff will come on soon."

Bridget took a drink from her Diet Coke and said, "Let's start at the Tapas."

"Okay. Now we have an hour to kill. I'll call in and give the general an update and see if she has anything for us." He dialed her number. She answered, and he gave her a brief account of events and the plan for the evening.

He closed the phone and Bridget said, "We need to talk."

"About what?"

"About us, about this job, about the future." She made a circle in the air and ended by pointing at him.

"I suggest we hold up on the talk," he said rubbing his chin. "Not because it's not important, but we'll have time later. We agreed to a partnership in the business, and the one topic I have to think about is that I'll have to take Laura on a full-time basis after the murders at my sister-in-law's house."

Bridget sat back and stretched in the early evening light. The sun reflected off her bronze skin, causing Matt to take a deep breath as if to inhale her beauty.

"Matt, I've given that a lot of thought and as you remember we killed the terrorists in Saudi Arabia and I thought your sense of revenge for the attack that killed your wife was satisfied. Am I wrong?"

Matt averted his eyes. Then he relaxed and took a couple of swigs from the Coke, trying to get his thoughts together before answering.

"You know that there are over one point four billion Muslims, of which eighty percent see America as hostile to Islam. Within that percentage, there is a very dangerous minority that either has, or wants to have, a small nuclear, chemical or biological weapon to use against us. These guys are basically Nazis in keffiyehs. All who do not give in to Islam must be killed, subjugated, or converted. You know, that's how they think. They also want to finish the Holocaust by destroying Israel—"

Bridget interrupted, "I want to know about your own goal in fighting these madmen."

"The bottom line is that we'll deal with radical Islamic terrorism until we defeat it. It won't go away if we ignore it. There are many who oppose this fight against these fanatics, but I don't want my daughter or my grandchildren to live in an Islamic America under mullahs and their Sharia laws. Never . . . not an America that looks like Iran. All wars are fundamentally about ideas, and the most determined always wins. We have to win this for ourselves and our children."

"You think that the most ruthless bastard always wins, because of the indifference of the masses in the beginning?" Bridget commented.

"Yeah. Peace activists always seem to demonstrate here in America, or in other democratic countries, where it's safe. Where are the demonstrators in Iran, Syria, or Saudi Arabia? Where are the so-called moderates? Why aren't they demonstrating in Iran and elsewhere? No friggin' way. They'd end up dead."

The late afternoon sun was setting, and shadows started

appearing on their faces. Both sat in silence as they took sips from their drinks.

"Thank you," she said. "I thought it was something like that, and not hatred because of what happened to your wife. I think we're on solid ground in our business, and we need to get going and find this Yuri. He surely went to some clubs, assuming he was in town at all. Time has to be running out. Let's go."

32

TWO DAYS AGO — WASHINGTON, D.C. — 4:30 PM

Mary Jean drove her new Cadillac, purchased the day before, to the office of SPAT, Inc. She wanted to see Julia and spend a few minutes with Laura. Julia had explained to Laura what happened in simple terms because the little girl had pestered her to death to tell her about it.

Mary Jean felt sure the child must still be traumatized by the murders at her former home. After spending ten minutes talking to the little girl, she asked Julia how things were going.

"We're getting along just fine. Matt is sure he'll be able to take care of Laura when he gets home, and I've volunteered to be the on-site baby sitter if required."

"It's apparent that's going very well. I'm glad for all of you."

The office phone rang and Julia answered.

"Well, speak of the devil," she said. "We're just talking about you. The general's leaving now. You want to speak to her?" Julia handed the phone to Mary Jean.

"Matt, I've been thinking about the meetings I told you about at the restaurant. Someone's giving the terrorists information, and I'm still concerned that you're being targeted. I'm going back tonight to watch my suspect, and I have the FBI on Fazio. It still may be nothing, but I'm in this until we find out who's orchestrating all these hits. Anything new there?"

She waited on Matt's response and then concluded, "Keep trying to pick up his trail. You want to talk to your daughter? I've got to get going."

She handed the phone to the girl. "Laura, your daddy wants to speak with you," she said, then gave her a little kiss on the cheek, waved good-bye to Julia, and left the office. She went to her apartment and changed for the evening's surveillance mission on Avery.

She arrived after dark, but found a place to park on the street and then walked a block to the restaurant. She managed to get the table in the cubbyhole again, from which she could see most of the patrons and the spot favored by Avery.

She ordered a gin and tonic and waited. A half hour passed. Another half hour, and she knew that something must have come up. Avery was supposed to be here according to his schedule, as he had nothing else on for the evening. Mary Jean could not sit there all night. After paying, she left the restaurant at 9:35.

On her walk back to the car, the wind chilled her to the bone and her skin felt frozen, so she decided to test the remote motor-starting device for the first time since taking delivery of the car from the dealership. She didn't know the exact range of the thing and tried from half a block away. Nothing happened. She stopped about a hundred feet under a streetlight and again pushed the button on her remote.

The Cadillac exploded into a fireball. Metal flew into the air, the heat and blast of the detonation sending Mary Jean flying. She impacted against a lamppost, where her lungs expelled all the air from within, and she felt pain as she rolled over on the sidewalk.

She didn't lose consciousness but felt blood pouring down her forehead and into her left eye. Sprawled flat on the ground, she moved her hand to feel her head. She found a cut on her scalp above the hairline that proved the source of the warm liquid on her face. She wanted to get up but couldn't catch her breath. Rolling over onto her hands and knees, she pushed herself up. Eventually, exerting enormous effort, she gained an upright position, leaning against the lamppost.

"Oh, shit," she exclaimed as she viewed her new car.

In the seconds it had taken her to focus on the event, she heard sirens coming in her direction. She didn't want to be here when they arrived. The attack was a direct hit against her, as the counter terrorist chief at the DIA. Someone had targeted her for elimination. Matt and Bridget weren't the only ones in danger now. She retrieved her handbag, swiveled and walked away, rounding the corner on her right at the first intersection. She took out her cell and dialed Mike Anthony.

"Hello, Mike. I need your help."

"What's happened?" Mike queried.

"Someone just blew up my car, hoping I'd be in it. I left the scene and need you to make some contact with the local police to get this painted as a stolen car that was burned by some teenagers on a joyride or gang-member initiation ritual."

"Why?"

"Because I waited at the restaurant for the man, but he didn't show. When I came out and remotely started my car, it exploded. I'm seeing a direct link," Mary Jean said.

"I see what you mean. If you're still in that area, there's a decent chance whoever did it is observing you. I'm on my way to the D.C. police. Try to see if anyone is watching or tailing you. Meet me at our usual place in two hours. That'll give me time to handle the scene with your car and take care of the reports."

"Okay. And . . . thanks." After she closed the phone, she felt like she'd recaptured some of her composure, but her hands continued to shake. She forced herself to focus on the situation. If the person who had tried to kill her remained in the area, she must try to identify him.

Mary Jean scanned around her immediate location and then surveyed the street. She saw no one peering in her direction. Many people passed by her and apparently hurried to the place where her car burned. A taxi came along the avenue. She stepped out and hailed it.

After she got in, she told the driver where to go and then began searching around to see if anyone had noticed her or attempted to follow the cab. As the taxi started to move, she picked out the Iranian diplomat as he turned the corner and observed her depart. A shiver ran up her spine. They had tried to kill her. Somehow they'd found out about her covert activity regarding Avery. She was right. It had to be Avery, but proving that would be another matter.

33

TWO DAYS AGO — SAVANNAH, GA

Matt and Bridget visited the Sapphire Grill, Vic's, Jazz'd Tapas, and the Alligator Soul, to no avail. The evening breeze from the ocean brought in a fresh smell. As they walked around the city, they both commented on the wrought-iron works of the downspouts on buildings and the semicircular stairways up to the entrance doors on many houses they viewed on the way to the restaurant. They ate at the 1790 Restaurant.

Matt ordered the lamb for himself, and Bridget opted for filet of sole. Matt squinted his eyes and peered through the slits at Bridget. "I must say, you do look beautiful even after a rough day of tramping around town in search of a demented terrorist. How do you do it?"

"I can't help it." She blushed a little. "You're just saying that because it's true," Bridget quipped. The meal arrived and they ate in silence for a few minutes. "So what do we do next?" she asked.

"I think we should continue to look in the night spots. Someone might have seen him. If we have no luck tonight, it'll be time to get the local FBI to assist in looking everywhere in Savannah for him. They'll have the same difficulty we're experiencing. As far as we know, he has no local contacts. No one here has ever met him. Snitches will be of no use to any agency, since they won't know this man." Matt stopped to sip his sweet tea for the first time. The waiter had called it the table wine of the South.

After wiping his mouth, he continued, "If they put the picture we have on TV, they'll get hundreds of calls that will lead nowhere and take a long time to investigate. No, we have to find him if he's still in town. So, after we finish dinner, let's head to a place called the Pink House. I understand they have a sort of nightclub."

"Sounds good. Let's go."

They arrived at the Pink House a little after 9:30. The entrance was on the south side of the building, and they went down stairs. On entering the room, the place appeared festooned with wall-to-wall bodies. In one corner, a small jazz group played and a few couples, packed on a minuscule dance floor, attempted to move in the confined space.

Matt eventually made it to the bar and ordered a drink. The barman came back after a short time and Matt showed him a photo. He asked him if he had ever seen the man. "He's a friend. We were supposed to meet here last night but we couldn't make it. I'm checking if anyone saw him."

"You a cop?"

"No. Not at all, just want to find him."

"Maybe Joan might've seen him. She's the photo girl. Ask her." Then he moved on. The orders for drinks were backing up even during this short conversation.

Bridget scanned for the photographer and finally spotted her at a table, making a pitch to capture the night on film for a young couple. She approached and waited until the two rejected the picture taking, but she noticed that the woman took their picture anyway. She heard her say, "In case you change your mind, I'll have it for you."

As the photographer moved from the table, Bridget repositioned herself to be in front of her. "How much do you charge?"

"Twenty-five."

"Okay, but I want you to see if you can remember this man." She handed over the old picture of Yuri with a fifty-dollar bill. The women glanced at it and then back at Bridget. Bridget said, "Yes, it's important that I find the scumbag. He ran off with some bimbo and left me with nothing. He's not even paying the child support, the dirty Russian bastard. I need to find him so I can tell the cops where he is."

The photographer looked back at the picture. "Sure, honey, I saw him in here last night with a young thing. I took a photo, but he didn't want to pay and tried to avoid the camera. Now I see why."

"Did you hear anything they said?"

"Some. She was from Atlanta and worked at an airport. They were talking about what she did, like direct planes or something. When I approached and took the shot without saying anything, he tried to cover his face. Told me to get lost. I'm glad he's your problem."

"Do you have it? So I can make sure it's him."

"Sure, honey. But it'll cost you for the picture." Bridget handed over the additional money and waited as the woman departed and came back in a few minutes with the photo.

"That's the bastard. Thanks," Bridget said and went over to Matt. "I think we struck pay dirt." She showed Matt the photo as she relayed what the photographer had overheard.

"Let's get this to the general. She should be able to identify the woman in the picture. She could be anyone at the airport, but if she's someone working with planes, she might be a federal employee. Good job," he said as he gave Bridget a high five. They left the bar and headed back to the hotel. There they faxed the photo to Washington and would DHL it in the morning. The fax machine display showed 12:10 a.m.

Now they had to bring the general up to date, Matt thought. They knew for certain of Yuri's presence in Savannah last night with a woman. According to the girl, he'd even talked with her about her job at an airfield in or around Atlanta.

Whoever killed Basam hadn't acquired the bomb, or Yuri wouldn't be acting like he had it. No, he still possessed it and would use it sometime in the future. There remained only one task —stop him.

34

YESTERDAY — WASHINGTON, D.C. — 12:20 AM

MARY JEAN ORDERED A CUP OF COFFEE. OUTSIDE, SNOW FELL AND presented the same sterile atmosphere as in the diner environment. The grill restaurant held only two other occupants, a young black couple who were apparently in love and unable to keep their hands off one another.

She waited on Mike Anthony. They had met here on occasion, and sometimes even this late at night. Based on the time he'd given her, he was long overdue. She forced herself to remain calm, because she had to talk with him. Pointless to call him, as he knew her location, and that she would be waiting, but something had obviously held him up. As she stirred the coffee with one sugar and no cream in it, the door opened, and Mike walked in.

He reached her table. "Shouldn't you go to see a doctor? That blood doesn't do anything for your red hair."

She smiled, "Thanks for coming. You seem a little beat yourself, and I'll get a medic to look at it later, but I don't think it's bad. You know how head wounds bleed. This one has stopped, and I can feel that it's only a small cut. Want some coffee?"

"Hell, no. I want to go home and go to bed."

"Okay, let's make it quick. What happened?"

"It took longer than I expected to get the stolen car story through. One detective there was a combat veteran, and he suspected more than a gang initiation. Just a minute, I need a drink." He went over to the bar and got a soft drink. After he returned, he continued, "What really happened?"

Mary Jean related all the events of the night and concluded with her observation of the Iranian diplomat as she'd left to meet Mike. She felt her head as it started to really hurt. She needed to take some aspirin, she thought.

"I'm waiting on the rest of the report I showed you. Maybe tomorrow. I'll let you know as soon as I get it. As far as your Iranian buddy, I think it's time I allocate some assets to finding out more about him. The fact that you saw him observing you justifies it. As head of the DIA counterterrorist operations, it's not a good thing to have an Iranian diplomat conducting surveillance on you ever again after what happened. Our legal mission is to monitor any suspected activity by diplomats. No need to mention the other thing for this to be a legitimate task. I'll get it going tomorrow. You get home and attend to the head."

"Okay, but I think there's more here than we are glimpsing," Mary Jean said.

"Maybe, and it's time for me to find out a few things," said Mike.

Mary Jean's cell rang, and she saw Matt's name. "Let me take this. You might want to wait a minute." She opened her phone and listened to the report from Matt, then told him to fax the picture to a number Mike had provided her. "I have a friend there who can help us get the identity of the woman. Good work. What are your plans?"

She heard his plan and then closed the phone. She glanced at Mike and gave a hand motion to the top of her head, "It's starting to hurt. I need to get some pills. Er... anyhow, they're in Savannah and have located a picture of Yuri and a girl from last night. She may be a federal employee if she works at an airport. We have to find out which one in order to help locate her. My people are on their trail, but they have nothing further to go on. They are planning to go to

Atlanta in the morning to take up the search there, assuming the bomb won't remain in Savannah."

"I'll get on the photo to see what we can find. Do you think Atlanta is the target of the bomb?"

"I don't know, but I agree that it's a more likely place than Savannah. I want to check, but I think the president is going there—maybe even tomorrow. I'll incorporate this into a briefing paper for him. I'll put in about the Russian team operating on our soil. At least we can let him make up his mind on the trip."

"You know how determined and stubborn he can be. He'll go no matter what," Mike said.

"I just don't want it to be his last trip."

RICKY JOBIN, AKA AL-BANNA, ARRIVED AT HIS APARTMENT WHILE MARY Jean and Mike met in the diner. Claude Moreau went to the kitchen to make some tea while Ricky provided some sweets in celebration of their successful mission. A third member of his cell, Maurice Levasseur arrived to join in the festivities. He had served as the driver on the operation to eliminate the general.

The phone rang before the tea was ready, and Ricky picked it up, answering with enthusiasm due to the high spirits they were both in after completing the task in Georgetown.

"You blundering idiot, you did it again," came the female voice over the receiver, loud enough for Claude, standing ten feet away, to hear.

"Watch your mouth, bitch. Who're you calling idiots? We did exactly what we were ordered." Ricky snapped as he nodded his head up and down toward Claude.

"You didn't kill her. That makes you an idiot."

"We weren't given the mission to kill the target, you sniveling bag. Our stated objective was to wire the explosive to the starter of the car. That's all you told us to do, and we did that."

"What the hell did you think you were supposed to do?" she thundered.

"We did what we were told to do. You instructed us to wire the explosives to the starter of the car and to get out of the area. We did exactly that. We heard the explosion when the car started. If she wasn't killed, that's your problem, lady. You go and kill her. We did precisely what we were ordered to do, and I don't want to talk to a woman again on this matter or anything else the leader wants done. He can call himself, but not a bitch like you. So get off my phone," Ricky said as he slammed it down.

The previous feelings of elation vaporized with that phone call. Ricky looked at Claude, who stood there dumbstruck. "What did you do?" he asked.

"I told her we are not taking instructions from a bitch like her, and it's time we acted like the warriors we are under the banner of Islam. Women have to know their place, and she's out of line giving orders to men."

"Do you know who she speaks for?"

"No. But ... ahh, I expect I'll be hearing from him soon. I'll tell him the same thing," said Ricky.

The phone rang, and he picked it up with a hello.

"Al-Banna," Rick said using his Islamic name in an authoritarian tone, He heard, "You exhibited rudeness to my assistant, who is only relaying instructions from me. I assure you she speaks for me in conveying my orders to you."

Ricky interrupted, forcing himself to refrain from yelling into the phone, "That may be true, but we're Islamic warriors and we don't take instructions from women. You're the one I was told to obey, and if you give me an order it'll be carried out."

"You listen to me. You will carry out the orders you are given by my assistant, or you will be dealt with in a very unpleasant manner. You have already been noticed for your failure in the attempt on Higgins, and now the failure tonight. Another fiasco will not be tolerated. You're in no position to make demands. Follow orders or you'll be in hell before you can rethink your stupidity in crossing me. Do I make myself perfectly clear?"

Ricky started to shake. His hand trembled and his breath came in short gulps. The bastard could do what he had threatened and Ricky knew it. "I don't even know who you are," he said in a sheepish intonation.

"That's right, and that's the way it'll stay. You recognize my voice from the tape you received from the man who indoctrinated you, do you not?"

"Yes, sir."

"That's better. I don't want to make a call to you again for something stupid that you've done. Send someone to take care of that general no later than tomorrow." The line went dead.

MARY JEAN ARRIVED AT HER CRYSTAL CITY APARTMENT THAT overlooked the Washington skyline. She could barely see the end of the runway at the Reagan International Airport on the Potomac. Her domicile exuded the epitome of modern-style black-and-chrome décor, including subdued indirect lighting.

She placed her purse down on the entryway table and headed for the bathroom to get some aspirin. *Three ought to do the job*, she thought, and after swallowing them, she applied a wet washcloth to her wound and cleaned it. In the mirror, she could see the small wound and put some Neosporin on it. Feeling a bit better, she went into the living room and poured herself a straight scotch with no ice from the small bar. She walked over to the sliding glass door, sat in a chair and viewed the beautiful scene of a peaceful and cold panorama of the capital. As she sipped her drink, she realized that the fears and troubles plaguing her had taken a greater toll on her clarity of thought than she'd previously understood.

The pressure of getting the demented Russian scientist turned terrorist, the president's scrutiny of her efforts to stop a nuclear attack on American soil, and the worry about her own health issue caused her more and more concern. She knew she might make judgment errors under such pressure. She had to make sure she did not. At least no one knew about her medical problem, since she had gone to a private doctor and not the military facility's medical personnel.

Matt and Bridget were on Yuri's trail, and soon they would catch him. If the FBI could get an ID on the girl in the photo, they would move in on her and with any luck get Yuri at the same time. Tomorrow the president would find out that she'd been the target of an attack, and she would have to appear to recount the event.

Mary Jean took a large sip of her drink. The chemo affected her life in many ways, and she didn't like it. The doctors had found a reemergence of the breast cancer that had been successfully treated five years ago. Her previous bout with the cancer had resulted in a lumpectomy. Afterwards, chemotherapy had proven successful but had caused sores in her throat and her hair had fallen out. She'd purchased a specially made wig so no one would notice. This round of chemo could be worse, and her stomach could get quite upset. She had studiously considered "alternative" palliatives, like marijuana and/or acupuncture therapy for the nausea and lack of appetite. Mary Jean had struggled with weight issues all her life, so a lack of appetite caused by the chemo could help her lose a few pounds, she mused.

This time the doctors recommended using chemo rather than doing a lumpectomy. They believed that would be the correct treatment. It might be the best remedy, but the side effects impaired her, even with the new pills to counter the effects. She knew she would beat it and then things would get back to normal, if what she did would ever be considered ordinary.

No more of that now. She focused her thoughts on Avery. Somehow he and the Iranian knew her plans, or perhaps they'd guessed her actions. They had been ahead of her, and after the failed attempt tonight they surely would try again. She would not run and hide somewhere else, but she would be prepared for them when they came. No doubt existed in her mind that the attack had been directed at her for checking into Avery. No other explanation seemed viable, not even the fact that she controlled the intelligence counterterrorist teams at the DIA. She was determined to catch him and then decide how to handle him as the president's oldest friend. It would be a delicate dance. She now knew he had somehow collaborated with the terrorists, and she would ensure he received justice for his treachery.

She just needed solid proof, and a plan.

35

YESTERDAY — SAVANNAH, GA

Colonel Anton Petrovich Ivanov slammed his fist on the table of the motel nightstand. That damn Igor. At least, he'd reported the Americans going to the house and leaving. He'd also related that the local police and military had arrived after they'd left the area. That meant they knew about Yuri and the address. Igor returned to their hotel room, went straight to the bathroom and stank up the place. Anton went outside with Ravshan to get fresh air.

"I think the Russian found the body, took the bomb, and escaped while our interpreter defecated somewhere. The bastard should have called to tell us about his sickness, and then I could have replaced him on the watch. He's not a soldier and doesn't understand the importance of being on duty and fully concentrating on the mission. I made a mistake in leaving him there."

"Colonel, there was no way of knowing that in advance. What are we going to do now? There don't appear to be any leads about where the man would go with the bomb," Ravshan said in Russian.

"Somehow our mission was compromised before we got here. I'll call the director now and tell him the situation."

Anton tried his phone, but the battery needed charging and the embassy had failed to provide a charger. He looked at Ravshan. "You had a phone that I saw you using last night on the way in from the airport. Does it work here?"

"Yes, sir."

"What do you use it for here in America?"

"Oh, not for talking, but I get emails and text messages from my friends back home, and it seems to function just fine. You can try to get through to Moscow on it. I believe it should work for voice."

Anton took the phone and dialed the number for the director in Moscow. Nikolai Vasilev came on the line after Anton told the secretary his name. "Well, Colonel, I expect you have succeeded by now. Report."

"Director," Anton said. He rubbed his hand over his head and tried to think how to put it. "The Arab terrorist is dead. We surprised him at the address provided by the defense attaché and he resisted. He died before he could give us any information. The weapon wasn't in his possession. The main target never appeared at the address. We have the location under surveillance, but a few minutes ago, the Americans showed up with police and military. We left before they found us. What are your instructions?"

"You are telling me you didn't get him or the weapon."

"No, Director, we did not," Anton said, knowing this was not going down well in Russia. "We arrived at the address as soon as possible and the man, Yuri Borisov, was not there. I'm in a foreign country to do one task, to conduct a search for the man here with no resources. If I am provided or can get information on his location, my team and I can accomplish the mission."

"Contact the defense attaché in three hours and he will have instructions for you. I'll get some of our assets to do some looking. They always seem to make a lot of chatter in certain areas before an event takes place. Maybe we can get an idea where they are targeting. No more excuses, you get him and the weapon or I'll ensure you'll regret your failure." The director hung up.

Anton gave the cell back to Ravshan and sat on the bed. As he did so, he heard the phone beeps, and guessed the sniper had received an email. The situation he found himself in could prove fatal to his career. The minister would hold him accountable for the failure to get the mad scientist and would ensure a quick end to his military service on his return to Russia. Immediate drastic action was now required on his part to get the bomb before it went off on American soil.

36

TODAY — ANDREWS AIR FORCE BASE — 7:35 AM

IT WASN'T COLD ENOUGH TO FREEZE CLAUDE'S SKIN, BUT DAMN NEAR. The frigid breeze rushed across the tarmac and slammed into anything exposed. The sun hadn't made an appearance over the eastern Maryland shore, and the cloudy sky prevented the normal bright light that preceded sunrise from illuminating the new snow covering the landscape. The first rays of day started to break over the eastern horizon as he drove to the air base in semidarkness, penetrated by the thousands of lights on the Capital Beltway around Washington. Uncountable minions drove their cars to an early morning start.

"Whatyadoing out here so early, Claude?" said the six-foot Air Force guard at the entrance to the hangar housing the president's plane. The man's black skin appeared encrusted with ice in the freezing conditions. Claude held up his pass for the guard to see, even though the guards knew him on sight.

Claude would have liked to tell him that this day he would fulfill the will of Allah, but he answered, "The office got a call from maintenance that there was a problem with the navigation electronics on the bird. So, here I am."

"Park in the visitor spot and go in to check in with the maintenance supervisor. I'll let him know you're here." He opened the gate, and Claude drove into the secure area with a sign that read "No Trespassing—Lethal Force Will Be Used." He knew the guards carried loaded weapons.

Claude parked the van in the visitor's spot and went inside. The warmth of the heated hangar enveloped him on entering, and he was glad to be out of the wind after the short walk from the vehicle to the hangar door. The Boeing 747 sat in the middle of the cavernous space, with light shining on it from every possible direction. As he walked toward the supervisor's position, he saw the various offices that coordinated the operations of the president's plane. Besides the mechanics' space, a designated area existed for avionics, tires, hydraulics, electronics, flight crew, catering, and fuel. The care they took of Air Force One, Claude thought, compared in almost every detail to operating a small town.

The head of maintenance, a short balding man in blue overalls, walked up to Claude as he approached and shook his hand. "Thanks for getting here so fast. We have a mission scheduled for the bird today, and the avionics boys say they detected a problem in the GPS nav equipment. The record shows that you came out here recently and serviced it, but something must be haywire. Go on over to their location and get filled in. We still have a few hours before flight time."

"No trouble," said Claude, giving the thumbs-up sign as he headed for the avionics area. He would take his time and get this right. The failure he had programmed into the unit four days ago now disrupted the GPS guidance system on the plane. He would take a few hours to evaluate what he already knew to be the cause of the problem. Whoever would observe him would get bored of watching his every move and would soon leave him alone long enough to upload his new program that would repair the nonexistent difficulty on the equipment. He knew; he would do more than fix it.

"Hey, Claude," an Air Force sergeant shouted as he approached him, walking across the concrete floor of the hangar. Claude recognized the sandy-haired, straight-as-a-rod figure of Sergeant Thomas Reed from his most recent trip to service the Bendix GPS navigation system on the plane. He remembered the sergeant had told him that he came from somewhere in Mississippi. Claude thought that accounted for the hard time he experienced in understanding him. "You was just out here to service this thing. What the hell did you do to it, man? The goshdamn thing wouldn't even turn on today."

"It was functioning properly when I left. You also checked it. So, we'll have to see what the problem is and fix it," Claude said with a smile and shook Sgt. Reed's hand.

"You want a cuppa joe 'fore we start?"

"That would be welcome. It's cold as... how do you say it here? A witch's tit, I believe," Claude smiled as he responded.

"You're right about that. Come on, coffee first and then you'll attack the plane."

Claude said to himself, "How right you are, Sergeant. How right you are."

37

THIS MORNING — SAVANNAH, GA — 7:35 AM

Matt hit the speed dial to the office, and Julia answered. "How's it going?"

"Nothing new. Laura is off to school. Also, we got a couple of email queries on our website requesting security evaluations. Most promising one is in New York. I sent a response to each and asked for more information, and I'll keep them on the hook till you get back. So what are you two doing down there?"

Matt heard Gandolf the parrot in the background. No profanity this time. "Well, we've found a lead on our man. We got a picture of the woman he accompanied two nights ago, and they're trying to get a name. Seems like she works at an airport in Atlanta. Could be the main one or one of the general aviation fields up there. Bridget and I are going to head for Atlanta. It seems the logical thing to do with the info we have. How's Laura doing?"

"She's fine. Meeting new friends at school, and that's taking some of the sting out of the nightmare she went through. When do you think you'll get back?"

"Don't know. Have to wait on the general to give us some assistance in finding the man. Do you have a Muslim friend up there to help us out?" Matt said and laughed.

"No. Don't know any," Julia replied.

"I'll call later to check on Laura after school. Till then," he said and disconnected.

"Is everything okay?" Bridget asked.

"Yeah. Nothing new at the office." He lay back on the bed. "You know, the more I think about this, the more I believe Atlanta is the target. What do you think?"

"It sounds right to me. If he's found a girlfriend who works at an airport... I think he'll use her either for entry to the airfield or to get the bomb on an airplane to explode it over a city. Like ... maybe Washington, or New York, or even Atlanta."

"Exactly what I'm thinking," Matt said. "He needs to move now. His buddy is dead, and I assume he knows that and that someone must be chasing him. He'll attempt to plant the weapon and then try to get away before someone catches him."

"The general hasn't gotten back to us, but going to Atlanta is the best lead we have. So let's get our butts in gear and roll," Bridget added.

They quickly packed their things and went to get the car. In less than fifteen minutes, they were on Interstate 16, headed for Atlanta.

ANTON ANSWERED THE CELL, WHICH DISPLAYED THE LOW BATTERY ICON. The voice of Major General Marshankin gave instructions in Russian.

"Colonel, the director orders you to go to Atlanta, Georgia. The intercept people picked up voice and electronic indications from the southern areas of the Confederation of Independent States that an attack of some type appeared to have been planned for that area. He said they viewed it as unusual to get intercept email from an American server being sent back to areas to the south of Russia. The intercepts originated from places in Turkmenistan, Uzbekistan, and Georgia." Anton knew these locations as all contained large numbers of Islamofascists and radical Islamists. The director coughed a few times before he continued. "The increase in traffic reached an inordinate level in the last twenty hours, and the evaluators at the headquarters had translated some of the phone calls and broken a few email intercepts, all pointing towards an attack on the American city of Atlanta."

"My phone is almost out of power. I'll go there and attempt to buy a charger at an electronic store."

"Try a Radio Shack," the Russian attaché in Washington said. "They will have what you need. Get a car charger so you can use it on the drive to Atlanta. You have to take your weapons, so travel by commercial air is out, and I can't get the plane that took you to Savannah back to you any faster than you can drive. So that you'll know, Colonel Ivanov, I'll inform the American military as soon as we finish. The ambassador will make a call on their State Department to deliver this same warning, that we have grave concerns that an attack will take place in a very short time on American soil by a terrorist who may be Russian," the defense attaché said.

"We're leaving for Atlanta now. Please try to get us more information on the location of our target. Maybe the American team has more intelligence. Could you attempt to get us an update on what they're doing?"

The defense attaché hung up and dialed Mary Jean.

38

THIS MORNING — DEFENSE INTELLIGENCE AGENCY — 7:45 AM WASHINGTON, D.C

MARY JEAN SPOKE WITH MIKE ANTHONY, WHO WANTED TO SEE HER THIS morning because he held the report she needed. They agreed to meet at noon for a light lunch at Landini's in Alexandria. Her secretary interrupted to say the Russian attaché wanted to speak with her. She answered it, "Good morning, Andrei. What can I do for you this morning?"

"Perhaps I can do something for you. Would coffee at the Old Post Office downtown be convenient, as soon as possible? I want you to know something at the same time my ambassador is delivering it to your State Department."

"I'm leaving now. Be there in twenty, twenty-five minutes. See you inside the main doors."

"Excellent," he said and disconnected.

Mary Jean arrived at the Old Post Office on Pennsylvania Avenue. Andrei greeted her and gestured with his hand for her to follow and they strolled over to a corner away from the pedestrian traffic.

"Sorry to rush, but I've been called back to the embassy for an emergency meeting. The subject will be the threat warning given to the State Department by our ambassador as we speak." He then proceeded to relay to her the gist of the intelligence information that would be passed. "Do you know, or are you able to tell me, what you are doing about the threat?"

"We have a team on the trail of Yuri Borisov," she said. "They're heading to Atlanta. They were able to find a woman he hooked up with and we're currently trying to identify her." Mary Jean shifted her position to take a quick look around to see if anyone was paying any attention to them. Satisfied, she resumed. "We believe she works at an airport in Atlanta, and he may be using her to get entry. The president will be in Atlanta today. I'm waiting on the result of the scans being done by various agencies that may provide us with concrete information on the identity of the woman. Then we'll attempt to get to her. Anything from anyone you may know in the area?" Mary Jean said.

"Nothing."

At that moment, Mary Jean's phone buzzed. She opened it to see a text message displayed on her screen. The picture had been identified as Marilyn Grosse, and her address in Atlanta was given. Her occupation was FAA controller at Hartsfield International Airport. The information provided the missing link on the woman, and she needed to call Matt with it. She did not notice that Andrei had also glanced at her phone display as he'd pretended to look around for anyone trying to eavesdrop on them.

"I have a name and address for the woman we're seeking. I'll get my team there shortly, and we'll see what she has to say. Thank you for the warning from your people. I'll keep you informed of what we find out," said Mary Jean.

"Always a pleasure to see you," he said. He moved off into the flow of people going and coming through the busy entrance.

Mary Jean dialed Matt's number.

"Matt, here's the address of Marilyn Grosse. She's an FAA controller at Hartsfield International." She gave it to him. "How long till you can get there?"

"We're already on our way to Atlanta, but it's a four hour drive. We'll push it and let you know as soon as we get there. Is the FBI going to be there before us?"

"No. I don't plan to tell 'em until you need help. You should be there before midday. I'm having lunch with my FBI contact in Old Town at noon. I'll call you after that."

"We'll get him, General. You can count on it," said Matt.

"I am counting on it," Mary Jean said.

AT ANDREWS AIR FORCE BASE, THE COFFEE BREAK ENDED AND CLAUDE took the thermos he and Ricky had packed with C-4, filled the remaining space with coffee to demonstrate to anyone watching that it was a real coffee thermos, walked over to the plane, and pulled the ladder over to the hatch below the flight deck. Sergeant Reed accompanied him. As he started to climb up the ladder with his instruments and his thermos, Reed pulled on his pant leg.

"Hey, man. No can take the thermos into the plane. Absolutely forbidden. Only your electronic gear to do the diagnostics. Sorry, but they're the new rules."

Claude knew better than to make a scene over the thermos, since he would lose, thanks to whatever security maniac had instituted the new procedure. Last week, he had been able to bring it into the plane and do the dry run for today's actual mission, but now he would have to improvise. This must be the will of Allah, and he would provide the necessary answer to his situation.

"I can't really drink it in the small space anyhow. Okay if I leave it here on the platform?"

"Sure. Go ahead and I'll check back in a while to see how you're coming along. Remember, this bird has to fly at noon to Atlanta."

"No problem. I'll get it done by eleven at the latest. I already suspect what is wrong, and I'll have to reformat the master disc and then run a few checks."

"Okay, man. Whatever you say. I don't understand any of that electronic stuff. Give me hydraulics and I know what to do," he said, giving Claude a broad grin. He did a military about-face, and walked away across the floor of the hangar.

Claude climbed into the belly of the aircraft and started his procedure for reprogramming the database, modifying a few items with ones he had created to ensure the plane would go to Atlanta International Airport. The thermos that contained the bomb he planned to connect to the system to enforce compliance on the part of the flight crew in landing at Atlanta International lay outside the aircraft. He went ahead and installed the warning not to deviate from the flight plan into the software.

When, or if the crew deviated from the direct flight plan Air Force One always received from the FAA controllers, then the designated warning would appear on their screen to inform them that a deviation of over five nautical miles or more would cause the detonation of three pounds of plastic explosives. The five-mile limit would allow for traffic approach control maneuvering at Atlanta, and it would be enough for them to signal the plane had a bomb on board. That would reinforce the need to land at Atlanta rather than going somewhere else to take care of the problem.

Claude concentrated on getting everything accomplished on time. He didn't know why it was so important for the plane to land at Atlanta. He didn't want to finish early in order to avoid any suspicion that only a small problem existed. What to do now that the bomb would not physically be on board? What could he do?

Then it came to him. Allah had given him this mission, and it would be his last. He felt prepared to sacrifice himself to destroy the president of the satanic U S of A. Yes, that crystallized as his only course of action. The solution to the problem now appeared simple, by the will of Allah, as he only needed to prove to these infidels that a bomb had been placed on board. They only had to believe it to ensure the success of the rest of the overall plan. Claude felt in his pocket for the key chain and clenched it in his hand. He held the means to detonate the explosives by simply pushing the panic and door buttons at the same time.

He finished the reprogramming at 10:30, and the crew performed a run-up of the engines and checked the GPS navigation system. Sergeant Reed took Claude to the snack bar, and they waited for the

Secret Device 187

test results. The plane radioed back that the system functioned satisfactorily and the presidential party was about to embark, for the flight to Atlanta. Claude finished his snack and drink and started to leave. Reed said to wait a few more minutes to confirm that the aircraft departed and that no more problems arose.

The president's plane departed the base reporting all systems operational. Reed thanked Claude and they headed for the door. Claude still couldn't figure out how to make them believe he actually had placed a bomb on the plane.

A roving air policeman had been on the other side of the hangar when Claude arrived. Claude walked toward the exit door as an air policeman and his guard dog came into the building. The dog went ballistic. It growled and circled Claude with it's fangs showing. The AP pulled his gun and pointed it at Claude. He searched the equipment box Claude had used for his reprogramming, and when he set the thermos on the ground, the dog barked and barked at it.

"You are under arrest," said the AP in a shaky voice. "How in the devil did you get it in here?"

Claude smiled, knowing that in his arrest, he had received a way to ensure the plan would work. He thanked Allah for this miracle.

39

THIS MORNING —WASHINGTON, D.C.— 9:02 AM

Major General Andrei Marshankin dialed the number of Colonel Ivanov as he walked outside of the old Post Office building. The clouds hung low over the capital, giving a feeling of more snow to come. A few pieces of paper swirled in the air next to the side of the structure in one of the little recesses near the entrance. The temperature remained in the high thirties, but the wind chill factor brought it down into the teens.

"Ivanov here."

"Colonel, where are you?"

"We're on the way to Atlanta. We should be there soon."

"I have an address for you. Get there fast, since the competition also has this information and will be acting on it as we speak." Andrei gave him the address and closed the cell. He hailed a taxi.

"Take me to the Russian Embassy."

Mary Jean watched as Andrei left the building and waited for a few minutes to observe her surroundings. No one paid any attention to her, and she headed for the exit. In her peripheral vision, she caught a glimpse of a man in a woolen sailor's cap looking at her. *Damn,* she thought, *I think maybe someone is following me.* She stopped and looked into the glass of the directory billboard. No, no one near her. Then she doubled back into the building—still no one. *Guess I'm jumpy,* she figured, *from those bastards that tried to kill me last night.*

She felt relieved. After a few seconds, she turned and headed for the exit. Outside, she decided to take a cab to Alexandria instead of the Metro. That way at least provided a different form of transportation from the way she'd arrived. It felt good to be in the groove again, practicing what many euphemistically called "the craft."

She felt elated to keep her hand in on the operational aspects of the agency, even though her specific responsibilities entailed handling the myriad details necessary to run a worldwide counterterrorist intelligence operation. She functioned on a daily basis as a manager, not really an operative anymore, unless something like Avery got her juices up, and her division heads actually handled the day-to-day decision making, except when she took an interest in a particular mission.

Mike Anthony sat at a table near the back of the Alexandria restaurant, and smiled when he saw her. He got up to shake her hand while giving her a light peck on the cheek.

"First of all, how's the head?"

"Not bad at all. Can you see anything?"

"Not a thing. You've got it camouflaged perfectly," said Mike with a grin. He held up a glass. "Water? I've got to go to a big meeting this afternoon on the other terrorist attacks we're experiencing all over the place." He scanned around. Even in the restaurant, she noticed he never let his guard down. "They're up to something big," he continued in almost a whisper. "I just know it."

"I think you're right, and I think I know what it is," said Mary Jean in the same low conspiratorial tone.

"Come on... give." Mike used a loud, guttural whisper.

"You were in on the meeting with the president when he ordered Matt to go after this guy Yuri, right?" she asked.

"Yeah," he said as he indicated for a waiter to come over. They gave their order for the lunch special of veal and asparagus with some sparkling water.

"So, since you gave me a report that never existed, I'm going to give you information I don't know." She waited as the server approached and poured the water. Once he departed, she continued in a barely audible tone. "My team has tracked the weapon to Atlanta, and the target was with an FAA flight controller from Hartsfield International Airport. Matt is on the way to get her now and find out what she knows."

"You want our help. I heard the president order us to assist if your man asked," Mike said.

"Not yet. I'd suggest you get some people alerted in Atlanta that we're working this. I read in the morning file from FBI that your guys are deep into an investigation on the bombing at Dobbins Air Force Base yesterday. How bad was it?"

"Thirty dead. The bastards snuck the explosives into the mess hall in a meat delivery truck. When they rolled the dollies into the center of the building, they exploded. The terrorists were suicide bombers, and we think they came from one of the nearby universities."

"Damn, Mike. What can we do to stop them? They're corrupting our kids at college. Look at the billions the Saudis are pumping into our higher education establishments. They manage the appointment of the chairmen of the departments they create, who may or may not be terrorists, and they teach or preach that we are the bad guys. Our schools do it to get the cash. What the hell are we to do?"

"You're preaching to the choir. The problem is, as I see it, the public doesn't know the extent to which these radical jihadists have infiltrated our society. We're trying to fight on the old system of an even playing field, and they've stacked the deck." The food arrived, and they remained quiet for a few minutes as they ate.

Mary Jean broke the silence. "This is really tasty. I was hungry. I'll run tonight to take off the calories." She said it in a halfhearted manner, and Mike smirked with his eyes lifted to the ceiling.

"I have a report that I never got for you and as far as I am concerned it doesn't exist." He reached into his inner jacket pocket and produced a one-page typed letter with a photo attached on the back.

Mary Jean opened the folded paper and started to read.

SPECIAL REPORT
FOR: DEPUTY DIRECTOR MICHAEL ANTHONY
FROM: SPECIAL AGENT THOMAS SYLVESTER

I followed up on the subject Julie Johnson. She married an Army paratrooper, Sergeant Richard Johnson, in the 82nd Airborne Division, stationed at Fort Bragg, NC, twenty-three years ago. From interviews, it appears they were a happy couple. Sergeant First Class Richard Johnson was killed in an airborne operation in Afghanistan.

The wife left Fort Bragg eight years ago, and no one here knows where she is today. Her husband did not reach twenty year's service, so there is no retirement check to go to his widow, and her present address or even a general location is not a matter of record with the Department of Defense.

The attached photo is from the DoD file for the last military ID card she was issued at Fort Bragg.

This completes the investigation here, and no further action can be taken.

Mike, you owe me a big one.

This is the only copy of this report.

Mary Jean gave him a grateful look. "Mike," she said, "it's wonderful to have old friends." She smiled ear-to-ear, her white teeth gleaming, and rotated the paper to view the attached photograph.

Her mouth dropped open.

40

THIS MORNING — ON ROUTE TO ATLANTA

MATT CALLED THE OFFICE. THE BRIGHT BLUE SKY SPORTED ONLY A sprinkling of puffy morning cumulus clouds above the hills ahead of them. The temperature on the car's outside thermometer read a pleasant seventy-two while Matt drove at eighty miles an hour on I-16. They passed Dublin, Georgia, and approached Macon, only an hour outside of Atlanta.

Julia answered his call.

"Anything new?" he asked.

"Not a thing. Laura is here before school. You want to talk to her?"

"Yes, in a minute. I want you to look up a name for me on the computer and double-check the address." He gave her the name and address Mary Jean had provided and waited. He heard the parrot and Laura talking in the background. It sounded like Laura's attempts to get the bird to eat something were not working.

"That name and address appear valid. What's the story?"

"We got the info from the general, and she's on the trail of someone we think might be connected to all this. We can't contact her again till after she has lunch in Old Town. So, when we get to Atlanta, we'll find out if this woman knows where Yuri is. She was with him in Savannah. We'll keep you informed. Please put Laura on."

Matt talked with Laura for a minute before she said she needed to run to catch the school bus. Matt said good-bye and ended the call.

"It's a current and valid address for Ms. Grosse," he told Bridget.

"How's Laura?"

"Sounds fine, but I have to see her to really get a handle on how she's reacting to the murders." After a minute he said, "The car needs gas, and I could use a drink. How about you?"

"Could use a pee break," Bridget chimed in.

Matt turned on the radio on the hour to get the latest news. Nothing good. Another terrorist attack on a bus of soldiers at Fort Benning near Columbus, Georgia, had killed four. "Do you think all these attacks in such a short time are a diversion to keep all the law enforcement agencies in turmoil and expending all their efforts on tracking down these bastards?"

"It's possible. They've been quiet for a few years, and now all of a sudden they're active all over the country, just when we know for sure that a madman has a weapon of mass destruction in the States. Might be more than coincidence. They're using the attacks to tie up all the federal law enforcement agencies and a lot of state assets too."

"Maybe their overall organization is orchestrating the multiple terrorist attacks to provide a cover for the main event," said Matt. He saw a gas station and stopped to fill up.

IN OLD TOWN ALEXANDRIA, MARY JEAN AND MIKE FINISHED THEIR lunch and gave one another a hug in front of the restaurant before going their separate ways. Mike headed down King Street, and Mary Jean started to walk up the hill to find a taxi. Again, she felt that someone was watching her. In order to satisfy herself that it couldn't be the same old jitters, she stopped in front of a store, went in quickly, and looked back out the front window. She watched for at least thirty seconds. Only a few people had ventured out in the cold.

Then she saw him.

He wore jeans and tennis shoes with a blue ski jacket, his head covered by a sailor's watch cap. The man stopped across the street to look in a window and stared into the window too long, way too long for a person to linger on a cold day. She decided to go back toward Mike. She started walking and that's when she saw a weapon appear in his hand.

She looked toward the back of a nearby car, where she saw a leg come around the bumper. Then the gun started upward in the man's hand. The assailant came completely into her field of vision as he raised the weapon to put a round into her at less than ten feet. She dashed around the back of the car. No question of accuracy at this range.

The gun came to a firing position. Their eyes met and she saw hatred, fury, and evil in his stare. The hatred remained on his face as his left eyeball exploded out of his head. Blood and tissue peppered Mary Jean's coat. She screamed. The sound of a weapon discharging reached her, but she felt nothing. Then the man toppled to the sidewalk, and Mike Anthony stood five feet away, his gun still pointing at her assailant.

She looked down at her clothes and almost fainted. The blood and mess almost made her stomach convulse. She controlled herself in order not to throw up. Her hands shook from her close brush with death.

"We gotta stop meeting like this," he said. "Who the hell is he?" He put his hand down to help her get up.

"Don't know, but I think he's been following me all day." She took a couple of big gulps of air to attempt to slow down her heart rate. "I sensed it earlier but spotted him before he opened fire."

"This will take some explaining. The deputy director is not supposed to be out shooting villains on his lunch hour. Let me handle the police," Mike said while helping her to her feet.

"Sure, you do that. I think this attack on me is connected to the attempt last night. Come to think of it, I'm quite sure." Mary Jean leaned against the car to recover her composure and tried to relax.

Her heart slowed with each inhalation. This was too much like her days in combat in the Gulf. She recalled the deaths and destruction she'd seen over there.

"Don't you want to know why I came back to save your ass?" Mike asked as he holstered his weapon. Sirens sounded nearby.

"Sorry, Mike. Of course, why the hell did you come back to save a damsel in distress?" Mary Jean tried to shake the crud that had come out of the dead man off her coat, without much success.

"For one thing, to pay you back for the last time you saved my neck, and for another, you forgot to take the picture that shocked you. I don't want to know why, because I sensed it was none of the FBI's business or mine. So I came to give it to you."

"Thank you for both reasons. Someday I may tell you about it, but not right now. Here come the local gendarmes. Someone called them with all the shooting."

"This was a robbery gone bad is the story we tell. I just saw this guy try to gun you down for your purse. Do you have an ID in that bag that's not really you?"

"Yes," she replied.

"Get it out. We don't want the world to know who or what you really are."

41

THIS MORNING — ATLANTA, GA — 11:00 AM

Yuri couldn't believe the luxury of the home in the Buckhead area of Atlanta. The mansion-sized house perched on top of a hill standing three stories tall, with a pool and a three-car garage, and even sported a small basement apartment for hired help.

She had invited Yuri to stay with her now that the husband had exited from her life. Yuri went around the house, observing the way wealthy Americans lived. The lower level sported a full bar and party area, complete with a sixty-inch flat-screen TV on the wall. Upstairs he found a kitchen that looked as if a master chef resided here. It contained the best Viking range and two Subzero refrigerators. The breakfast table, at the far end of the kitchen overlooking the pool in back, bore a country design.

The rest of the main floor consisted of a dining room and living room area with a grand piano. Off the main room, a screened-in porch almost as big as the inside room looked over a manicured lawn. The master bedroom, down a small hallway off the living room, contained its own separate screened-in veranda. The entire house overflowed with art and antique furniture.

Yuri came back from his walkabout in the house and they sat in the kitchen, having coffee and lemon squares purchased earlier at a Starbucks.

"You like the place?" she said.

"It's better than anything in Russia. You Americans certainly know how to live well." Yuri stuffed a large part of the square in his mouth.

"We've had a great time for a few days, and I know you said you were coming to Atlanta to meet someone to find a job here. What do you plan to do?" Marilyn queried. She sat back in her chair and took a sip of her coffee, waiting for an answer.

"The man I'm supposed to link up with is looking for a physicist in nuclear engineering to assist him in developing a new method of using atomic energy. He contacted me on the Internet and arranged for the meeting. I have to check my email and let him know I'm here. He'll tell me where I need to go."

"Let's finish our coffee, and while you're doing that, I can get ready to go to work. Will you be able to stay tonight?" Marilyn got up and did a sensual would-you-like-to-get-your-hands-on-me? walk over to Yuri. She put his hands on her breasts. "They'll miss you if you say no."

He squeezed her and massaged her for a few seconds when she sat on his lap. Then he said, "I'm sure I can come . . . back. I have to get on the Internet now and see what is planned for me. If nothing today, then we can—what did you call it? Play around, before you go to work."

"Great. Now I'll get my things ready, and you do your Internet browsing." She got up, put her coffee cup in the trash, and headed for the master bedroom. Yuri watched her go and pulled his computer from the knapsack he'd carried in from the car. He'd left the case that contained the atomic weapon in the trunk of her car, and Marilyn had said nothing about it when he'd helped her carry her suitcase and his duffle bag into the house.

He went outside to the small patio deck off the kitchen and started his computer. In a few minutes, he connected to the Internet and opened his email. After the decryption program ran, new messages from Fatimah appeared for him. The first contained a response to his demand for payment before conducting the operation to set off the bomb.

"Money request met. Deposit made to account this day. Instructions to follow."

Yuri went to the bank's website and checked on the deposit. The money now showed in the account provided to Fatimah in Savannah. He electronically moved it into another account at the same bank in case they got some idea of withdrawing it at a later time.

The second message from Fatimah rendered a shocker.

"Target arrives Hartsfield International at 1430 hours local today. Ensure package is delivered by 1440 hours local. God is Great.

Fatimah"

Yuri smiled. This was more like it. They had given him everything he demanded, and now he simply needed to set off the weapon and get out of the country. Better yet, he could stay here and hide for a while with his ability to access millions to live any lifestyle he desired. He could disappear, and the Russians would forget about him in time.

The next email he sent updated the control group at Fatimah:

"Will accomplish mission today. Plan to arrive at airport before 1430 hours local and place instrument in the tower. Will contact you after to confirm, and expect transfer of remaining money to my account. The Russian."

Yuri realized that by now they must suspect that Basam was not the one writing the messages and that it must be him. He didn't care, and maybe it was better that way. He possessed the knowledge for which they now paid. Maybe they would need to do it again at some point in the future.

The mission parameters required it be accomplished today, and only three hours remained to set it up. He held the ace in the hole. Now he knew a way to access the airport and get the bomb into position. The Americans didn't even know it existed. With Marilyn going to the airfield and working in the tower, getting the case there would accomplish his objective. If possible, he wanted to place it at the top of the tower, since the destruction area would be greater in proportion to the height above ground at which the detonation occurred, but if not at the top of the tower, anywhere on the airfield would completely obliterate everything within a four-mile radius. After setting the timer, he would take her car to get a safe distance away.

An hour and a half remained before she would leave for work. He went back to the bedroom, where she stood in a bathrobe, unpacking her suitcase. *What a beauty*, he thought as he walked over behind her and reached around to hold her. She straightened up and took her time as she opened the robe.

She slid around in his arms and put hers around his neck. After giving Yuri a passionate lingering kiss, she walked backwards toward the bed. She pulled him down on top of her near the edge of the bed, with her hands still around his neck.

Afterwards, Yuri rolled over to take a rest, and Marilyn headed for the shower. He dozed off for a few minutes and woke to hear her on the phone out in the living room.

"You're not going to believe what I did over the last few days. I can't believe it myself."

Yuri walked quietly down the hall to listen.

"I met this guy named Yuri in Savannah and he screwed my brains out. I can't get enough of it. Honey Jo, can you believe it? Come in at two and we'll meet in the break area and I'll tell you all about it." She considered for a few seconds, then said, "Okay, I have to get a move on if I'm going to be there earlier. See you there."

Yuri went back to the bedroom, got dressed, packed his duffle bag and placed the pistol in his belt on the small of his back donning a light windbreaker to help conceal the bulge. After a few minutes, Marilyn didn't reappear. He went to find her, but before he did, he took her cell phone out of her purse and turned it off as a precaution, since the time for action loomed only a few hours off. He didn't want any unexpected events. Then he went to find her.

After searching in the house, he went to the garage. There he saw the trunk of the car open. He tiptoed over to the car and when he reached the vehicle, he saw her bend over and reach into the trunk.

She started to open his case.

42

THIS MORNING — INTERSTATE 16 — 11:44 AM

Colonel Anton Ivanov sat in the passenger seat of the silver Mercury Sable rented in Savannah and observed the topography of the land. An old infantry soldier, he visualized the type of military action that would be needed to conquer this sort of terrain. It would take a bloody campaign, the American Civil War had proven that.

The coastal plains of Georgia slipped behind them, and the rolling hills they now passed through, created by the various ice ages that had sliced valleys in the earth, appeared covered mostly with woodlands on this monotonous stretch of rural countryside the interstate traversed. The bright clear day did nothing to improve his disposition.

Ravshan drove as they rushed toward Atlanta. They traveled in silence for almost an hour. Anton's mind focused on capturing the mad Russian, thereby ensuring acquisition of the weapon. That crazy traitor had actually betrayed the motherland by selling out to radical Islamists. Anton's duty and his career rested on his ability to retrieve the bomb. How could the security services have allowed this creep to get by their scans? How could they not keep track of him? The military knew they'd let go a man capable of making an atomic weapon. Ivanov knew the answer—money. There wasn't enough of it to cover everything. Surveillance on every unemployed, highly technically trained individual couldn't be done.

Anton had fought for Russia in Afghanistan. That country, a cesspool of humanity one step out of the Neanderthal age, consisted mostly of knuckle draggers with no ability to think or to see reason. The Russians had offered them a way into the present century, and they'd preferred to ride camels and horses while attacking tanks. Anton had received three wounds fighting these tribesmen, and when the government had decided to leave that desolate and impoverished country, the Koran-thumping bastards known as the Taliban had soon taken over and plunged the whole area back into the Stone Age. But they didn't seem to care.

A musical sound in the car whipped his focus back to the present. He shifted in his seat and turned to Ravshan with a questioning look.

"It's just an email coming in on my phone. I'll view it later," said Ravshan.

Anton calculated the time to be early evening in Moscow; the director should still be in his office.

"We've got to stop and get gas and a map. I would like to use your phone once again to check in with the director."

They stopped at a filling station. Ravshan read his message and deleted it, then handed the phone to Anton. Ravshan got out to pay for the gas and to obtain a street map of Atlanta.

The director came on the line. Anton said, "We are within an hour of being at the address we have for our man. Your assistance helped to get us the location. Do you have any further instructions?" Anton played to the man's vanity and hoped his reporting on the current situation would mitigate the failure in Savannah.

"This is welcome news. The defense attaché in Washington also informed me that the Americans may be ahead of you. Take care of the problem and get the goods back here. Call me when you have accomplished your task." The director hung up.

Anton realized from the director's tone of voice that he'd somewhat softened his previous position, and things might work out after he recovered the bomb. All that remained for him to do was complete this mission successfully, and the whole event in Savannah would be forgotten. The director must realize that what had happened there wasn't under his control and that the information had been too old by the time they were able to act on it. On one hand, only a few knew the operation in Savannah hadn't worked out, but on the other hand, if he succeeded, only a very few would know that too. At least in the latter case, he could plan to retire in less than a year.

Ravshan got back into the car after pumping the gas. He started the engine but did not put the car in gear because he heard Igor in the backseat, tapping his hands on the back of his headrest.

Another car pulled into the gas station while Anton was speaking on the phone to Moscow. Igor almost came over the top of the seat to tap the colonel on the shoulder as Anton gave the phone back to Ravshan.

"Sir, look over there. The people in that car over at the far pumps are the ones I saw leave the house where you killed the Arab."

43

THIS MORNING — OUTSKIRTS OF ATLANTA— 11:44 AM

Matt pulled into the filling station south of Atlanta to take a break and to gas up the car. They both got out to stretch their legs, and after Matt filled up the car, they moved it to a parking space in front of the convenience store. Inside they got some drinks. In less than five minutes, they returned to the car and got back on the road headed to Atlanta.

"You've been very quiet. What's on your mind?" Matt said.

"Well, we've had all this time on the drive up here, and I've been thinking about us."

"What have you thought?"

"I realize we're not rushing into any relationship. Not really. We've been together for over a year in the same unit and gotten to know each other over a long period of time. You see what I mean?"

"Yes," Matt said. He had waited a few seconds before responding, trying to imagine where this was going.

"I'm wondering if you're ready for a long-term commitment for us to work together?"

"I don't know if we've gotten that far."

"No. No, I don't mean it as a pressure for you to do anything at this time. It's more of a thought process I'm going through. Remember, we promised to be open and honest. You asked, and I told you what I was thinking. I still want to go to get my degrees when my enlistment is up."

"That's being truthful. I really think we should postpone this talk till after this mission and then take a day to communicate about what each of us might see happening in the future."

"Okay. Right now I've got the GPS map programmed to take us to the address. I do think we can work in the field together. I have to go in order to keep saving your ass," Bridget finished with a wide grin on her face as she punched him in the shoulder.

They were so involved in their conversation that the silver Mercury Sable that pulled in, clearly visible in their rearview mirror, went unobserved as they left. The traffic density increased when they exited off I-16 and joined I-75. Even an amateur could follow someone on this overcrowded interstate. Matt followed the directions given by the GPS for the next half hour. As they neared their destination, Bridget got out her weapon and rechecked it, put an extra magazine in her coat pocket, and then checked Matt's, just in case he needed it as soon as they exited the car.

"Really a swanky neighborhood. Money, money, and more money," Bridget uttered as they approached the address.

"Our man must have hooked himself a winner in Savannah to get into one of these," Matt said. "Wonder if she knows anything about him other than a bar pickup?"

"We'll be there in two blocks, so we can ask her."

They now traveled on city streets. When they were only one street away from the address the general gave them, Matt picked out a car following them and told Bridget.

"I'll keep going . . . no, wait the car turned off. False alarm," he said.

"No one else could know about this woman. There should be no one after her but us." Bridget got out of the car as Matt cut the engine in front of the address. "What a mansion. If she's got a hubby, he must be loaded and out of town, or maybe she's divorced or having a quickie weekend with our man."

"She could have inherited it. You're right though, she didn't buy this on an FAA controller's salary," said Matt.

They walked up to the door and rang the bell. After waiting two minutes and ringing again, they decided to walk around the house. They went to the back by the pool, where Bridget pushed on the back door, and it opened. "Let's go," she said.

Methodically, they searched each room but did not find the woman or Yuri. Lastly, they went to the garage, but they saw no car.

"Look here. Duct tape on the floor. Stuff scattered on the workbench. What do you make of it?"

"Not enough information," said Matt. "Let's go back inside and check again."

As they searched, Matt picked up the landline phone and hit star 69 to redial the last person to phone this number.

"Hello, sugar," came the female voice with a Southern inflection. "What's happened for you to call again so soon? That stud balling you again?"

"Ma'am, my name is Matt Higgins, and I'm a federal agent. We are looking for Marilyn Grosse."

"What? What are you?"

"Please listen. I'm a federal agent, and we have reason to believe that Marilyn is in grave danger. You answered like you're an intimate friend. Do you know where we can locate her?"

"No, but she's supposed to meet me at work a little before two."

"At work? Are you an FAA controller?" Matt waved at the phone and gave a thumbs-up sign. He thought they might have an absolute lead in this person.

"I been one for eight years. What the hell is going on?" came the response.

"Could you give me your name?"

"Honey Jo Stevens. Now what is going on?"

"We have reliable intelligence that a terrorist is in Atlanta. Your friend may be in danger from the man she's with. We believe he is one of the terrorists. Where is she supposed to be at two?"

"The supervisor wants us all in early today to do the turnover before the president gets here at two thirty, since he's landing at Hartsfield instead of Dobbins, and none of us has ever handled Air Force One. I told Marilyn to get here then and I'd meet her in the snack bar."

"The president is arriving at fourteen hundred thirty hours," Matt said. "That's only two hours from now. If you hear from her, please contact me or have her contact me immediately." He gave her the number.

"'You're for real. Holy shit! . . . Okay, I'll try to call her now on her cell. I'll call you if I get her."

Matt didn't get a chance to confirm her cell number because Honey Jo disconnected. Matt stared at the phone and told Bridget what Honey Jo had said. "We've wasted an hour here. Yuri must be on his way to the airport if Marilyn's going to meet Honey Jo at two. I bet he'll use her to get into the airfield." He rotated to face Bridget, "We have to warn the President and call—"

Then he saw the three men standing behind Bridget, with one weapon pointed at her head and the other two aimed straight at him.

44

BUCKHEAD AREA, ATLANTA, GA — 12:46 PM

MATT STARED AT THE THREE MEN. BLACK SHIRTS AND BLACK PANTS showed a lack of sartorial imagination, but their weapons, easily recognized Glocks, left nothing to visualize. One of the men started to move towards them and indicated for both to raise their hands. As he passed Bridget, she grabbed his arm and flipped him over her shoulder. She did not know more armed men stood behind her. One of those men, with instant reflexes, hammered her head with his pistol, and she went down in a heap.

Matt felt rage, hatred. Bridget's slumped body spurred him on to go after the bastard who'd hit her. He charged at the man, hitting him in the jaw with a crushing resonance. Then he swung his foot up to get the second in a powerful tae kwon do move. The last man slammed the pistol into Matt's skull as he rotated from the kick. He felt a searing pain in his head, and then everything went black.

He sluggishly opened his eyes after deciding to wait and not indicate he was conscious. Let them talk first. They didn't want to kill him, since they could have shot both of them when they had come into the house. He guessed the attackers had come in through the same door he and Bridget had used.

Still unable to move, he felt the assailants search him. They removed their weapons and placed them on a side stand in the corner of the living room. Not a word passed their lips.

Matt regained full consciousness and realized he couldn't change position. His hands were securely bound, as were his legs. He found he couldn't turn or move his head in any direction.

Maybe they were terrorists coming to assist Yuri. No, if they were, they certainly would have killed them. Maybe they were home invaders after any valuables in the house. That didn't fly either. They operated like professionals in the way they had handled Bridget and then his attack on them. They wanted them alive. But why?

"Captain Higgins. I know you can hear me. Don't play the fool."

The voice sounded Russian, Matt thought. He opened his eyes, but his hands and arms, ankles and knees remained tightly taped to a chair. Tape encircled his neck. Bridget moved and he felt her in the bonds that connected their necks. Someone had done a first-class job binding them together and to the chairs so completely they couldn't move anything except their eyes and mouths.

"Captain Higgins, we are not here to harm you, but to retrieve some property we believe is ours. Where is Yuri Borisov?" asked the oldest of the three men standing in front of him, his eyes unblinking. He had short-cropped salt-and-pepper hair, a face like a bulldog, and a superbly toned physique.

Matt guessed they must be Russian intelligence. First of all, they'd called him "Captain," his rank in the military, and second, they knew about Yuri. He didn't know how much of the phone conversation they'd heard before he turned around.

"How is Bridget?" Matt asked.

"The sergeant is fine, and not damaged any further than her injury from her futile attack," the leader said.

Matt recognized him as the leader of the three. Must be a senior intelligence officer, either civilian or military. He knew Matt and Bridget had been military, and that must be from the briefing the Russians had received after they'd spoiled the attack by the Saudi terrorist. That group had attempted to use the weapons Yuri constructed to destroy the West's supply of oil from the Saudi Arabian oil fields.

"I asked you a question. Where is Yuri Borisov right now?" The tone demanded an answer.

"I'll ask you one. How did you find us here?"

"You are not in a position to ask questions. But, I'll tell you very quickly, and then you'll tell me what I need to know. I have to stop the man. You can't. So, your help is essential. Do you agree?"

Matt knew when the time to compromise had arrived. He sat on the losing end in his present situation. He had little choice but to go along, at least temporarily, so he barely moved as he nodded his head.

"One of my men here saw you leave the house in Savannah that we knew Yuri Borisov used. You didn't act like police, so I reasoned you were intelligence officers after the same thing as me. We followed you here in your car. Fortunately, we heard you talking on the phone. We now know he'll be at the airport at two. Where is Borisov right now?"

Damn, Matt thought, *he's right.* Someone had followed them in Atlanta. He needed to focus on what he would tell this man. He didn't actually know the location of their target.

"I would tell you where he is if I knew. I don't. I know he'll be at the airport at two, and the president of the United States is due to arrive there at two thirty. You have me at a disadvantage, and I assume you don't want the bomb to go off or you wouldn't be trying to get this Yuri," said Matt as he tried to turn his head without success. These guys knew their business. No way could they get loose from these bonds quickly or easily.

"So your president will be at the airport about the same time as you think Yuri will be there. Thank you, Captain. That's all I think you can tell us. We'll leave you now."

"Cut us loose and we'll help," urged Matt.

"I'm afraid not. You might assist, but then again you might impede us. We have a mission, and I'll not allow anyone to compromise it. I'll see to it that you are released in a few hours." He signaled for his men to follow him, and they left.

Matt struggled with the restraints, to no avail. Bridget began to move. She came around in a few minutes and Matt filled her in.

"How will they get into the airfield?" Bridget asked.

"I don't know, but that man is resourceful. We have to get ourselves out of here." They both struggled but remained unable to move even a fraction of an inch. After a minute, they stopped the struggle and confessed to the futility of continuing.

Time passed, and the clock on the wall showed one fifteen.

"Do you hear something?" Bridget said.

"No."

"Listen, someone's using a key in a door. They opened one lock and are opening a deadbolt."

They both moved their eyes as far as they could to see the figure of a beautiful black woman come into view.

"Cut us loose, please," said Matt. "Who are you?"

"Honey Jo."

45

TODAY — ANDREWS AIR BASE — 1:25 PM

Claude didn't move when the air policeman pulled his gun and ordered him to raise his hands. He complied and waited. The policeman searched him, but found no weapons. Sergeant Reed approached from the other side of the hangar.

"What's going on here, Airman?"

"My dog reacted as trained to the presence of explosives. I have to take this man into custody until CID can get here."

"The Civilian Investigation Division won't believe this happened in the president's airplane hangar. Call your Secret Service contact for instructions," ordered the sergeant. "Besides, the man is leaving and no bomb or anything else has gone off."

"I have my orders, Sergeant. Please help me escort him to a room where he can be interrogated," the policeman said.

"Follow me and I'll call the Secret Service."

He picked up his gear, and they led Claude across the expanse of concrete in the hangar to a room near the maintenance section. The small room contained only a table and a three steel chairs. The grease monkeys used it for a break room. Oil rags lay in the corner, and a picture of an earlier Air Force One, the venerable Boeing 707, hung on the wall.

Claude sat in one steel-framed chair and put his hands on the top of the folding table. They left him there and closed the door. He now had the time to finish his plan. There would be a few minutes at least before any Secret Service agents appeared, and he must convince them that a bomb actually existed on board Air Force One or the overall plot would collapse. He firmly believed that and planned to sacrifice himself to ensure the operation succeeded. Allah had picked this time to test him, because he knew in his heart that he could not fail.

They had allowed him to bring all his equipment and the thermos into the room. What fools. He checked his pocket one more time to make certain it contained the key ring. It felt light in his hand. He would tell them the story, and he now knew how to convince these infidels that he told the truth. To lie for the sake of Islam was not only allowed but also encouraged if it brought success to the warriors of the faith.

His watch showed a quarter to two when the two agents entered the room. The bald-headed one with the regulation suit for the service that identified him as law enforcement was obviously the one in charge. The other was a young man, maybe late twenties, sandy-blond hair, with a small nose and foggy blue eyes. Both said their names, which Claude failed to even pay attention to, and sat down, dragging up two of the folding chairs. The young one picked up the thermos and placed it on top of the table.

"Mr. Moreu," the older agent said, "what do you have in the canister?"

"I have coffee in it. If you like, I will pour you some to drink," Claude said in a straightforward manner.

"We'll take it downtown to get it analyzed since the dog indicated it contained explosives. If it doesn't, we'll return it to you here and apologize. In the meantime, I'm afraid we'll have to detain you until we know, because if there are explosives in it, you will be going away for a long time."

"In that case, I can save you a lot of time," said Claude. He retrieved the key ring from his pocket and raised it in front of the agents, making no big show of it, and twirled it as a means to calm himself. He flipped the keys back and forth as he held the activator between his thumb and index finger, a nervous plaything.

The young agent got up and stood by the door. He inserted one hand into his suit coat and waited. The older one said, "Go ahead, Mr. Moreau."

"The reason your dog reacted to some form of explosive is simple. While I worked on the plane for over two hours today, I placed a bomb on board that will detonate if that aircraft deviates from its preprogrammed course to Atlanta by more than five miles. It'll explode if the pilots attempt anything other than a landing at Hartsfield International in Atlanta."

"You're joking," said the older one. He put a big smile on his face.

"You stupid pig, I'm not. The device is in the nose compartment. Its detonation will take off the front end of the aircraft, and there will be no way to save the plane. The pilots will most likely be killed, and all of the control surface interfaces will be destroyed," said Claude as he raised his head and stared at the agent.

The older one reached across the table, grabbed Claude by his shirt, and pulled him clear across the table right up to the man's nose. "You piece of shit. Why would an asshole like you do something like that?" he roared into Claude's face.

"It's the will of Allah that the man and this government perish from the face of the earth," Claude responded.

"Oh, shit. You're one of those. Go tell operations," he ordered, and the young man left to comply. The door shut. The agent's fist sent Claude flying back across the table and toppling over the chair to the floor. Still holding on to the key ring, Claude looked to see what the man planned to do next. He watched him come around the table.

"Don't hit me again. You will regret it."

"How, you sanctimonious piece of bacon fat? I'm going to fry your ass."

"To make sure your people believe the message the other agent is sending I'm going to sacrifice myself, and you will go to hell while I'll enjoy the fruits of paradise. Just as the Prophet promised."

The agent reached down, jerked Claude to his feet with the key chain still in his hand, and reared back to deliver a knockout blow.

Claude smiled at the agent. A second before receiving the blow that would have smashed his face, he felt the detonator in his hand and pressed the buttons.

46

ATLANTA, GA —1:45 PM

"Honey Jo, help us."

"How?"

"Go to the kitchen and get a knife to cut the duct tape," Matt ordered.

"Wait just a minute. Who are you?" queried the tall black woman in jeans and a white blouse.

Matt tried to wiggle a little to face her better but couldn't move. The duct tape held him fast. "I'm the federal agent who called you a few minutes ago. Please get us loose. Can you see if my partner is all right? I think she's passed out again."

Honey Jo walked over in front of Bridget. "She's not looking well. Not totally here yet. Looks like she passed out. Now, big boy, I did something for you. Now you tell me what is going on."

"Miss, you've got to get us free. Your friend's life now depends on us."

"Sure, that's what they all say when they want you to do something. I don't even know if you are what you say you are, and until you tell me what's going on, you is staying right where you is." She walked over in front of Matt. He saw her neck decorated with a three-layered gold necklace, and a gold comb held her hair to the side.

He could see she wasn't kidding, so he decided to tell her enough to get out of the bonds the Russians had put on them. Time was now against them, and if he didn't get moving, the terrorist could set the bomb off and kill millions in a metropolitan area like Atlanta, and the president of the United States.

"Okay. There's a Russian with a bomb, an atomic weapon, like I told you before. We think your friend got mixed up with him somehow, and he's using her. The target might be the airport where you both work. We must find her. We found the man's accomplice dead in Savannah and we believe he might be the one responsible. We really believe your friend is in grave danger."

"Shit, you're serious."

"Yes, and we're working under the direct orders of the president. I have identification in my—"

"If you are such special agents, how's come you is tied up?" she said with a sideways grin. "Seems to me you ought to have the bad guys tied up."

"Honey Jo, cut these ties now."

"Nice try, boy. But I don't take orders well."

She walked around and stood in front of Bridget. She shook her, then slapped her. "Come on, baby, wake up."

Bridget groaned and tried to move her head. She said, "What happened?"

Honey Jo bent down in front of her face. "What's the Russian got?"

Bridget tried to look up, but the tape prevented her head from coming up. "A bomb," she said in a groggy manner.

"All right, Mr. Special Agent, you are probably telling me some of the truth. I'll go get a knife." She headed to the kitchen.

"Bridget, are you all right?"

"Got a whopper headache, but yeah I'm okay. What's going on?"

Matt brought her up to date on events and finished as Honey Jo entered the room. She walked over to Bridget and cut one arm free. That left the two tied together by their necks, all legs and thighs tied to the chairs and their hands still wrapped in duct tape. Bridget still couldn't function at her peak and took the knife in her hand as Honey Jo bent over and placed it there.

"You'll get yourselves free. I gotta go."

"Wait, we may need your help," Matt said.

"I ain't staying here. You do what you's gotta do and so will I. She's my best friend and that's why I comes over to see what you were talking about. You'll be free in a few minutes, but I've gotta go help my friend." She ran out of the room, and he heard the front door slam a few seconds later.

"Bridget, can you cut us free?"

"She didn't cut all the way through. I'll have to force it apart." She made a hard, jerking effort. The tape didn't give way. After a few more attempts, the ripping noise of the tape separating filled the air. "There, at least my right arm is free."

Bridget placed the knife under the restraint on her left hand and tried to slice through it. "Damn, she must've given me a butter knife. This one couldn't cut anything. She stood above me, and maybe it cut for her but I'll try to punch through and then rip it apart."

Their heads bobbed up and down with her efforts. The tape around their necks nearly strangled them with the effort she exerted. The Russians had looped the tape at least twice around their necks and crossed it behind their heads. It took a few minutes to get her left hand free.

"I'll try to cut the tape around our necks and then I can get my legs free."

"We're being defeated by the clock. They have a half-hour head start, and it'll take us more time to get out of here. The president is due to land at two thirty and it's a quarter to two according to the clock on the wall. It'll take us at least a half hour, or more to drive to the airport. Got to get a plan together. Need to call for help on this," Matt said.

It took Bridget a few more minutes to get their necks free, and then more time to get her lower legs released and come around to cut the bonds restraining Matt. The kitchen wall clock showed one minute after two when they finally broke free.

Matt rushed over to get his phone. He dialed and thought of what to say.

Bridget watched him. "What are we going to do? Do you have a plan?"

"Yes."

47

WASHINGTON, D.C. — 2 PM

"What's going on, and where are you?" Mary Jean said with no preliminaries when she answered her cell.

"We're in Atlanta, and a Russian team got the better of us and tied us up," he said in an opening release of pent-up frustration.

"Slow down and tell me."

He did. It took only a minute for her to get the details and his request to get his new plan into action.

"Get moving to the location you gave me and I'll have it on the way in two minutes," Mary Jean ordered. She closed her phone. Mike Anthony stood near her and she told him what had happened.

"Damn. I'll get hold of the Secret Service and give them a rundown on what we think is happening."

Mary Jean dialed her phone and told the person who answered her name and rank. She waited for the officer on duty at the National Military Command Center in the Pentagon to verify her identity. When he did, she gave him her request.

"I need you to send the backup helicopters in Atlanta that are there for the president's visit to a city park location I'll give you. Two of my operatives will be there, and you must get them to the control tower at Hartsfield International at once. The man they will pick up is Matt Higgins. He will be in charge and is under the direct orders of the president. Do you understand?"

"Yes, ma'am."

She gave him the location of her team.

"Wait one, General." In a few seconds he came back. "I checked with the general officer on duty and we can have the assets you requested on station in ten minutes, but he wants to speak with you."

The next thing Mary Jean heard was, "General Bergermeyer, this is General Forsman. Why do you want me to send that asset to your man?"

"General, that man is the president's own operative, and he is trying to stop the detonation of an atomic weapon in Atlanta when the president lands. I need my request acted on now. Use me as the scapegoat if anything goes wrong, but I need it ASAP."

"Is that Matt Higgins you're requesting the assistance for?"

"Yes, it is."

General Forsman said, "I remember when he was my student and we shared that terrible day on 9/11. He's a special man. I'll order what you asked for, ETA ten minutes. When it's over I'd like to talk to him. Good luck." The phone went dead.

Mary Jean breathed for the first time in what seemed like forever. Now she dialed Matt.

"Your helicopter will be at the location requested. It should be there in less than ten minutes."

MATT SHUT THE PHONE. "WE'VE GOT TO MOVE. A CHOPPER WILL PICK us up about a half mile from here at the park we passed coming into this area. How are you feeling?"

"My head is still hurting like hell. I want a chance to return the favor to that goon," Bridget said, rubbing her hand over the back of her head.

Matt helped her to the door. "You know, we wouldn't have a quick way into the airfield if the chopper wasn't coming. The woman has a pass and the code to get in. Yuri must intend to have her get him into the airport." He stopped to open the door for Bridget. "How do you think the Russians are planning to get in?"

"Don't know. Hopefully, they won't . . . or will get hung up . . .or security will respond if they try to break in," said Bridget.

"I think you're hurt too bad to go on. You should stay here."

"No friggin' way. Let's go," said Bridget, moving to get into the car. "We have weapons in the trunk and we need to get them."

He opened the trunk. "Here's yours," said Matt, "and I'll take the rifle as well." He handed her a weapon.

They arrived at the park, where they heard the chopper blades whipping the air in the distance. Both glanced up to see the approaching helicopter.

"I see you called for a limo," Bridget jibed.

"Yes, but I forgot to wear my tux," he said with a smile and touched her shoulder. "I don't want you to get hurt."

"I know, but we both took this job on and we'll both finish it."

They walked in a crouch to the UH-60M Blackhawk Sikorsky helicopter to get on board. This chopper, Matt knew, delivered more power, had enhanced capabilities, with outstanding survivability in combat, and was the all-around best choice for a military utility helicopter. This bird, the latest and greatest, was on duty to support the president's trip to Atlanta.

Matt showed the pilot his credentials, and they boarded the chopper. Once seated, Matt took a headset and talked to the pilot. "Get us to the control tower at Hartsfield International as fast as you can."

"I can't go there, it's restricted airspace, sir."

"Didn't you get a directive from the national command center to follow my orders?"

"Yes, but that's illegal with the president landing there soon."

"Mister, I'm giving you a direct order on behalf of the president to proceed directly to the control tower at Hartsfield by the most expeditious route. If you have a problem, you can get it from him, followed by a summons for your court martial for disobeying a direct command from the commander-in-chief. Am I clear?"

Matt took off the headset and dialed his cell. The pilot nodded his head, and the chopper then lifted off the ground. He heard the president answer his personal cell.

"Hello Matt. What's happened?" the president said with his Virginia intonation.

"Mr. President, I think you should not land at Atlanta. I'm sure that there will be an attempt to detonate an atomic device when you land. We know they got it into the country."

"We're only a few minutes out. What proof do you have, Matt?"

"Sir, we don't have much time. I've tracked them from Savannah to Atlanta. The trail ended at the home of an FAA flight controller. I believe the Russian kidnapped or murdered her to get access to the control tower. They know you're landing shortly." Matt was gasping for breath and tried to speak over the noise of the helicopter's rotors. He continued, "The man has the weapon with him. Bridget and I are on the way to the airport to intercept him."

Matt waited. The president remained quiet. He must be on hold, he thought, as the President didn't come back for a couple of minutes. Then he heard, "Matt, I can't turn the plane around just yet, and I'm relying on you. If there's an atomic weapon in Atlanta you must find it before we land." The phone call ended with the president hanging up.

"He won't turn the plane around," he said to Bridget. "What the hell is going on?"

Bridget grabbed his shoulder and talked into his ear to reduce the noise interference inside the helicopter. "There must be more to this than we think. We've got to get to that control tower and get that weapon."

Matt sat back and hoped the pilot could get them there in time to prevent a catastrophe.

48

ATLANTA, GA — 2 PM

The cell on the driver's belt chimed on their way to the Atlanta airport. Ravshan looked at it. "This has to be for you, Colonel. It has the director's phone number that you called on the ID." He handed the phone over.

Andrei took it and heard, "Is this Colonel Ivanov?"

"Yes," he answered to the female voice of the director's secretary. Then he heard the voice of the director.

"Colonel, what's the situation? The president wants an update before he makes a decision on what to tell the American president, if he has to tell him."

"We are in close pursuit of Yuri Borisov. We know where he's going and we believe his goal is to set the weapon off when the president lands in Atlanta, in about a half hour. We're attempting to intercept him in a few minutes." Anton didn't want to say anything else for fear the director might try to orchestrate his plan to take credit and maintain deniability if it failed.

"I'll inform our president of your actions and expect to hear from you in a few minutes on the successful conclusion of your mission. You understand what failure means." The director disconnected.

Anton put down the phone and stared out the window. The

bastard remained in Moscow, making sure his ass stayed covered if this operation went south and that Anton would be the scapegoat. Politicians were all the same—slimy, two-tongued lying bastards. If they ever did what they ordered military men to do there would be no wars, no nuclear confrontations and possibly no terrorists trying to placate political masters by their actions. Then again, maybe not, since human nature still would not change.

He turned his head back to the front of the car he said. "We've got to get to the entrance of the control tower. We passed signs for the airport on the way in. How long to get there from here?"

"Best guess would be ten minutes," Ravshan said. Igor sat in the back and said nothing.

They pulled off the interstate onto the airport road and followed the sign to the cargo area. The control tower appeared in the distance, but Hartsfield International Airport covered 4,700 acres and employed 53,000 of all types needed to operate an airport of this size.

As they drove around the outer road, they passed cargo airlines loading docks, a Georgia Power truck with two men in yellow jackets laying out cable beside the road, and four yellow DHL trucks. They eventually drove by the gate that displayed an "FAA employees only" entrance sign. It led into a three-story parking garage with elevators to the top, and after passing the garage, they could see a one-hundred-foot walkway to the entrance of the tower door. The gate to enter the garage had a security box to allow access to the workers. Anton assumed the tower would have one also.

"If we try to crash through there, the alarm will sound, and they'll be on us with many weapons before we can get to him, if he's here," said Igor.

"We know that, and we don't plan to get killed here," Ravshan said. He looked into the backseat, and starred at Igor in the rearview mirror.

"Turn around and go back the way we came," Anton ordered. Ravshan accomplished the maneuver and proceeded past the FAA entrance for a quarter of a mile.

"I want you to pull up behind the Georgia Power truck. We will capture it and take those two workers as prisoners. I'll force them into the back of the van, and we'll take their yellow jackets. Igor, you drive the van back to the FAA entrance. Ravshan and I will get in the back, secure the men, and take their garments. No killing. We don't want a trail of blood to follow us." Anton drew his weapon as the car pulled up behind the van.

Anton and Ravshan got out and approached the men. Less than five feet away Anton showed the gun and said, "Don't move. We will not harm you if you do as you're told. Get into the back of the van." He pointed with his weapon, and Ravshan stood beside him in a manner that hid the weapon from any passing car. They were lucky. No vehicles passed as they forced the two men into the van.

Inside, they took off the worker's yellow safety jackets, tied the two up with wire they found in the truck, shoved rags into their mouths, and secured more wire around their necks and heads. They couldn't move, run, or make a noise with the bonds in place.

Igor got into the driver seat and turned the van toward the FAA gate. A red car was entering the FAA area, and the gate closed behind it. The car disappeared into the garage as they stopped the van next to the security box.

"Now we get out and pretend we are working on the security box. Take some of their wire and tools and place them on the ground near it."

In less than a minute, they appeared to be fixing the security system at the gate. Anton continued, "Someone will come by to go in, and I want Igor walking up and down on the road about fifty meters from here. As soon as the car arrives, you come up on the side away from the security box, where the person will be inserting the card to get in. Ravshan and I will take them from the open window side, but just in case, I want you to be ready to point a gun at the driver from the passenger side. Any questions?" Neither indicated they had any. He and Ravshan put on the yellow vests of the power workers as he finished talking.

"We force them to drive in and park. We put them in the trunk after tying them up with wire from the truck, then we head for the tower with their security pass to gain access."

They both nodded and Igor started to walk off as a car approached and slowed to turn in. "Get ready," Anton commanded. He checked at his watch, which displayed 2:00 p.m. He realized this would be close.

The car rolled to a stop by the security box, Anton and Ravshan pretended to work on. The driver rolled down her window and looked at the two. She shook her head and said, "Hey, you boys is at the wrong place. We have our own security people to handle this box."

Anton produced the gun and pointed it straight into a young black woman's face.

49

ATLANTA, GA — EARLIER AT 11:44 AM

Yuri reached behind his back and under his shirt to where he hid his pistol as he approached the car in Marilyn's garage. He stayed his hand as he saw she hadn't opened the case, "I was looking for you," he said in a loud voice.

She seemed startled and raised herself from the bent-over position in the trunk of the car. "Sorry, I came out here to find my sunglasses before I go to work. I thought I might've left them in the trunk when we unpacked the car. By the way, Yuri, what's in the case? You didn't take it in, so it must not be clothes."

Yuri moved his hand from behind his back and reached out to touch her cheek. As he did so, he used his other hand to fondle her.

"Come on. We just got out of bed, and I have to get ready to go to work. What are you going to do?"

"I need to get to downtown Atlanta to meet my contact. We have been communicating on the Internet. Why don't we get ready, and I'll take you to lunch on the way to your job, and then I'll get a taxi to my meeting?"

"Will you tell me what it's about at lunch?"

"I promise. Let's get moving."

She gave him a kiss and broke the embrace as she headed for the door into the house. Yuri glanced at the case and noticed that the latches remained closed. She hadn't seen inside. He shut the trunk and tagged along after her.

Yuri paced back and forth while he waited for her to finish her makeup. He sat down and retrieved his laptop, sending an email to Fatimah on his location and his intention to be at the airport at 1400 hours local. The weapon would detonate at 1440 hours.

Marilyn walked out of the bedroom, and they headed for the red Lexus at 11:45.

"Why don't we stop and get a light lunch at my Italian place not far from here?" Marilyn asked.

"Sounds good to me. I'm getting hungry. What time do you plan to get to your work?"

"About two or a few minutes after. I'm going to meet my friend, Honey Jo, before we go on duty to have a girl talk. Of course, I won't mention you." She giggled.

At the restaurant, Marilyn ordered for both of them and then sat back in the booth and asked, "What are you doing in Atlanta, and what's with the case?"

Yuri used the time to deliver the plausible explanation he'd devised earlier. "I have a meeting with the deputy director of Georgia Power to discuss a refinement to the nuclear generators they use to produce electricity."

"Wow! You really know about nuclear reactors? I thought you were kidding before."

"Well, yes. I worked in that field in Russia. During my time with the department there, I developed a system to increase the output of the nuclear generators by between four point two and four point nine percent." Yuri smiled as he finished this point.

"Doesn't sound like much. A few percentage points," Marilyn said.

"Believe me, it's a quantum leap forward. An increase of one half of one percent could save the company millions of dollars and give them a greater profit margin."

"What's that got to do with the suitcase?"

"In the case, I have a small mechanical model needed to produce the results I told you about."

"Why, once you show them the model, they'll know how to build it, won't they?" asked Marilyn. She moved aside to allow the waitress to put the food in front of them.

"Not really. The model could be copied, but without the mathematical formulas and the coefficients, they would not be able to make it work."

"So, that's your game. You'll sell the information to make it operate?"

"Something like that," Yuri responded. He took out a cigarette and lit it. She had said she didn't mind.

"Will you make a lot of money?"

"If they buy it, I'll become a millionaire." He realized that she could be influenced by that prospect, so he would not mention his secret millions.

"When do you meet with these guys?"

"At three this afternoon."

"I'll tell you what. We'll go to where I work. You take my car and go to the meeting. Then you can pick me up after ten and let me know if you're a millionaire."

"That would be super. Thank you. I'll do that." Yuri could almost see the wheels rotating in her head as to how to land a millionaire, but he'd just removed the last obstacle to getting into the FAA control area to place the bomb.

On leaving the restaurant, Marilyn drove the car to the airport. It took thirty-five minutes, and she arrived a minute before two at the security gate to the FAA area. She rolled down the window and inserted her badge into the slot, and the gate opened. She went under the overhang entrance to the three-story parking garage and pulled into a space near the elevator.

"I can take the elevator up and you can take the car."

"Does that badge get you into everything around here?"

"Not everything, but it gets me into all the FAA facilities." She reached over and gave him a kiss. "Good luck with your meeting, and

I'll be at the gate for you to pick me up at five minutes after eleven. Okay?"

"Sure," he said. They both got out of the car and met at the rear bumper. Another kiss, and as Marilyn started to go, Yuri pulled the weapon and hesitated a second. *No, don't kill her*, he thought. She might be useful in his getaway after he set the bomb, since he planned to get as far away as possible in thirty minutes. That was the time he'd planned to set on the atomic device. He took a step after her and slammed the barrel of the pistol into the back of her head. She went down. He rushed to the driver's side of the car, as the keys were in the ignition, found the button to open the trunk, pressed it, picked her up, and put her in it. After retrieving the case, he relieved her of the FAA ID badge, slammed the trunk lid closed, and headed for the elevator.

Yuri checked for surveillance cameras and didn't see any. They must not consider this an area that requires oversight, he thought, but he observed a camera on the gatepost where she'd slid her badge to gain entrance to the garage. Reassured, he walked to the elevator, pushed the button and waited. He knew what he must do. Get to the tower. Get inside and up to a high floor. There he would set the timer for thirty minutes.

The president's plane would be on the ground and he would be on I-75 going south. Thirty minutes would allow him ample time to get out of the danger area, and he would continue on to Florida. Then he thought better of taking the elevator and decided to take the steps. Someone might get into the elevator with him and not know him as an FAA employee. He walked a few feet to the right, pushed open the door to the stairwell, and started up the three flights of stairs, unaware of the Georgia Power truck that pulled up to the security gate.

50

HARTSFIELD INTERNATIONAL AIRPORT, ATLANTA — 2:02 PM

Igor opened the passenger-side door and jumped in, pointing his weapon at the black woman. He could see the fear in her eyes. Anton and Ravshan got into the backseat. Anton heard Ravshan's cell phone beep with an incoming email, and he glanced over to see him look at it, then quickly put the phone away.

"Drive into the garage," ordered Anton as he placed the barrel of his pistol against her head.

"Ooooh!" Honey Jo started to do as directed. "What you want?" she screamed. Fear showed in her eyes, which looked like they verged on popping out of her head.

"Shut up and just drive to the entrance to the tower," commanded Anton. He saw her name on the badge that hung from her neck, Honey Jo Stevens.

"It's on the top floor of the garage, but you have to walk to the tower," said Honey Jo as slow as she could, apparently trying to stop her voice from trembling.

"Then drive us to the closest place we can get out and go to the tower," Anton said.

He could see the woman's hands shook, but she'd started to regain some composure, and that might be a problem. "Listen, lady.

There's someone trying to set off a bomb at the tower today. We're here to stop him. So don't fight us. You're in no danger."

"Don't exactly look like that to me," said Honey Jo as she clutched the steering wheel with both hands.

"We'll only tie you up till we get the bomb, and then we'll leave. That's all we're going to do. I can't take a chance that you won't alert people to our presence," Anton said.

"Hell, I wouldn't tell a soul. Who the hell are you anyway? FBI? You sound foreign."

"I'm sure you won't tell, but I still have to do it my way."

They approached the top of the garage and discovered three free parking spaces.

"Pull into that space," commanded Anton, pointing to one of the empty places.

After she parked the car, Igor reached over and took the keys. Anton and Ravshan got out of the back, and Anton opened the driver's door. He took Honey Jo's arm and pulled her from the car. Ravshan put a piece of the duct tape he'd pillaged from Marilyn's garage across her mouth. Then he bound her hands behind her. Anton took the FAA ID badge and placed it in his pocket. All of this happened in less than thirty seconds.

"We can't leave her here. We should kill her," Ravshan said.

"We'll take her into the stairwell and tie her up there. I don't think any Americans use them, as most of the one's I've seen are fat and overweight," said Anton. "At least now we have a car to get out of here, and we're not going to leave a trail of dead Americans."

Anton checked his weapon and the others did the same, and then Igor shoved Honey Jo toward the door to the stairs. Anton led the way. He opened the door to the stairs and saw a half set of stairs going up and out onto a path that led to the tower. He also saw a man lifting a case as he cleared the top step.

"I think I saw our man," he said loud enough for the others to hear. Then he pointed to Honey Jo. "Tie her to the rail and follow me."

Anton ran up the steps and out onto a concrete area that provided a path over to the control tower. He could see airplanes taxiing on both sides of the tower. The noise of the jet engines filled the air but weren't deafening because of the vast distances between runways. The wind blew hot air around, causing Anton to gag a little at the heat emanating from the acres of concrete.

He looked out on the walkway. There he saw a man walking towards the tower with a large case rolling behind. "Stop," he yelled in Russian. The man turned, looking shocked to hear his own language. Anton recognized the face of the man—Yuri.

He watched as Yuri started to run toward the tower. "Stop or I'll shoot."

Yuri looked over his shoulder as he ran toward the tower. He could easily see Anton with his weapon drawn. Anton heard his two men coming up the steps. He raised his pistol, took aim and fired two rounds. The first one hit Yuri in the right leg, the second in the center of his back. The force of the bullets sent him tumbling forward as a misty spray of pink filled the air around Yuri. After impact on the concrete, he lay sprawled on the path to the tower, still clutching the handle of the case.

Anton deliberately moved up, keeping his weapon trained on the fallen Yuri as he reached down to pick up the case. As he did, he heard a pistol shot ring out from behind him. He jerked his head around and saw Igor collapse to the ground, the man's face obliterated from a bullet entering his head from the rear. Ravshan stood there with his weapon now aimed at Anton.

51

ARMY HELICOPTER — 2:06 PM

Matt looked out the open door of the chopper as it raced toward the control tower. He had to stop Yuri. The Atlanta airfield came into view, seeming to stretch for miles in all directions, runways and planes everywhere. His cell rang.

He didn't check the caller ID and experienced mild shock when his daughter's voice came on the phone, "Hello, Daddy. Where are you?"

"I'm in a helicopter and I can't talk now. Please put Julia on the line."

The parrot squawked in the background, "Pretty Laura, feed me," and then Julia said, "Sorry, but she just had to call you. I hope it's okay."

"Forget it. Right now I need you to tell the general we have the terrorists in sight at the control tower in Atlanta. We're approaching in a helicopter and should be there in less than two minutes. I'll call you when this is over." Matt closed his phone and told Bridget about it.

"You love your daughter and she loves you," Bridget said.

"I know, but my mind is on the mission and getting us out of it alive. Remind me to call Julia when this is over and talk to Laura for a few minutes."

"See, you sound like a tough guy, but you're really a softie at heart." Bridget pointed to the tower just then, and Matt saw a man going from what he took to be a parking garage and walking to the tower pulling a case by hand.

"Might be our man," he said to Bridget. Then he looked again and saw three more men exit the garage onto the walkway. The first one fired shots at the man with the case, and then shot the other man. He then aimed the gun at the man going for the case.

"What the hell is going on?" Matt said. The helicopter was now on its final approach to a landing at the tower and descended to two hundred feet. Over the headphones, he heard the pilot disregarding the tower's warning to leave the restricted area. The chopper would touch down in a few seconds right by the tower.

"Get your weapon out. Whoever's down there is playing for keeps. You go out the other side, and we go to the front of the chopper and try to capture the man who now has the case. Shoot first if in doubt. We have orders to get the weapon."

"Fine by me," Bridget responded. She checked that a round was in the chamber of her weapon.

Matt instructed the pilot to stay on the ground and wait for them.

The helicopter came straight in and made a small adjustment into the wind before it landed, putting Bridget on the side with the terrorist. Matt jumped as soon as the skids touched the ground. Simultaneously, Bridget sprang out from the other side.

In the last seconds of the flight into the tower area, the situation on the ground changed. The one man standing on the walkway saw them exit the helicopter. He fired at them. Bullets hit the helicopter. One hit Bridget as her feet touched the ground.

On the walkway, Anton stared at Ravshan as the helicopter

approached the airfield. He started to raise his weapon, but Ravshan fired first. The bullet hit him in the chest, causing him to spin around to his left and drop the case as he fell hard onto the footpath and felt the concrete smash into his face. He lay crumpled on the hot surface and tried to rise but couldn't. Searing pain stopped him, but he could hear running feet. A hand turned him over, and he looked into the face of Ravshan.

"Why?" he uttered.

"Why? I'll tell you why. I'm the backup for the man you just shot. I've known his every move for two days from my control group from emails. You see, I'm a Muslim, and I have a jihad to perform here in this place. I'll be in paradise in a few minutes, as soon as I set the timer on the atomic bomb. I'll go to Allah with an expectant heart. You'll go to hell."

He took the FAA ID from Anton and placed it in his pocket. Then he looked at the fallen man, spat on him, and said, "You're an infidel and you subjugated my people for centuries. Now it's time for us to spread the word and laws of Allah to the whole world. The destruction of America is our primary goal, as it's the main enemy. Today I'll deal a mighty blow to destroy the Satan in this world."

Ravshan picked up the case. He aimed his weapon at Anton to finish him off, but he noticed the thump, thump of a helicopter's rotor blade nearby and turned toward the noise. Barely a hundred meters away, he saw the well-known outline of a Blackhawk sit down not fifty feet from the tower, and people started to get out of it. He opened fired at them.

He must stop these infidels and then set the timer. He knew how to set the timer from the emails he'd received during the entire mission from Fatimah. The last message had told him that pursuers approached in a helicopter. All he had to do was get inside the tower, as high up as he could, and open the case to set the timer for one minute. The whole place would be vaporized. At this exact moment, he needed to stop these intruders and make it to the control tower.

He fired three more bullets at the chopper and then saw a figure get out. He took aim and fired. The bullet hit the target and it went down. Then another figure appeared on the other side of the craft, and the man shot at him. That man ran toward him. Ravshan took careful aim and fired. The target stopped and fell.

Good, he thought as he grabbed the case and headed for the tower door.

MATT SAW BRIDGET FALL AND HE ABOUT LOST IT. *SHE'S HIT! DAMNIT.* He shook his head as if clearing water from his hair in a swimming pool and looked toward the man shooting. He didn't doubt that he would kill the bastard who had shot Bridget as he ran toward the target, firing as he went. A bullet zinged across his scalp on the right side, slightly above the ear. He fell down and the blood rushed out of the head wound. It flowed into his eyes and he became blind for a few seconds. *Get up*, he told himself. *Forget the pain. Wipe the blood away and get moving. Kill the man who shot Bridget.*

Matt forced himself to get up. The chopper was only twenty feet away, but the man ran toward the tower door. *Think.* Then he urged himself to move and go for the rifle in the chopper.

He rushed to the chopper, jumped on board and retrieved the sniper rifle. As he scrambled into position, he gave the "go up" sign to the pilot. The chopper started to lift off, and Matt stretched out on the floor to use it as a firing platform. Of course a helicopter was not the most stable platform in the world, with the bouncing of the craft under the rotors, but it gave him the advantage of height. He would be looking down on his target. The blood rolled down from the wound and obscured his vision. He wiped it away and addressed the sights on the weapon.

The rifle was pressed snug against his shoulder and the sights lined up on the man whose hand extended to put the pass into the security pad to enter the tower. Matt took a breath and let out a little. He had to do this slowly. No hurrying or he'd miss. The rifle recoiled. The round missed the target and hit the tower above the man's head.

Come on, he told himself. *Take it easy. Squeeze the trigger*, "Squeeze, don't pull it," he said as he exhaled in sync with the word coming out of his mouth. The man swiped the pass and bent over to get the case while he held the door open. Matt let out a little more of his breath and aimed. *This is for Bridget*, he thought, and with effort, he kept the sights aligned on the target's head. The pain from his head wound forgotten, he squeezed the trigger.

The wall splattered with red behind the man's head. The target crumpled, blocking the door open. The case lay on the ground beside him.

"Put me down," Matt ordered the pilot. He reached the ground in seconds and raced to Bridget. She rolled up, holding her right shoulder.

"I'll live. Help me up," she said.

Matt helped her up and held her for a second. He realized the importance of getting out of the area with the bomb before anyone learned of its existence. They went up to the walkway. Bridget went over to the man called Yuri. He opened his eyes.

"Why did you do it?" she asked.

After a short pause, he said, "Money." He held out a set of keys. "Get her out..." Then he stopped breathing and his head fell to the side. Matt didn't take the keys. They dropped to the ground as his attention swung toward Bridget.

Bridget stood over Yuri's body, but Matt now raced to the tower door, the man he had shot no doubt dead. He recovered the case, searched the man for ID, and took the cell phone he found. Then he walked back toward the wounded man, trying to roll over near where Bridget stood over Yuri's body. Matt took a clear look at the man. He recognized him as the one who'd tied him up at Marilyn's house. His wound gushed blood. Matt ripped off his shirt and pushed it against the wound. With medical help, he would probably survive, Matt guessed.

"Who are you? Don't lie or I'll finish you off."

"Colonel Anton Ivonov, Russian Army Intelligence, and I believe you are with American intelligence."

"Colonel, let's get you on the chopper and get out of here."

Matt sprinted back to the steps, where the last man lay on the ground. The exit wound had taken most of his face off. A quick check of the stairs showed some movement. He held his pistol out in front and descended the steps. At the bottom, he found Honey Jo tied and gagged. He untied her and removed the tape from her mouth.

"Thanks," she said.

"The favor is now reciprocated. You didn't see me. Your captors tied you up, and you managed to get loose. You heard gunfire but didn't see a thing. Do you understand?"

"Yes, but..."

Matt ran back and helped Bridget down to the chopper. He then carried the colonel and laid him on the aircraft's floor. Bridget seated herself, but Matt thought she might faint, because her head flopped to her shoulder. She rolled over and landed in a prone position on the floor.

The case with the atomic bomb remained. Matt ran to get it. With no idea if it was armed, he grabbed it. With all the exchanges of the thing, he guessed that no one had armed it. Not an EOD man himself, he didn't have the explosive ordnance demolition training to even attempt to do a disarm procedure on an atomic weapon. Better to get it out of the area. An EOD team at the air base could handle it. After taking a last look around, he jumped on the chopper with the bomb and gave the pilot the order to get them to a military hospital ASAP.

The pilot told the tower he intended to depart to the west and lifted off without waiting for clearance.

52

AIR FORCE ONE — 2:25 PM

AIR FORCE ONE CONTACTED THE TOWER AS DIRECTED BY THE CENTER.

"Atlanta tower, this is Air Force One, Outer Marker at three thousand."

"Air Force One cleared to land on runway 9 left. Wind 090 at 6."

There would be no further communication with the aircraft from the tower unless some emergency occurred.

On board the aircraft, the president said to Avery, "Well, Dean, I guess the bomb won't go off. We've stayed within the five miles, but I still want to get off this plane fast."

"I concur," Avery said.

The president's private cell phone rang. Matt's number appeared on the display. On opening the phone, he said, "What's happened?" He listened for a few seconds and then said, "Thanks, Matt, I'll be back in Washington later tonight. After you take care of Bridget, I want a full briefing on what happened. Give her my best, and thanks."

He closed the phone and told Avery everything had been taken care of and no bomb would go off on the ground. Dean's face showed some confusion, so he explained that the people he'd sent on the mission to stop the terrorist from detonating an atomic bomb had captured it and eliminated the terrorists."

Avery looked relieved but bewildered. "I'm glad." The president had no way of knowing about Avery's previous warning.

"The nation saved from a nuclear blast . . . and we're safe. Let's get to the dedication, and then I have to put on a bold front for the governor here to get him reelected. All in a day's work." He walked toward his seat on the plane and ran his right hand over his hair in a vain attempt to flatten it down.

ON BOARD THE HELICOPTER SPEEDING TO THE MILITARY MEDICAL facility at Dobbins Air Force Base outside Atlanta, Matt made the call to the president and brought him up to date on all that had happened.

On the floor, the Russian colonel groaned with his eyes open. "What's happening?" he said in a grunting voice that conveyed the pain he was experiencing.

"You're on the way to a military hospital. We needed to get out of the airport before anyone discovered that we were both chasing an atomic weapon. Did Yuri shoot you? How come one of yours held the bomb and shot at us?" Matt leaned down close to the colonel to hear his response.

The colonel took his time before he described what he'd witnessed after he'd arrived at the airport. From her prone position, Bridget heard the story and shouted, "Your own fucking man shot you and tried to blow us all up!"

Matt raised his hand to try to calm her. He needed the information to inform Washington. "Whose phone is this?"

"It belonged to Ravshan, the man who shot me," replied the wounded officer. His eyes slowly closed and he lost consciousness.

Matt opened the phone and saw a text message on the screen.

Intercept team in helicopter coming after Yuri at airport.

"Bridget, these bastards knew our every move and kept their man informed of our actions."

"How?"

"I don't know, but I have an idea how to find out. We have to do it before this phone is turned off. I'll take care of it after we get you to the medics."

The pilot told him they would land in two minutes, and the emergency medical teams awaited them there. As soon as the chopper landed, the medics placed Bridget on a stretcher and headed for the entrance of the hospital. The colonel came out next and they rushed him inside. Matt followed and tried to get in with Bridget.

"Young man, we need to see to that wound of yours," said a nurse, blocking his path.

"Not now. I'll be back, and then you can check it."

The nurse told him he could stay in the waiting area and she would come to get him as soon as they could. He knew protesting would produce no results and returned to the waiting area, but soon went outside to make a phone call. This had better work, he thought.

THE HELICOPTER LIFTED OFF FROM THE AREA OF THE HARTSFIELD control tower as Honey Jo emerged from the garage steps. "Oh my God!" she repeated over and over. Her hands went up to her mouth in horror. She rush walked toward the tower, took out her cell, and dialed airport security. Every controller knew the number by heart, in case a crew experienced a situation needing armed assistance.

While waiting for the phone to be answered, she skipped past the man with no face, toward a man lying facedown with his hand out. She could see a body holding open the door to the tower. "Oh my God," she almost shouted as she took in the carnage. She glanced down at the man lying next to where she stopped.

"What you got there?" she said. She thought it looked like Marilyn's key chain with the miniature red BMW on it. She reached down and picked it up. Surely it must belong to Marilyn. Honey Jo got through to security and told them that bodies lay outside the control tower. She learned they'd already sent people from calls by others.

To go back down to the garage to find Marilyn's car seemed like a good idea. She hadn't answered her cell in hours. After walking down all three levels searching for the car, she located it on the ground floor. A thumping noise came from the trunk. She opened it with the remote key, and her friend Marilyn appeared bound and gagged.

MARY JEAN BERGERMEYER REMAINED WITH MIKE ANTHONY. They drove away from Alexandria once Mike had handled all the police details of the shooting in broad daylight in Old Town Alexandria. Her cell phone rang.

"Matt, what's happened?" she queried.

Matt gave her the details of the events at the airport and the trip to the medical facility. "General, I have the cell phone the terrorist was using to get his instructions. It's still on, and I can read his messages. I think it means the decrypting program is active. If the phone were switched off, we would probably never get the code to reactivate it. Do you think our friends at NSA could help here?" Matt didn't know what that entailed but he didn't have anything else to go on.

"You've done marvelous. I'll get my friends at the FBI to get on the scene at Hartsfield. They'll know what really happened and will help. I'll call you back in twenty minutes. In the meantime, see if you can find a secure telephone on the base, and get me a report on the medical conditions as soon as you hear anything." She disconnected and told Mike what the situation was. He started dialing on his cell phone, and Mary Jean dialed her friend, Admiral John Kidd, the director of the National Security Agency at Fort Meade, Maryland.

MATT REQUESTED A SECURE PHONE AND LEARNED ONE RESIDED IN THE office of the commander of the hospital. He went to the emergency room area to wait. He needed to know about Bridget's condition before he did anything else. In ten minutes, the nurse came out to tell him that a sedated Bridget rested in a private room.

"How is she?"

"In decent condition. She's young and strong, but she probably will take a long time to regain full use of her arm," said the nurse while leading him to the room.

"How's the other man?" Matt asked.

"Not so good. If he makes it, it'll take a long recovery." The nurse stepped aside at the door, and Matt glanced in to see Bridget propped up in the bed and asleep. He went in. Her shoulder was all bandaged up and the color missing from her face. *I know Laura likes her. In the last year of training for missions, she has become my best friend and now...*

He reached down and held her hand.

His cell phone rang and Mary Jean said, "Go to a secure phone and call this number." She gave him a number and said good-bye.

53

USAF MEDICAL FACILITY — 3:42 PM

Matt used the secure phone to call Admiral Kidd.

"Hello, Captain, or should I say Mister, now that you're in the undercover business. I hear you did noble things today to save the president, and now you have a special cell that we need to get info from."

"Yes, sir. Thank you. I've recovered a phone I believe the terrorists were using to communicate. It's still on, has two bars of power showing out of a possible three." Matt spoke directly with the admiral and remembered he had spoken with him before, during the recent adventure in Saudi Arabia.

"Don't turn it off. I have an Air Force technical sergeant coming to your location now. He'll plug in a power cord and connect a computer to the phone, and the data will be sent here. My people will use that to back trace who sent the message. We'll be able to send a code to all the servers that were used to learn who received any information from the same source that sent data to the phone you have. Then we'll know where the computers with the messages are located."

As the admiral finished explaining the methodology of the

tracking system, an Air Force sergeant entered the room and smiled at Matt while holding up some cables.

"I believe your man is here. Nice to talk to you again, Admiral."

"You take care of yourself and that lovely young lady. Is she going to be all right?"

"Yes, she is. Good-bye, Admiral. Here's your man." Matt handed the cell phone to the sergeant and watched while two different cables connected it to some sophisticated device. Then, he realized, at that moment the phone's brain wound its way to Fort Meade.

Nothing more he could do here, so he returned to Bridget's room. He reminded himself to check on the Russian colonel in a while. Then he sat in the single metal chair in the room, exhausted from the ordeal, ignoring the loss of his own blood from his bullet wound, and waited for Bridget to open her eyes.

THE TECHNICAL ANALYSTS SECTION AT FORT MEADE RECEIVED THE DATA from the phone and went to work. They had initially estimated calculated four hours to complete the task for the admiral. The experts used the deciphered phone's internal system to backtrack along the text and email trails. They found the node that had sent the text messages and then followed all the transmissions from the originator to all the recipients of those messages. They managed to implant a minuscule program in each of those receiving units to order those devices to send all information in their databases from the original sender to Fort Meade. This plan gave them the ability, along with other technologies, to be able to locate the unique identifiers of each piece of equipment that had received the original messages. In the end, they would know where each instrument was located and who owned the receiving cell phone, laptop, or mainframe.

As this was a priority assignment, the analysts used the most powerful computers available to the NSA. The banks of computers comprising this super monster covered over thirty thousand square feet and contained their own air-conditioning system. The mainframe would take less than five minutes to accomplish what they wanted once the parameters had been established and fed into the supercomputers. After two hours of analysis, they inputted the data to the computer. Less than five minutes later, the machine gave them the answers to all their questions. Three hours and forty-five minutes after receiving the task, a report of their findings reached the desk of the director, Admiral Kidd, at 8:12 p.m. He called Mary Jean.

"I've got what you want, and it's a doozy. Sending it by secure fax to you now. It's your business, but you'll probably need the FBI on this one. Good luck."

"Thank you, Admiral. I really appreciate it," said Mary Jean.

"Just a show of what we can do together, young lady. Also, I should warn you that the targets might find out we tagged them if they possess sophisticated protection devices. Probably won't, but you never know in this ever-changing electronic age."

"I'll take you to dinner for your help," Mary Jean offered.

"I'd love that. When?" He pushed a little here.

"Sunday okay?"

"Pick you up at seven," said the admiral, hanging up the phone with a toothy grin. The push had worked. He thought about Mary Jean for a few minutes until the next crisis landed on his desk. This evening he would go home around midnight for a few hours sleep before being back at work at six in the morning.

MARY JEAN VIEWED THE FAX FROM ADMIRAL KIDD. SHE FELT JUSTIFIED. Avery was in it up to his impeccable hairdo. Then another name and number hit her with the force of a fast-pitch baseball, confirming the earlier information from the FBI. The Iranian diplomat had masterminded the plan, as most of the messages had originated from his office.

She picked up the phone, called Mike at the FBI, and told him what she knew. "We need to coordinate our plans on this one. There are some areas you and your people ought to handle, and two I need to do by myself."

"You know the president is on his way back to D.C. right now?" asked Mike.

"What time will he get to Andrews?"

"An hour and a half from now."

"Do you have enough to nail Avery?" said Mike.

"I'll have to think on it. But the other people on this list are fair game for you. Some might be terrorist cell leaders or members. That's enough for you to investigate. The Iranian is in your arena, since you're responsible for diplomats. I'll secure-fax this over to you in a minute."

"What are you going to do about your man?"

"I've got an hour to think about it. Let me know how you use this info, will you?"

"Of course, I can't tell you officially. Take care." He hung up.

Mary Jean sat back and pinched her lower lip between her thumb and forefinger. This fax presented a major problem, and decision time was now, without delay. The stakes demanded immediate action, and her job entailed making the decisions, doing the dirty work, and smiling when necessary. She made her determination, got up, grabbed her coat, and headed for the airport.

She fabricated a story that her niece planned to visit tomorrow for a day, then called the SPAT office from her car, hoping Julia might be there. Matt would probably call her to tell her about Bridget. Mary Jean bet she'd waited at the office to hear any news.

When Julia answered, Mary Jean heard Laura and the parrot talking to one another. The parrot wanted Laura to feed it.

"Hello, Julia. It's Mary Jean Bergermeyer."

"Have you heard anything from Matt? How is Bridget?"

"Nothing new. He told me she's resting and will be all right. He said he talked to you, so you know about as much as I do." She slammed on her brakes to avoid an accident when someone ran a red light. Recovering quickly, she continued, "I'm calling to see if I can have Laura over tonight to visit with my niece to make up for the visit that never happened last time."

She heard Julia talking to Laura, and then, "Laura said she would like to do that."

"I'll pick her up in a few minutes. We'll go on to the airport to pick up my niece. The two of them should have a great time together."

"Okay, I'll have her ready when you get here." That ended the conversation.

Mary Jean smiled. The second part of her new plan was now complete. The first part had started earlier, when she'd ordered Matt to get to Washington on a military jet.

54

ON BOARD AIR FORCE ONE — 8:23 PM

DEAN AVERY AGAIN FELT IMPORTANT, AFTER THE PRESIDENT HEAPED praise on him a second time for his assistance on the policy speech delivered in Atlanta. Subsequently, he settled into his seat after visiting with his old friend and boss. It felt comforting to be liked, and it felt even better to be alive. The threats he had been warned about had not materialized. He figured that he should be dead now, as the Iranian had warned him not to go on the plane. No matter, he would give his life without hesitation if it proved necessary in the attainment of their long-term goal, the conversion of America.

All these years, no one had suspected him. He had always conducted himself in a careful manner, but lately some things did appear to have slipped just a little. Ever since he had met Julie again, things seemed to get disjointed from the totally organized and predictable life he had led for so many years. She was the same as when they'd attended college. Those were the days. They'd loved, walked, converted to Islam at the same time, and thought they would be together forever. He started to recall the events that had led to their breakup, but his phone rang, interrupting the nostalgic trip.

"You've been discovered," said the voice of the Iranian.

"What?"

"They have breached our security and found out the names of all my contacts. Our analysts assure me they did this less than an hour ago."

"What are your instructions?"

"You are probably not in a position to eliminate today's target while on the plane. When you get back, go to the Islam of America camp in the Blue Ridge Mountains near Charlottesville, Virginia." The specific directions followed. "You will be met there and provided for. If you stay in Washington, there will be a public trial sooner or later, and all our connections will come out, damaging you and our cause."

"I understand," Avery said and closed his phone. The world changed in a few seconds from an amazing place at the pinnacle of his influence to a disaster. Now it became necessary for him to run, at least for a while, until he could figure out what his future held. As soon as the plane landed, he would get Julie and head for the safe hideout. His connection with the radical Islamists and the jihadists could never come out, or the public image damage would be disastrous for the cause. First he took out a pen and wrote a note on a plain piece of paper.

"Mr. President. I hereby resign my office as national security adviser, effective immediately." He signed it and put it in an envelope, planning to hand it to the president's aide when he deplaned, with instructions to give it to the president in the morning. The president would want to know where he was when he didn't arrive for the early-morning intelligence briefing.

With only a few minutes before landing, Dean Avery looked around at the symbols of power displayed in the aircraft, the Great Seal of the United States, the Presidential emblem, etc., for the mightiest nation on earth. Someday soon, they would all come down and be replaced by the green banner of Islam. He maintained no doubts about this, and he would go undercover to work for that goal. All the secrets of the great Satan were in his possession, and his knowledge could enhance their efforts to achieve an easier victory. They would protect him to get at that trove of information.

The plane landed and taxied to its parking space. The president deplaned first, and then Avery gave the envelope to the aide. He descended the steps last.

On the tarmac, Brigadier General Mary Jean Bergermeyer greeted him. Matt Higgins stood at her side. What in blazes was she doing here? She couldn't already know about him. Not this fast. The Iranian had called only a few minutes ago, and that would provide him time to get away. He raised his hand in greeting. Might as well gut this out, he decided.

"Mr. Avery, a word with you if I may," the general said.

"I'm in a bit of a hurry. The president wants me to meet him at the White House as soon as possible to discuss some issues. You understand?" he said in a conciliatory manner.

"I understand perfectly. This'll only take a minute." She took him by the arm and led him away from the few people standing around chatting after a ride on Air Force One. Matt waited out of earshot.

"What's this all about?" he asked.

"Don't play stupid, you fucking traitor. You're guilty of treason and I'll prove it." She spat the words at him.

"Whatever do you mean?" he continued meekly trying to attenuate her animosity. *My God, she does know*, he thought.

"Listen to me, you piece of shit. You informed the Iranian diplomat of the movement of the president's special team of Matt and Bridget to Texas. You knew the location of the terrorists' attacks we've been experiencing over the last two weeks in advance and did nothing to stop them." She moved right up to his face, stared hard at him and appeared to want to hit him.

He stepped back, "You're crazy, General. What proof do you base these accusations on?"

"When I have all the proof, you will be charged with high treason by the attorney general. You and your girlfriend set my people up to be eliminated, assisted a terrorist to import a weapon of mass destruction into this country, and knew about the plot to kill the president on his trip to Atlanta today."

"All wild accusations that you will regret making after I talk to the president about you. You won't have a job tomorrow morning," he said, stiffening and standing tall.

"Let me assure you, mister, you won't when I'm through. You'll be ruined."

"If you're through making accusations, and don't have a warrant for my arrest on these ridiculous charges, I have a job to do, General. Good night," he concluded, then swirled away from her and walked to his car.

MARY JEAN STOOD ON THE TARMAC UNTIL HE DROVE OFF IN HIS CAR. She smiled. She had him. His act hadn't fooled her. Fear had permeated his eyes, and he'd started to perspire under her accusations. Her plan continued to take shape. Keep the pressure on him. She rejoined Matt and told him, "I believe the Iranian will have to take care of Avery, not because of his value to the cause but the damage he would do to it if he were brought into a courtroom. We will see in a short time."

Time to move. She ran for her car, where Matt's daughter, Laura, waited. Matt kept up with her to the car and then called to get an update on Bridget's condition, and also asked the nurse, "How's the colonel?"

"The doctor talked to me and says he'll recover but will require extensive rehab. He won't be able to move for at least a week," the nurse said.

"I'll see the Russians are informed," Matt said. "I'll tell them what we know and what happened, then find out what they want to do with him. I'll tell you when I get back there in the morning, and I can't wait to get Laura home."

He hung up and looked at Mary Jean.

"The plan is in motion," the general said. "Don't forget. Without your efforts to get Yuri, we would never have gotten this far. From here on, I think it will be automatic. All we can do now is wait."

Mary Jean got into the car with Matt and told Laura that Bridget was okay. She would be back in a day or two. Laura gave a big smile and said, "I miss Bridget." She hugged her dad.

Then Mary Jean started the car and raced back to the office of SPAT, Inc.

She wanted to watch her plan materialize.

55

WASHINGTON, D.C. — 10:31 PM

Dean Avery raced to his home. He called Julie and told her what had happened.

"What are we going to do?" she asked.

"You're coming with me. He has a safe house arranged for us and we'll continue the struggle from there with a support team to help us. We'll disappear for a while—but we'll be working together, and no more subterfuge about our relationship. I want you with me."

"When will you pick me up, or do I meet you somewhere?"

"Are you at home or your office?"

"Office," she said.

"I'll be there in thirty minutes. We'll go in my car, since I know where we're going and it has a GPS to get us there."

"After all these years, we'll be together. I'll be ready. I don't have to go home. I'm prepared now to start over." She hung up.

At his house, Avery got the clothes and personal things he needed, and with two suitcases in his car, he went to get Julie.

She waited for him in the front of the office and as soon as she saw his car, she rushed to get in. Avery drove the car off at a fast clip but didn't peel rubber on his acceleration. After they went a few blocks, he told her where he planned to go.

"I don't care, as long as we're together," she said.

MATT AND MARY JEAN WATCHED FROM DOWN THE STREET AS AVERY drove off. She called Mike, "Did you get the tracker on the car?"

"Sure did. Before he left the airport. We'll know where it goes. Anything happening?"

"He just picked up Julia. Now we've confirmed the identity of the woman in the burka. Matt is taking this hard. She fooled him as well as all of us."

"I can't believe the bastard pulled it off for years. The president will have to know about this. You going to tell him?"

Mary Jean responded with, "Tomorrow morning. I'll get Admiral Kidd to go with me to lay out what happened with the terrorist attacks, the atomic bomb, and Avery's treason. He'll take it as hard as we did when we saw the names on the list."

"What about the kid?"

"She's with us. Matt and I have sort of been driving this course of events, and so far it's working as planned. Let's just hope it keeps working. Your people go along on this?"

"Hell yeah. We're preparing to take down some of the ones we know for sure participated in the recent attacks. This presented us with the breakthrough we needed," he said.

"What are you going to do with the ringleader?"

"I'm proposing we do nothing. They'll change their codes as soon as they figure out we hacked them, but I'd guess he's taking orders from someone higher up. He's the middleman, and he's a diplomat with immunity. We'll get all of the worker bees in the net this time and leave the queen where we know to watch. Thanks for everything. I've got to go to coordinate a hit in northern Virginia. Talk to you tomorrow." He was gone, and Mary Jean gave a little chuckle to herself. She felt a rush of adrenaline knowing that they would soon take down the bad guys.

"Mary Jean, why are we here at Dad's office?" asked Laura, who looked out the window. That brought her back to an immediate problem. She would get someone out here to secure the place and make sure the computer and phones reached the NSA for analysis. All this would be used to build the legal case against Avery.

"I'll tell you in a few minutes. Now I believe it's time for me to take you to my place and for your father to go to be with Bridget."

She smiled at Matt, dreading the consequences of how Julia, the Julie Johnson of the FBI report Mike Anthony gave her, would act on being captured. Over the years Avery had taken them all in and this woman had provided all of Matt's and Bridget's details to her controller at the Iranian embassy. She had almost gotten them killed on at least two occasions, with Bridget taking a bullet the last time. She was the Islamist from hell, mused Mary Jean. She had existed for years as a spy for the terrorists and as a traitor. If she let him, Matt would terminate both of them on the spot. Mary Jean had decided her plan might accomplish the same thing, because they can't just have intelligence officers going around killing the national security advisor. No, the proper thing for them to do entailed getting a warrant. Then they would plod down the cumbersome legal trail to getting a conviction. There might be another way, she mused, all in all a better way.

Mary Jean knew, at least the US abided by its own laws in such cases—no summary executions by the white hats and that sort of capsulized the general rule. Tonight she wanted to go down a different road.

AVERY SPED DOWN I-66 TO THE TURNOFF FOR US-29 AND TOOK IT TO Charlottesville. From there he went west on I-64 to Virginia route 635 and 151 to Nellysford. They stopped once for gas outside Charlottesville and arrived at the location he had received from the Iranian at a few minutes after midnight. The road sign showed an arrow pointing to the right, and above it read "Islam of America." He carefully pulled onto the small dirt road and followed it for a quarter of a mile. The only light came from his headlights.

He rounded one last sharp curve, and four men stood blocking the road in long white robes and white sock-type caps. He drove up to them, cut the motor, left the lights on, and got out.

The cold chill of the nighttime mountain air hit him. The temperature registered at least twenty degrees below that in Washington.

"Mr. Avery?" asked the first man.

"Yes."

"We've been expecting you," came a voice inflected with an accent from somewhere on the Indian subcontinent. He moved up to Avery and shook his hand. Not over twenty, Avery thought, as he viewed the youth who had only a small beard, his clothing hanging loose on his slight frame. The color of his eyes remained out of sight, but Avery guessed they were black. Then his greeter saw another person in the car. "We weren't expecting anyone else."

"There was no choice but for her to come with me. We work together and were both compromised today. I'll see that it is approved tomorrow by the embassy," Avery said with a little too much force.

"I see," was all he got in reply.

Another man stepped up, tall with a long black beard and a bulging stomach that rounded out the front of his white robe. "If you would follow me, we have a cabin arranged for you. Our instructions were that you were to be separated from all of us and away from the body of our students here. We have a cabin further up the hill that no one goes to except the leaders of this mosque. Follow me, and leave anything you have. It'll be brought up later."

That's more like it, thought Avery. *Now we're getting the respect we deserve for all we accomplished for the cause.* He went back to the car and opened the door for Julie. "Come, my dear. They have a place for us further up the hill. Our things will come up later."

Julie got out of the car and walked beside Avery. "How far is it?" she asked.

"About a quarter of a mile," answered the big man, "but it is not passable for a car. So we need to walk up the hill. We have flashlights and a lantern for you to use in the cabin tonight."

"I should've worn tennis shoes or hiking boots," Julie said.

"Don't worry. After tomorrow, we'll be well taken care of, and we'll provide the cause valuable information. So come along until we get some rest," Avery finished.

"Excuse me," said the young one, "but I'll catch up with you in a few minutes." He ran off in the direction of a building to their left.

They continued up the hill for what seemed like a long time. Julie huffed and puffed because of her out-of-shape body. As if by magic, a cabin appeared in the woods with a small open area in front of the porch. He and Julie huffed and made loud exhalations indicating their fatigue. "We'll have beds to sleep in, and tomorrow we'll get all this sorted out," promised Avery. On entering the building, they realized the one-room structure was constructed of logs and had no electricity, but they observed that it did contain two beds.

In less than five minutes, the young man reappeared at the cabin door. He gave a nod and said, "I have news for you."

They approached him as he stood in the doorway to hear what the man would say. Avery and Julie were both hit over their heads with flashlights. They tumbled to the floor. It took the men less than a minute to tie their hands behind their backs, and then tied ropes around their upper bodies to keep their arms securely fastened against their sides.

Avery came out of his dazed condition first. "What are you doing? You know who I am. What's going on?" he shouted. They pulled him to his feet.

No one answered him. Julie made complaining sounds on the floor and they stood her up. They stuffed cotton into their mouths. Avery tried to get it out so he could reason with them. This whole thing surely must be a mistake. Struggling proved useless. He couldn't dislodge the gag.

The men then forced them out on the porch and shoved them

along a path that led up the hill. After ten minutes of this, Julie couldn't go on, and a man picked her up and put her over his shoulder. They came to a cliff that plunged fifty feet straight down into a gorge. The man dropped Julie to the ground and then forced Avery to his knees.

The young man spoke. "Your car is being driven down I-81 and then up into the Pisgah National Forest in North Carolina. All of your possessions and your prints are in the car. When they look for you, they will be searching hundreds of miles from here. You, however, will be here."

He ordered one of the men to place Julie on her knees beside Avery. They took out a video camera with a light and started to record.

The young man stepped in front of the light and started to speak. "Hold the filming for a minute. Avery, I called the embassy while you were climbing up to the cabin. I'm telling you this so that you will know I'm speaking with the authority of the control group at Fatimah from Iran." He stopped and pushed his hair back. The darkness of his skin and the light from the camera confirmed Avery's guess that his eyes were black, but now they were two sparking onyx stones. "Start the camera," he ordered.

The whir of the camera broke the stillness of the otherwise silent night. A wood owl hooted in the distance and the bushes behind them moved, probably a fox out for an evening rabbit hunt.

"The will of Fatimah is that you will sacrifice your lives in the name of Allah and for his honor. The events of today are irreparable. You will be caught and brought to their justice system. It will dishonor all Muslims if you are made to talk, and you would be compromised in the end. The faith is supreme, and your deaths will ensure no disrespect will be brought in the name of Allah. Your duty has been performed and your place in heaven is assured. All Islam thanks you for what you have done and what you have sacrificed. Go to Allah."

The big fat man whipped a curved sword from behind his back. Avery heard the whoosh in the nanosecond before the leading edge of the speeding blade touched his skin and continued on until his head rolled off his truncated body. In a heartbeat, the sound of the blade swished and took off Julie's head. The camera caught it all.

Only the piercing cry of a bird, a chuck-wills-widow, filled the night.

EPILOGUE
SPAT, INC.

MATT, WITH ONLY A SMALL BANDAGE OVER HIS WOUND, BROUGHT Bridget into the office after the Marine Corps aircraft delivered them to Washington from Atlanta.

"Could you get me a drink? I need a beer," Bridget said.

"Sure. How are you feeling now that we're out of the military-controlled medical and flight services?"

"I'm really all right. The shoulder is stiff and gives me a little pain, but nothing I can't handle."

"We're alone for the first time, and I have to tell you, we make a great team."

"You are so right, but I've lost too much function to be out in the field with you. I'd be a liability."

Matt put his hands in front of his face like a stop sign. "I didn't ask you to go on a mission. Not yet, anyway." He smiled as he said this.

The office door opened, and Mary Jean and Laura came in. "Glad to see you both. How are you, Bridget?"

"Daddy, Daddy!" Laura ran to her father's arms. He swooped her up.

"Fine, General," Bridget said.

"Congratulations."

"Daddy, can Gandalf stay with us?"

Matt nodded.

"I should leave you two alone, but I wanted to show you the paper." Mary Jean handed over the Washington paper with a story on the front page of the resignation of the national security advisor and another article that stated the FBI had successfully raided an apartment in Seattle and killed three terrorists in a gun battle. Another FBI raid in northern Virginia had resulted in the death of Ricky Jobin following a high-speed chase after his wounding of a federal officer.

They both read the article, and Mary Jean said, "I thought you might want to know that the Seattle raid produced a computer with invaluable email addresses and some names that will give us an edge in monitoring their activities. The FBI displayed no intention of taking prisoners if they resisted. My friend over at the Bureau is overjoyed at the outcome of the raids."

The phone rang and Laura picked it up. "Hello," she said. She listened and then smiled. She looked at her father and said, "A White House man wants us to come to dinner. He sounds nice."

Matt took the phone from his daughter. "Hello?"

"Matt, you two did a superb job in Atlanta," came the voice of President Brennan, "and your daughter sounds like a fine young lady. Is Bridget recovering from her wound?"

"Yes, Mr. President, she is," he said so they would all know the caller. "General Bergermeyer is also here."

"Excellent. Excellent. Now I need to thank you in person and congratulate you both. Please join me for dinner at eight this evening in my private dining room. Bring the general, because a foreign government has requested some help and I think you're my man to assist them. This will be something completely different from this last adventure, and I pray not as dangerous."

"Ahhh," mumbled Matt trying to figure out a response.

"At eight," said the voice. Then he heard the dial tone.

THE END

Thank you for reading **Secret Device**. If you enjoyed the book, please **tap here to leave a review on Amazon.**

BOOK 3: *Secret of the Thorns* **is now available on Amazon** in eBook, paperback, and audio.

FREE NOVELLA: To receive your free copy of the exclusive Donavan Adventure series novella *Secret of the Assassin* (not available anywhere else), visit **tomhaase.com/assassin**.

SECRET OF THE THORNS (EXCERPT)

THE DONAVAN ADVENTURE SERIES (VOLUME 3)

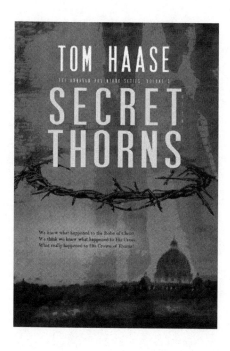

PROLOGUE

September 12, 1683
Vienna, Austria

THE CLASH OF STEEL, THE CLANGING OF AX BASHED HELMETS, AND THE smell of splattered blood still lingered in the nostrils of John III Sobieski, King of Poland and the overall commander of the multinational Christian forces. The triumphant royal banner, carried high by the king's bloodied standard-bearer, flapped behind. Sitting on his black stallion, the king scanned the area, searching for his captain of the Polish heavy cavalry, the Husaria.

He sighted the gore-covered captain, and shouted, "Cheslaw, round up all our men and secure the abandoned wagons. Keep everything." The man's loyalty and the sovereign's trust in him never wavered. More than once Captain Cheslaw had saved the king's life on the field of battle.

"Yes, my lord." His battle hardened captain galloped off to obey the command.

King John watched his valiant subordinate ride away and took one last approving gaze over the battlefield devastation. The priests gave the dying the Church's last rites. The dead were placed in wagons for burial. With clenched eyes, in an unsuccessful attempt to wipe the crimson-soaked scene from memory, he turned his steed toward the bivouac area. His standard-bearer and personal guards followed.

Reaching his tent, he dropped his dented shield on the ground. King John forced himself to move one leg out of the saddle. When it touched the ground, he gritted his teeth against the pain shooting through his back. He'd deflected a heavy strike to his shield during the battle, but the blow had left lasting effects.

Inside his headquarters, he discovered a delegation from the city of Vienna awaiting his return. They stood before him with their hands clean, while his troops' dripped in blood.

"Your highness, we are eternally in your debt," the senior Austrian alderman said, making a respectful bow. The rest of the delegation followed suit by bowing low. "Without your intervention against the Islamic invaders, the Saracen army would have destroyed our city...you are the savior of all Europe." The alderman rose and faced King John.

He examined the groveling nobleman, as he stood there clothed in his finery. The king clenched his fist. Why had he bothered to come to the aid of such cowards? All of Europe might well be better off without these sniveling weaklings. They failed to fight yet waited for someone else to save them. If the Pope and the Holy Roman Emperor hadn't pleaded for his help he would have let them rot in their besieged city. As it was, he'd given his word to save them and despite his feelings the king could not break his word.

"Our Emperor, Leopold I, wishes to welcome you in triumph tomorrow," exclaimed the head of the delegation. "He requests that you follow our defense force commander in a tribute parade."

"The devil take you, I say. You and your commander can..." He paused to regain control of a temper about to explode. Unclenching his fist, he lifted his hand to stroke his salt and pepper beard before massaging his sore neck. He wanted to strangle these ungrateful bastards. They planned to put him behind the do-nothing defender of the city when he and his cavalry were the ones who charged into the mightiest army ever to assault Europe. The invading Muslim forces would, without doubt, have destroyed Vienna had his ferocious and bold attack into their ranks not routed them.

"Your commander and defense forces shall follow me and my men!" King John declared.

"But sire," the alderman sputtered. "He is our military leader."

"And I am the victor, not he. I led my army of 70,000 men against twice as many Muslims and defeated them. I will lead my victorious troops through the streets of Vienna at ten in the morning. I expect every citizen to be out to welcome them. Good night, gentlemen." He turned and strode into his private quarter of the massive tent.

After a few minutes, he heard Cheslaw outside. "Your majesty?"

"Enter," he commanded.

"Sire, we have secured the wagons the infidels abandoned in their flight and I placed them under guard." Cheslaw, the captain of the cavalry, remained at attention after speaking. His face splotched with blood and his chest armor displayed dents from blows suffered that day.

"At ease. Tell me, what is in the wagons?" King John asked.

"There are eight holding gold and silver coins. I believe they used these treasures to buy items they could not steal on the march."

Delighted to learn about the gold, King John smiled, and then sat down on a wooden chair covered by a sheepskin. The money would provide a way for him to pay his men. Perhaps he could even undertake improvements he longed to carry out in Warsaw. "Anything else?"

Cheslaw nodded. Relaxing his rigid stance, he said, "A wagon full of manuscripts. I cannot read all the texts. There is Arab scribbling on most of them, but some appear to be Latin or Greek. One of our priests examined them and speculated the documents may be booty from the fall of Constantinople."

"Well done. Keep the guards on the wagons and have them start for home at first light. Prepare the rest of the troops for a parade through the city at ten and then we will continue toward home. We have been away long enough."

"I will attend to it." Cheslaw made a slight bow of his head and started to turn.

King John stopped him. "Wait. I wish to keep what we need to pay the troops tomorrow. Transport the rest to Warsaw. Put the remaining gold in my personal wagons and give the manuscripts to some scholar or monk to untangle. I cannot procure money for paper manuscripts. To me, they are worthless except to start hearth fires."

He noticed Cheslaw smile as he turned to depart.

1

Present Day
Ethiopian Desert, The Temple of Isis – A Greek Archeological Site

With her small brush, Bridget Donavan swept the sand away from a line of the ancient Greek text engraved in the stone before her with strokes not unlike those of an artist. Every day for the last two months had been the same, clear and stifling hot. The tablet rose eight feet above the sand and rock surface of the desert floor. The artifact hadn't always been so exposed. Many weeks of careful excavation led to this point.

Bridget kneelt and then squinted her eyes, straining to read the weather worn text near the base. Taking a small notebook from her back pocket, she then copied the recent uncovered Greek writing. At the end of the day, she would transfer it to her computer as she did every day as part of her university project.

Something made her pause while reading the text on the stone. A prickling climbed the back of her neck. Something was wrong. Bridget realized it was the lack of noise. No clanging of picks off stone, no helping voices. She could hear no sound, something she was not accustomed to from the helpers on the site. The silence disturbed her.

Sweat trickled down her face and fell between her ample breasts. Her sweat drenched shirt clung to her back. Salty water streamed off her forehead stinging her eyes. Her trained combat senses now screamed an unmistakable warning.

Before she could react to her instincts, her satellite phone rang, startling her. This phone was her singular way to communicate with the outside world and it to her. She stood up as she rubbed the sweat from her eyes, and then grabbed the phone from her belt.

Bridget walked toward her small equipment table and looked at the phone. The caller ID on the face of the phone read 'Unknown'. Scanning the area, she looked for her helpers, but saw none.

The phone rang again, nagging at her. She calculated that it must be evening back in the States and the project manager at the university was the only one who ever tried to reach her. She intended to start her vacation tomorrow. Maybe he wanted to wish her a safe return to the States.

Bridget punched the talk button. Before she could get out a hello, the sound of her brother's voice boomed from the other end, "Bridget, you're not going to believe what I found!"

She hadn't heard from Scott since attending his doctorate graduation. She tried to avoid hearing from him. Not after what he'd done. Her presence at the graduation was for the family's sake. Bridget didn't even want to think about Scott. Someone in the family must've sent him her phone number in case of an emergency.

"Hello to you too, Scott. Where the hell are you? And why are you calling me?" As she spoke the last word, she heard a shuffling noise behind her, the sound of someone running in the sand.

Whirling toward the unexpected noise, she confronted an African man holding a machete. He stopped his running, seeming surprised she'd heard him.

"Bridget." Scott's voice called her name over the phone.

"I'm busy now, Scott. Gotta go," she shouted as she disconnected and then dropped the phone on a small oblong table holding her archeological hammers and brushes. The large African man now charged toward her, swinging the weapon, slashing the air, eyes wide open, whites showing. He screamed a loud belly-wrenching cry that made no sense to Bridget.

Her heart pounded as the man closed the distance. She froze for a millisecond, sensing her death could be just seconds away. *Move*, she commanded herself, *you've been in combat before, now move!*

As the man rushed headlong at her, time seemed to slow and Bridget noticed every tiny detail. She saw that her attacker stood about her height but where her frame was slender his maybe a hundred pounds over her weight. She could smell the stench of sweat and alcohol like a bow wave before him. Tattered remains of a military camouflage uniform barely covered the lower half of his body.

Come on, stupid. Move! The words screamed in her brain again.

Her initial shock melted. Just as the attacker reached her, she managed to sidestep his lunge in a rapid, yet fluid, movement. At the last possible second, she reached out and grabbed the man's extended arm. With all her strength she twisted it, thereby maximizing the use of his forward momentum. He howled in pain. The weapon dropped. She used her instincts and stuck out her foot to trip him while using her left hand to force him to pitch forward, bellowing as he did.

She breathed a sigh of relief now that her hand-to-hand combat training she'd learned in the Army kicked in. She now operated on automatic just as she did in the Iraqi desert during the war.

Did the African have a gun? She scanned him. No, none visible.

She scooped up the weapon, turned, and in one swift movement faced the machete-man, swinging the blade at her attacker. As he tried to regain his feet, she struck. The steel sliced a path across his stomach. His earsplitting scream of pain reached her as she again searched for a gun. None. He curled up, holding his stomach, a river of his blood flowing out.

Bridget needed to take this opportunity to flee. The grueling heat and her sweat didn't enter her mind in the excitement of the fight. Her instincts told her to get away. Run. She understood one thing for sure, getting out of here would be the best part of valor. She clenched the machete tight, noticing the bright red blood on the shining blade. It didn't bother her as much as the fear that the next blood let in this desert might be hers. Her anger boiled against her attacker. She was certain that he would've raped her if given a chance. But before she took more than a few steps, a second man appeared, taller, healthier and white.

God, what now? A white man. He must have spent time taken care of her workers or he would have attacked her with machete man.

This man held a knife. *Shit, I hate knives*, she thought.

The knifeman grinned at her, teasing her with a long-bladed hunting instrument.

She knew his type, him and his African buddy. They were rampant brigands, killers. These scoundrels were the worst dregs of devilish trash in this area of the world, outcasts from both ethnic groups. She knew they would kill anybody, especially Americans, to obtain a few dollars.

The knifeman stopped a few paces in front of Bridget. She could see two parallel slash marks on his chest from at least one previous knife fight. He swished his blade back and forth in his hands. She backed into the small table next to her on which rested equipment for excavating the site.

The attacker's grin showed her his few brown-stained teeth. Her mind registered that he missed half of his left ear. He hopped a few steps to the right and then back. He seemed to delay his thrust as if waiting for machete-man to sneak up on her backside. He must not realize that she was the one who now held the machete behind her back, and his comrade not in any condition to help.

The heat of pumping blood flooded her face, she could feel the rush and knew the complexion of her face would now match the fiery red color of her hair. Her eyes darted around.

Where in hell are the men I pay to work on this dig?

She realized she wouldn't be getting any more help with this thug than she'd gotten with the first.

"I'm going to have fun with you, big tits," knifeman said.

"I'm going to cut yours off, you bastard. Come at me if you dare. I'm ready," she shouted as her anger reached a pitch and rage took over. She swore no man would do *anything* to her again without her consent.

But rage wouldn't help her fight. Bridget knew she must clear her mind. She took a long slow breath, remembering again her army training. This was going to be the real test of her martial art skills. Just focus on one thing—killing him. Kill him fast and don't hesitate.

With his right arm raised, slashing the blade through the air, the knifeman started forward taking his time, as he emitted a loud guttural sound.

The sun gleamed off the blade and reflected into her eyes. Blinded for a second, she felt a visceral, gut-wrenching fear of impalement. Don't think of what they might have done to the helpers. Don't remember the unfulfilled plan to get a gun while out here in the desert alone. Concentrate on killing this thug before he gets me first.

The knifeman started to lung. Just then her cell phone rang. His eyes slid over toward it, distracting him for the microsecond Bridget needed. She bent low. With his attention on the phone, she sprang forward with the point of her machete slicing into his chest. Thrusting upward with a twisting motion and then jerking the blade out, she used her momentum to spin toward a new sound behind her back. The machete-man she thought she'd dealt with rose and held a hand to his stomach wound. Would he try to attack again?

Bridget wasn't taking any chances. She stalked toward him with her weapon held high. She'd finish both these bastards.

At the sight of her, the man turned and, with something between a stumble and a run as he held his hands over the deep wound to his stomach, he disappeared over a sand dune. She let him go.

Stopping to recover her breath, Bridget let the sun beat down on her. The intensity of its rays pounded without mercy in the afternoon Ethiopian desert, but in that moment it emphasized her feeling of aliveness. Thank God for her military training. Her life hadn't flashed in front of her during the moments she thought they might impale her, so maybe it wasn't her time. Thoughts like that were helpful after the fact, but didn't do her any favors during the fracas.

God, she had killed this man. Bridget stared down at the bloody corpse and tried to regain some composure. It didn't feel like the killing she experienced in combat, in the heat of a firefight. Her hands started to shake and she felt nauseated. Her stomach gurgled and she swallowed hard to keep whatever remained of her breakfast down.

The cell phone rang again. She bent down, recovered it, and then pushed the talk button as she sat down on a nearby rock.

"Come on, sis. What's happening?" Scott demanded.

Bridget scanned the area for other attackers in the vicinity. Holding the phone, she walked toward the main camp. In the distance, she noticed her hired hands flat against a sand dune. The outlaw renegades must have gagged and tied them up. Without doubt they had forced them down to ensure no noise of alarm came from them until after they attacked her. She remained behind at the site to close up for this season after her fellow American coworkers departed for the States. The attackers knew the remaining local assistants would own no valuables.

"Bridget. Answer me."

"Sorry, Scott, uh...a few things I had to deal with here. Why are you calling?" she asked between large gulps of air.

Bridget didn't want to scare her younger brother with the details of the attacker's demise. She might still be angry with him, but her brother, the academic, would freak out at any hint of violence.

"Where are you?" he shouted.

"Not so loud. I can hear you, dammit," she said. "I'm on a dig in Ethiopia, deciphering some old Greek inscriptions on a temple to Isis near Gortas. What about you?" Her eyes wandered to the six beautiful columns with quadrangular capitals supported by the head of Isis, as a Denderah, visible from where she stood. No need to mention them. He wouldn't have a clue what she meant.

"I'm in Warsaw," he replied. "Listen, I've found some old — I'm not able to decide any specific dating, but ancient— and maybe original—manuscripts in Greek and Latin. The curator, Mr. Wozniak, doesn't even know about these texts. He thinks they're all written in Arabic. Could be King John brought them back to Warsaw after the Battle of Vienna."

Bridget remained silent as she thought about the implications of Scott's words.

"Do you hear me?" he demanded in an impatient tone.

"Yes," she said. "But I'm having a disbelief moment. My skepticism meter is on red. Go on," she ordered, glancing in the direction the attacker fled to make sure he didn't return. The blood trail clear and the man must be losing a lot of it. Nevertheless, she kept the machete at hand.

"Someone buried these documents in the bowels of Warsaw's national museum and the curator, an old friend of my college mentor, asked me to take a look at them. The Arabic writing alone is from the seventh to the ninth century. I'm still working on dating the Greek and Latin. But it's earlier."

"My God, Scott, you're not for real?" Bridget's voice conveyed her misgivings. Could her younger brother find something so significant in his first summer after graduation? Even if he could, and she doubted it, she didn't believe it would make any difference to his career. She again scanned in the direction the attacker fled, but saw nothing.

She also used the moment to realize that from her own experiences, she knew that the *old boys* of the academic world would endeavor to cut Scott out of any credit for any discovery he might make.

"I'm calling you," Scott continued, "because I also found two pages of Latin text that begins, *Ego Petrus, Apostolus Jesu Christi* (I am Peter, Apostle of Jesus Christ). Do you realize what that could mean, sis? This text could reveal whether Peter admitted Jesus married the Magdalene, that he faked the resurrection, or he had a son. I know that sounds crazy, but others have postulated such things. This document might confirm or forever silence the speculation. How about that?"

Bridget rolled her eyes upward, trying to think of a way to counter Scott's claim. She didn't believe what he said and he hadn't convinced her of anything. He needed to be much more careful of such wild academic claims. They could ruin him or get him killed by some religious fanatic. She waited for him to continue.

"I'm more intrigued by the Arabic texts," Scott said. "Something like those could potential cause a significant change in one of the world's major religions — even start a war in Islam. Christianity might get a jolt from something Peter wrote if any of this can be authenticated."

"Don't get carried away," Bridget said.

"Tone down your disbelief. Believe me, it's for real," Scott continued. "The curator doesn't know what I've found. This is my doctorate field. I know what I'm talking about and I need your help."

She ignored his request and moved over to her truck where her assistants lay tied up on the ground. They had surrendered as soon as they saw the renegades, fearing for their lives.

"I don't see how this is possible. Not at all." She held the phone in her left hand and sliced the binds holding her helpers. She then stuck the blood soaked blade in the ground. "Besides, why should I help you? I don't even like you anymore."

Once she set free all the helpers, she signaled to them to get the truck ready to leave as she continued her conversation.

"Come on, sis, give me a break. Please forget what happened. Would you quit bringing *that* up? It's old news and never was all that big of a deal. But this— this is important." He paused to let his plea sink in. "Listen, the real mystery is the Greek texts. These are, by my best guess, hundreds of years old. They may be copies of some more ancient text."

"No big deal?" she shouted back at the phone. Scott would never get it. He'd betrayed her and that betrayal he now called no big deal?

"Think about getting a look at the Greek manuscripts," he tempted her. "They're right in in your area of specialty.

The mention of Greek manuscripts sent her mind into hyper drive. Scott knew Greek and would be able to tell if they were old writings. If they were some lost or to date unknown ancient texts, this discovery could end up being a feather in her cap as well.

"Do you have copies of all these papers?" she asked.

"No. I plan to copy a few more pages, but tomorrow I can examine all of them again. I'm meeting with the curator and the museum archeologist this evening. He's going to tell me how he made the discovery of what he believes are old Arabic scrolls." Bridget now noticed his voice sounded louder in his anticipation of learning more.

"Make sure you ask questions. Don't just sit there and believe everything they say. Remember, they're after money and credit for any such find," Bridget said. She clenched her hand into a fist and banged the side of her leg. He needed to understand the stakes here.

"I believe some of the Arabic parchments may be translations from Greek documents we know about from references by others. They may be the transliterations, or in some cases exact translations, of the originals into Arabic." He stopped. She could almost hear the gears spinning in his head.

"What? There's something you're not telling me?"

"There's a map and I believe a detailed listing of a treasure. I... don't know how to figure out...the code on the map, so—"

"This can't be. They're probably fakes, including the Arabic text. You can't believe they're authentic." A plan blossomed in Bridget's mind. The ride to the airport would take three hours and from her previous departures, she knew that the last plane left around nine at night. And if she thought about it, she wanted to make sure Scott didn't get himself into any danger. She remained furious with him but he remained her baby brother. If anyone killed him, it was going to be her, not some stranger. Bridget thought about her brother's piercing black eyes and his long, black hair that no one could convince him to cut. His natural olive skin made him a handsome fellow in anyone's book.

Yes. A trip to Warsaw appeared in order.

"Where are you staying in Warsaw?" she asked.

He told her the name of his hotel.

"This better not be a wild goose chase...or should I say wild text chase," she warned.

"All I can say," Scott continued, "is they look genuine to me. I've handled these types of texts before in our national museum and know what they look like and how to handle them—which, I might add, they are doing a poor job of at this museum. But you're the best person I know who has the Greek knowledge and is an ace at figuring out puzzles. I know for it to be real we must have them authenticated."

She could hear his rapid breathing as he continued, "Someone will need to discover the location of the treasure. You were always the genius in that area. I need your help in this. It may be an extraordinary find. We have to be the ones who discover this historic and potential multi million dollar treasure."

"They'll think the writings of Peter are the most important, but I think this map is. There are but two pages of Peter's writing — let's say his gospel. No one knows about it. Even the curator missed it because he thinks all the documents are in Arabic. Can you come? Do you believe this is happening to me on my first—"

"You're losing your objectivity. But the remainder of the text has to be found. Two pages do not a gospel make. Calm down. You probably have nothing but a mythical treasure and some fake Latin and Greek documents. How in the hell could they be in Warsaw? No historical proof suggests such a thing. Wait a minute." She heard a beep from her phone. On examination of the display the battery low light blinked.

"My battery is running low. Don't tell anyone anything. Don't say any more. Keep those pages in a safe place. I'll be there." She disconnected and shook her head in wonder. What the hell had little brother gone and done?

This discovery would make both of their careers and might even provide world-shattering...*hell no. Stop it. That is too far down the road. Get real, girl.* She punched the end button on the phone, and moved toward the truck, determined to protect Scott from making a fool of himself. If what he said proved true— but no, it couldn't be.

She needed to convince him to drop the matter before he lost credibility. If he became associated with such a find and it proved a forgery or a deliberate fake, he would be ruined and become the laughing stock of the experts in his Arabic and Islamic studies area. Her little brother might mess up his new career before he even got started. She must prevent that catastrophe, no matter what happened to her before.

As she travelled to the airport, she took the time to wonder about the attackers. Were those brigands who just after money or something else? One white man seemed very strange. She would have expected two Africans. Besides, why would they raid an archeological dig where no one kept any amount of money?

That might mean they weren't after money. What if someone had sent them to kill her?

2

Warsaw National Museum – 3:34 p.m.

When Scott hung up, an uncomfortable sense of doubt wormed its way into his brain. He should be more skeptical, his sister right. As a trained academic, he must force himself to slow down and not believe his assumptions without scientific proof, or at least a rational explanation concerning the discovery of the documents.

He returned to the museum archives and delved into the writings. Scott lost track of time. He jumped when the door swung open and the curator entered. His half-rim glasses made Scott smile. The man looked and played the part of an old-world museum curator down to the ivory-tipped cane and his flowing snow-white hair.

"Well, young Scott. What do you think of the documents?" The curator's Polish accent acute when he spoke English.

Scott couldn't put his finger on it, but something didn't seem right with the curator's demeanor. A normal curator would exude delight at the find before revealing everything to the world. But Mr. Wozniak had kept the knowledge of the discovery to a select few. On the other hand there were, after all, the authentication problems and that must weigh on the curator's mind.

"It's an amazing find. Have you determined how they came to be here?" Scott asked.

The curator poured himself a cup of coffee from the side table, took a drink, and flipped his white hair back over his head and out of his eyes.

"The museum archeologists, under the supervision of Cezar Zamoyski, our distinguished head of that department..." He stopped and wiped the sides of his mouth with a paper napkin before continuing, "After examining the chest I found, he concluded it may be part of the booty our king brought back to Poland. You will remember that John III Sobieski saved Europe from the Islamic invasion by defeating their army at the gates of Vienna in 1683. He brought much of the spoils of the battle, including gold and other items, back to Poland. Many believe he gave valuable manuscripts to a monastery, but we always supposed that to be a tall tale to increase the king's stature. Now, however, we may have located at least some of those lost documents."

Scott took off his small reading glasses. His eyes were good at distance, superb, in fact, for weapon shooting on the pentathlon team at university. For up-close reading he often needed glasses, mainly in dim light.

"That would explain all these Arabic texts," Scott said. "I would like to hear the story of how you discovered this treasure. I believe these documents contain the writing of the Prophet Mohammed, and perhaps a large section of the Koran. I suggest you do more examinations to determine the exact age, but my first guess is you may have an early copy or even perhaps the originals based on the writing style and some of the archaic words used. It could help me date the Latin and Greek texts." Even as he slipped up, Scott damned himself. He did not intend to mention those at this time.

Wozniak's eyes narrowed as he fixed a stare on Scott.

"I didn't know there were any Latin or Greek texts. I only saw Arabic writing." The curator then took on an affable smile. "My secretary just copied the manuscripts blindly, ensuring no damage occurred in the process. May I?" He reached for the copied document.

Scott handed him the Latin text. As he examined it, the curator's face glowed in excitement. His eyebrows rose as he continued to read. Scott assumed, in a predominately Catholic country like Poland, most of the older people probably received schooling in Latin during their academic years. Mr. Wozniak mumbled as he translated the text, and then looked up, a grin on his face.

"Scott, do you realize what this is?"

"I can, however, recognize the first words, 'I am Peter the apostle of Jesus Christ' I believe is what it states."

"You haven't told anyone, have you?" Wozniak asked.

Scott knew that years of scholarly research were needed to validate the find but the publicity for the museum would provide worldwide recognition. The curator, for some reason, seemed determined to keep his secret from the world.

"Can you read any of the Greek documents?" Wozniak asked without waiting on an answer to his first question.

"No, not really," Scott admitted.

"Let me call Cezar. He's an expert," the curator said, referring to another museum employee Scott saw a few times but never met.

After making the call, he returned and soon a large man entered he room.

"What have you got now?" Cezar demanded.

Wozniak introduced Scott. Scott told Cezar of the Latin and Greek text and what the Latin text said.

"It can't be a gospel according to St. Peter, can it?" Wozniak asked.

"I doubt it," Scott chimed in, trying to mirror some of Bridget's skeptical outlook.

"Wait just a second," Cezar's voice boomed. "If I recall, there exists one reference of such a gospel from the second century. A Gnostic named Marcion provided the first list of books he felt appropriate for a New Testament. It contained a short list of books and the single time this gospel was mentioned and then dismissed as an error on the part of the writer. In reality, the first officially sanctioned list of books in the New Testament was by Irenaeus of Lyon. But there's no mention made of a gospel by Peter. Church leaders solidified Irenaeus's index in the fourth century. St. Jerome persuaded the church to adopt the list of books listed by Irenaeus as the inspired word of God."

"You tell me that a gospel by St. Peter could exist? I don't believe it," Wozniak said.

Cezar looked at each in turn, and then said, "Many in the past believed the Popes kept selected documents in their personal possession and this one you uncovered might contain instructions given to Peter by Jesus. Some might even speculate it's a secret the church doesn't want anyone to learn." He rubbed his chin, then reached for the document on Scott's table.

"Like what?" Scott asked, raising one eyebrow and shaking his head in wonder as Cezar picked up the text.

"Maybe Jesus didn't rise from the dead or ascend into heaven, maybe he married and lived happily ever after, or maybe he was gay. How the hell would I know?" Cezar asked with a wave of the hand. "It is possible that someone at the Vatican might know about it. I doubt they would ever admit to its existence at this late date."

"Why didn't the world know about this gospel, or more accurately, this so-called gospel, if it even existed before now? Where has it been?" Scott asked.

"Remember the Goths in the fourth century overran the Roman Empire and the Popes felt they had to send their treasures off to the safest place in the Empire. Well, at the time, that place was Spain. Rome was subsequently sacked. Later the Moors overran Spain. And all records over the following centuries were lost. It happened to many other documents as well."

"If there was a gospel, Cezar, it would have been in the Bible," Wozniak said.

"When St. Jerome persuaded the Pope to adopt the current Bible," Cezar said, pointing at Wozniak, "he didn't know about a gospel by Peter. There were plenty of gospels at the time to choose from to go into the New Testament but the list from Lyon emerged as the winner. You have to remember the Pope made the final decision on the books in the New Testament and if he had a private gospel from St. Peter he could have manipulated its absence no matter what Jerome wished."

"Someone would've been looking for this over the years. People would have known about it," Scott said with defiance in his tone.

Cezar put the document down. He walked over to the table with the coffee, turned and looked at Wozniak. "You have anything to drink besides this thin liquid piss you call coffee?"

Wozniak tapped his cane on the floor. "Come on, Cezar, tell us. Haven't you archeologists looked for such a thing?"

"From time to time over the centuries scholars did bring up the subject of this Gospel of St. Peter, but they presumed it lost, if it ever existed. Some researchers in the Renaissance era decided to take up the search but after years found no trace or evidence of its existence. No record of such a gospel remained in Rome and the retreating Muslim army destroyed most church records in Spain."

He stopped and took a drink from his cup. He walked around the room and came to face Scott.

"Over time," Cezar continued, "scholars just dismissed a gospel by Peter as a myth or as something lost forever. Rumors existed that some important documents accompanied the Muslim army in its attack on the gates of Vienna, but no facts ever emerged concerning that."

"So you believe this gospel could be the real thing?" Scott asked.

"From what we know," the rotund archeologist pulled his jowl cheeks up into a disturbed smile, waited a few seconds, and then said in a deliberate manner, "it is possible. That's all I'll say."

"Detailed examination should prove its authenticity or that it's a forgery." Wozniak swayed back and forth using his cane as a fulcrum. "But a find of the Gospel of St. Peter and of the original Koran could impact the world's great religions and would have monumental importance to both."

"We must leave for another meeting. Please excuse us, Scott. I'll see you at five. We'll talk more then," Wozniak said. He grabbed

Cezar by the arm. The man spit the coffee back into the cup and the curator led him to the door.

After they'd left Scott alone, he continued to examine the manuscripts. The next time he glanced at the clock, it showed almost five. Scott started for the curators' office, anticipating learning the more about the discovery of the documents.

END OF CHAPTER 2

Secret of the Thorns **is now available on Amazon** in eBook, paperback, and audio.

ABOUT THE AUTHOR

TOM HAASE is the author of the Donavan Adventure series and Chuck McGregor Coastal Adventure series.

Tom had a thrilling experience when he jumped out of an airplane for the first time as an Army paratrooper in the 82nd Airborne Division. During his distinguished 28 year military career, Tom lived in Korea, Nepal, Ireland, Greece, England, and Cyprus. He had the honor of commanding a firing battery in combat in Viet Nam and representing the Department of Defense as a United States diplomat and Defense Attaché in four embassies. After retiring from the U.S. Army as a Lieutenant Colonel, he flew as a commercial pilot for a regional airline, and was rated to fly the Boeing 737.

Now, instead of flying airplanes or jumping out of them, he writes complex, fast-paced adventure novels to thrill readers.

He lives in Savannah, Georgia with his wife, Kate.

To learn more about his latest books, please visit tomhaase.com.

facebook.com/authortomhaase

twitter.com/tommhaase

Made in the USA
Columbia, SC
26 November 2021